# PRAISE FOR PRIDE LEADERSHIP

For nearly two decades NGLCC has been the business voice of the LGBT community, helping empower and elevate our business leaders worldwide. *Pride Leadership: Strategies for LGBTQ+ Professionals to be the King or Queen of their Jungle*, by NGLCC-certified business owner Dr. Steve Yacovelli, speaks to the importance of fostering the next generation of leaders in our community to ensure our social and economic progress continues moving forward toward opportunity and inclusion for all.

*—Justin Nelson, Co-Founder & President,*
*National LGBT Chamber of Commerce (NGLCC)*

*Pride Leadership* not only focuses on what I, too, feel are the most important leadership traits for anyone—authenticity, empathy, communication, courage, relationships, and change—but it sheds insight on these topics with a positive, engaging voice. Here's to every LGBTQ+ Leader taking a look at—and applying—the concepts in this book.

*—Mike Dilbeck, Certified Speaking Professional and Fundraiser*

Exploring leadership from a queer (LGBTQ+) perspective can be a challenge. There aren't many role models when you're an "outsider" or an insider within a marginalized group. The gifts our communities' experience can bring to leadership are not well articulated in the mainstream, but Steve Yacovelli has the chops to put all the pieces together. Read, then go forth and LEAD!

—*Jamison Green, PhD, President, Transgender Strategies Consulting, LLC; author of* Becoming a Visible Man

There are a lot of "leadership" books out there today, but none come to mind that speak directly to an LGBTQ Leader. In *Pride Leadership*, Steve not only speaks straight to our community (so to speak), but does so with empathy, passion, and practical wisdom. An enjoyable yet thoughtful read, I highly recommend this for any LGBTQ person wishing to amp up their leadership game.

—*Gina Duncan, Director of Transgender Equality, Equality Florida Institute*

Being an inclusive leader is so important, more now than ever before. For an LGBTQ+ Leader, understanding your power and influence in leveraging empathy, being authentic, managing relationships, and the other competencies Steve shares in *Pride Leadership* are great revelations for emerging leaders, and good practical reminders for experienced leaders. I highly recommend this fun, informative, and engaging read for any LGBTQ+ Leader.

—*Jon G. Munoz, Vice President, Global Diversity & Inclusion, Hilton*

Leadership books and courses are often designed to speak to the talents and cultural sensibilities of only a select group of society. Not only do we need to transform how we look at leadership, we also need to create models that resonate with emerging communities. *Pride Leadership* is a wonderful tool not only for LGBTQ leaders, but for anyone who wants to connect, serve, and empower today's emerging workforce.

—*Dr. Joel A. Brown, Chief Visionary Officer,*
*Pneumos LLC*

---

This book explores the power in embracing our true identities and harnessing that power to be genuine leaders. There is no more need to be the leader we thought we needed to be. Instead, we get to be the courageous leaders we deserve to become.

—*Dr. Christopher Zacharda, Director of Student Conduct,*
*Tulane University*

---

An accessible and essential read. Leadership in action. *Pride Leadership* is filled with resonant examples and exercises to teach profound lessons—to and about ourselves. It will teach you to think like an inclusive leader.

—*Ingrid Galvez Thorp, Co-Founder of Thorp, LLC,*
*a business management strategist specializing in human resources:*
*Organizational and Leadership Development*

*Pride Leadership* offers tactical and measurable strategies for LGBT+ leaders in the workplace. The six leadership competencies—specifically, authenticity and empathy—are spot-on and can lead both LGBT+ and Ally leaders to success.

—*Wes Werbeck, COO,*
*Out Leadership*

Dr. Steve Yacovelli has focused appropriately on leading with authenticity and integrity. These dimensions of leadership are critical distinguishing characteristics, and must be taught to and learned by leaders. As a skilled leadership development facilitator, Steve captures the essence of how the LGBTQ+ community can benefit from practical lessons in being the best leader possible. Steve's life lessons—framed from personal and professional experiences—are open, honest, and from the heart!

—*Don Stenta, Assistant Vice President,*
*The Ohio State University Alumni Association*
*and Distinguished Adjunct Professor,*
*John Glenn College of Public Affairs*

Under the Obama Administration, the federal government was tasked to develop ways to be more inclusive to the LGBTQ+ communities. I developed the Many Faces One Dream (MFOD) tour for the U.S. Small Business Administration (SBA) to answer that charge. One of the pillars of MFOD was the LGBT Business Builder, connecting entrepreneurs to SBA's business development resources to include access to capital. In addition, we focused our messaging on "Leadership" being the key ingredient to success. We encouraged entrepreneurs to tap into their greatest resource—Leadership—and we would connect them to powerful networks to help them succeed, scale, and grow. *Pride Leadership* will serve America's LGBTQ+ entrepreneurs very well. It is the perfect handbook for all leaders to follow.

—*Eugene Cornelius, Jr., Senior Director for Strategic Alliances International Council for Small Business (ICSB)*

---

You have to see it to be it. Yet far too many LGBTQ+ entrepreneurs, executives, and employees alike are hard-pressed to identify out and proud possibility models crushing it in business. *Pride Leadership* offers the elixir guaranteed to encourage more rainbow family members to step out of their closets and onto their leadership thrones. Treat yourself to a healthy dose of professional development you can take with you on your next road trip, and enjoy the transformation.

—*Rhodes Perry, MPA, Founder + CEO of Rhodes Perry Consulting, bestselling author of* Belonging at Work, *and podcast host of* The Out Entrepreneur

---

Thoughtful, helpful, and wickedly enjoyable. If you lead any team, business, or organization, you'll get a lot out of Steve's insights found in *Pride Leadership*. Plus, it's pretty darn fun to read.

—*Casey Nicholaw, Tony Award-winning Broadway director/choreographer*

The experience of being in the LGBTQ community has been such an unexpected professional gift, in that I have gained so many skills through my efforts to be authentic, to connect with others, and to bring my full self to every interaction. At a time when so many are still closeted at work, this book provides encouragement and inspiration that identity can be a powerful engine of our success!

—*Jennifer Brown, Founder and CEO, Jennifer Brown Consulting, and author of* "Inclusion: Diversity, the New Workplace, and the Will to Change" *and* "How to be an Inclusive Leader"

# PRIDE LEADERSHIP

# PRIDE
# LEADERSHIP

Strategies for the LGBTQ+ Leader
to be the King or Queen
of their Jungle

Steven R. Yacovelli, Ed.D.

PUBLISH
YOUR
PURPOSE
PRESS

For permission requests, write to the publisher, addressed "Attention: Permissions Coordinator," at the address below.

Publish Your Purpose Press
141 Weston Street, #155
Hartford, CT, 06141

PUBLISH
YOUR
PURPOSE
PRESS

The opinions expressed by the Author are not necessarily those held by Publish Your Purpose Press.

Ordering Information: Quantity sales and special discounts are available on quantity purchases by corporations, associations, and others. For details, contact the publisher at the address above.

Edited by: Heather B. Habelka
Cover design by: Rocío Martín Osuna
Typeset by: Medlar Publishing Solutions Pvt Ltd., India

ISBN: 9781946384775 (print)
ISBN: 978-1-946384-68-3 (ebook)

Library of Congress Control Number: 2019902815

First edition, June 2019.

The information contained within this book is strictly for informational purposes. The material may include information, products, or services by third parties. As such, the Author and Publisher do not assume responsibility or liability for any third-party material or opinions. The publisher is not responsible for websites (or their content) that are not owned by the publisher. Readers are advised to do their own due diligence when it comes to making decisions.

Publish Your Purpose Press works with authors, and aspiring authors, who have a story to tell and a brand to build. Do you have a book idea you would like us to consider publishing? Please visit PublishYourPurposePress.com for more information.

# DEDICATION

This book is dedicated to all the LGBTQ+ advocates out there striving to make the world just a little bit better-er.

From the lesbian leading their workplace LGBTQ+ Employee Resource Group (ERG), to the gay man starting a Gay-Straight Alliance at school, to the senior transgender executive paving the way for other trans folks in their workplace, to the gender fluid health care worker sharing their perspective on how the department can be more inclusive, to the bisexual co-worker educating their peers and being visible to others; these are the folks—much like you, dear reader—who are making change for the better.

Keep it up …
make change …
and have a little bit o' fun in the process!

# CONTENTS

Contents

CHAPTER FOUR

## The Shiny Unicorn That is You: Being Your
## Authentic Self . . . . . . . . . . . . . . . . . . . .77

CHAPTER FIVE

## Roar Like a Lion: Having Courage . . . . . . . . . 111

**CHAPTER SIX**

# Yielding the Magic Fairy Wand (or Sword) of Empathy . . . . . . . . . . . . . . . . . . . . . . **147**

### CHAPTER NINE
### Getting in Shape: Shaping Culture. . . . . . . . . 251

## CHAPTER TEN

## CHAPTER ELEVEN

# FOREWORD

F ORGING YOUR PATH as a leader is a challenge for anyone, and being an LGBTQ+ leader has added challenges but
also immeasurable rewards.

As an LGBTQ+ leader, I've known the challenges that we face
as well as the lessons and skills that being part of our community
can teach. When I think back to coming out while leading my
college football team at Bloomsburg University of Pennsylvania,
I knew in my heart that I needed to be true to myself, but knowing
that did not make it any easier. Not knowing how others would
react or if my coach and those I respected would support me and
how my truth would impact my role as team captain all ran through
my mind. While it took a lot of time and a lot of strength, I dug
deep and shared my authentic self with those around me and found
love and support along the way. Sharing and then persevering has
taught me how to lead and shaped me into who I am today.

Flash forward to pursuing my law degree at Michigan State
University. Thinking about those I would one day represent helped
me to further develop empathy. I value that my experience may not

be the same as those around me and the notion of "putting myself in someone else's shoes" has helped me to see things from other perspectives. This has allowed me to step up and lead groups of people from differing backgrounds and ideologies around a common goal. As someone who was often seen as "the other" because I was raised in a military family and moved 17 times, or because I was an out football captain, I recognize that perspectives and ideologies will always differ from mine. Most recently, I recognize this from across the proverbial aisle. To this day, having empathy for others is a cornerstone to how I engage my constituents and those with whom I work.

As a Pennsylvania legislator, the best way to get things done is through leveraging relationships. As a lawyer and a gay man, I've known that building relationships with those around you—be they friends or colleagues—allows me to not only leverage my empathy ("Hey Brian, how do you think they are looking at this situation?"), but be conscious and respectful of the fact that my way of seeing the world isn't the way others do. I constantly ask myself how can we move toward and find common ground to make things happen. Building relationships as a leader is building trust, and I've found that through listening, leveraging empathy, and finding common ground I can be a more impactful leader than if I'm closed off and focused on my own agenda.

If you know me, you know I'm passionate about equality and fairness, especially as it relates to our LGBTQ+ communities. When I think about culture, I think about it including everyone and all people have a place—and a voice—at the table. As an LGBTQ+ advocate, I strive to make sure that we all have equal footing and that passion for cultural change is something that all

LGBTQ+ leaders can embrace to help better position our community for tomorrow.

Through my experience as faculty of the Center for Progressive Leadership and the National Campaign Board of the Gay & Lesbian Victory Fund, I work with LGBTQ+ leaders from all walks of life. When I think of the traits necessary to excel in leadership, it takes the balance of everything that Steve outlines in this book.

So, enjoy the stories, advice, and perspective in Steve's book; as I can attest that being authentic, having courage, being empathetic, cultivating relationships, fostering an inclusive culture, and effectively communicating to those around you are indeed the bedrock for effective and inclusive leadership—whether you're a member of the LGBTQ+ community or not. Also, find the courage to reflect on yourself, your current and aspirational leadership behavior, and how you can best move those to be even more effective. In order to make change, move the fight equality forward and make the world just a little bit better, we need **you** to become one of our thoughtful, dedicated, and fearless leaders!

Lead on, fellow Community members!
*Pennsylvania State Representative Brian K. Sims*

# PREFACE

......................................................

*"LGBTQ+ people have a natural ability to be effective, authentic, and empathetic leaders; they just have to tap into that natural instinct and believe in themselves to channel their super powers."*
– Dr. Steve Yacovelli
(yeah, that's me, The Gay Leadership Dude!)

<u>P</u>roactive Communication • <u>R</u>elationship-Building • <u>I</u>ntegrity, Authenticity, & Courage • <u>D</u>eveloping Culture • <u>E</u>mpathy

## First Off: Why the Heck is Steve Writing about Leadership for LGBTQ+ People?

Lemme 'splain, Lucy …

I've been a professional communicator all my career: from working in marketing to corporate training to leadership consulting to change management … all my paychecks over the years have been because of some job where I learned to talk goodly and communicate effectively. And I've seen how the power that this, coupled with other traits or competencies, has separated the manager from the leader within the workplace (or—let's be honest—the corporate "jungle"). I also did a little bit of studying on these concepts, with an undergrad degree in Speech Communications-Public Relations, a Master's in Educational Policy & Leadership, and a Doctorate in Education (and I definitely have the student loan debt to prove it!).

And, as a member of the LGBTQ+ Community since getting my card in 1994, I of course have experienced my career through the lens of being a gay dude. And, throughout the years, I've tried to give back to our Community through volunteer work, political actions that move our collective equality forward, and have, in general, been a "boots (heels?) on the ground" for our march toward fair treatment in the workplace and well beyond.

A few years ago, it hit me that—as a member of the LGBTQ+ Community—there's some common experiences we have faced together. While I will absolutely admit we all have our own experience and context with which we look at the world (more on bias and unconscious bias later!), as a collective Community, we have many shared traits/skills/experiences. Duh: that's what community means!

So, I started to think about us as a Community and our shared experiences through the lens of what I see that makes someone very effective as a leader in the workplace, it hit me: LGBTQ+ folks—in general—naturally have a lot of the skills it takes to be effective leaders. Whether that's having empathy, being authentic, or knowing how to communicate effectively to a variety of audiences, through our shared journey we've had practice in many of these areas. And we can channel that awesomeness into being a more effective and inclusive leader in our respective workplaces—and beyond. And thus *Pride Leadership* was born (cue "Circle of Life" music and picture me holding up this book on Pride Rock now).

## W.I.I.F.M. and Steve's Not-So-Hidden Agenda

When I first learned how to create training programs for the adult learner, one of the first terms I was exposed to was W.I.I.F.M., pronounced *whif-em*. W.I.I.F.M. stands for What's In It For Me? As an instructional designer (yes, that's what they call folks who make those training classes you may or may not like going to), you always needed to explicably identify the W.I.I.F.M. for the folks who are sitting in your training classes. So, I want to share what I think is the W.I.I.F.M. for you as a reader of this book.

First, I suspect you fall into one of two camps:

1. You're just venturing into your own leadership development journey and want to start to understand what competencies you may want to focus your energies on to develop and grow; or
2. You already have some semblance or knowledge of your leadership competence and you just want to grow it even deeper.

Regardless of where you are starting on your leadership journey, I hope that you learn to identify/appreciate not only your natural skills in being an effective leader as an LGBTQ+ person, but also garner some tips and tricks on how to further develop those skills and begin to apply those strategies in your everyday leadership life.

In addition, my really big desire is that—in some small way—I can help you be a more effective LGBTQ+ Leader and that you take those skills and help move our world forward to be more inclusive. Whether that's assuming a leadership role at work and being sure your organization is more inclusive toward LGBTQ+ peeps, or taking a leadership role within a group that focuses on LGBTQ+ equality, or volunteering somewhere in your community to provide that LGBTQ+ perspective, I truly hope you apply what you learn in this book to make our world a little bit better.

## How I've Built Our Leadership House

As you go through this 1,000+ page book (made ya look! Did you quickly go to the back of the book and see how many pages are there?), I'd like you to be aware of how I've structured each chapter:

1. We start with a real-life story on LGBTQ+ Leadership ... whether they be awesome-sauce success stories or some crash-and-burn failures in leadership, I think it's important to hear from others besides me (we'll call these **Jungle Love: Pride Leadership in Action**);

2. We'll define stuff (so we're on the same page ... literally) and provide some context on the topic of leadership competency and what I've found to be current or pivotal thoughts in each topic;

3. I'll pepper some reflective questions (called **Drone Perspective: Reflective ?'s**) at the right spots to get you to think about your own LGBTQ+ leadership path and how it relates to the topic at hand

4. I tie each leadership competency to concepts as mentioned in *The G Quotient* research (more on that later); and finally

5. There's prescriptive steps or actions you can choose to take in order to be more effective in that particular leadership competency (appropriately called **"Mane" Development Strategies**, because, you know, lions!).

Some things we'll chat about are concepts and ideas I've seen within my twenty-five-plus years of creating and facilitating leadership workshops for clients (both internal and external to the organizations). Whether it's the Fortune 100 media/entertainment company (run by a rodent) I've worked with, to a very "big blue" Fortune 50 tech giant; from a national not-for-profit professional association supporting libraries, to a major philanthropic foundation trying to eradicate malaria and other great improve-the-world-initiatives; there are so many similarities in the challenges that leaders have in all the groups I've played with not to notice a pattern. Other topics are just concepts or books I've curated as "best practices" over the years and happily share those concepts (with appropriate credit to each originator!). Note: I get zero kickbacks with any of the best practice concepts from others; I've just found their stuff to be awesome and applicable in today's workplace jungle.

In addition, the topics themselves really, really dovetail together. It's impossible, for example, to talk about organizational culture (Chapter 9) without talking about cultivating relationships (Chapter 8); so many of these concepts overlap. To me, though, that's the cool thing: as a leader you aren't developing these skills or competencies in a vacuum, but collectively building them together to strengthen your awesome LGBTQ+ leadership self.

## "Don't Take That Tone with Me, Steve!"

If you're one of the people reading this book who I personally have the pleasure of knowing: THANKS FOR BUYING (unless I somehow coerced you or I gave you a freebie, or you gave birth to me—thanks, Mom and Dad!). Now, if you know me, you'll definitely hear my voice in this narrative. I tried to write as I speak about these topics, with a little cheekiness sprinkled in to hopefully make the experience enjoyable. If I don't know you, well, I hope someday we'll say a hello.

There're many folks who approach leadership (or any learning aspect for the workplace) in a serious manner. Sadly, I think this turns some folks off of the learning process and frankly doesn't make the content stick very well (trust me: I'm a doctor … of education at least). I've been teaching many of these concepts for years and have found that even the most uptight executive wants to have some fun. By making this book a little more conversational, it is my intent to not only make it into "edutainment" (or entertaining), but also—hopefully—help make the concepts stick through the use of stories, anecdotes, and some verbal silliness.

I take your being an effective and successful LGBTQ+ Leader very seriously, but I don't take myself as such. Hopefully that transfers in the pages that follow.

## Your Job as a Reader, Skeeter

As you go through this book, I've tried to insert some ideas and thoughts for you to take away, maybe give yourself some homework, but generally reflect on your own leadership style—what's working or what could be a little bit better. As you read, see if you agree with the concepts presented. Do you have a different experience that would perhaps make your perspective on the topic different than mine? Great! If not, how does what we discuss relate to you?

The challenging part of this being a book (and not a class, webinar, or face-to-face coaching) is that it's very one-sided: Steve's side (with some special guest stories and experts sprinkled in). We don't get the chance to engage in dialogue, talk about how your perspective is different than mine, and learn from one another. Sorry about that.

But that doesn't mean this book is meant to be passive; on the contrary, I'd like you to engage and reflect on what it takes to apply these leadership concepts to your world (or as I like to say, your *context*). How will you make even just a few changes in your approach to leadership after picking through this book?

That's your job ... should you wish to accept it.

# Why'd You Say it THAT Way, Steve?

## First and Most Importantly, Why Do I Use the Term LGBTQ+?

I tried to be as inclusive to our wonderfully diverse Community as I could. Some folks use the acronym LGBTQIA to specifically include our intersex, asexual, and ally family, or some further separate it out using the LGBTTTQQIAA acronym to focus more specifically on our transsexual and two-spirit family members as well as separate the identifiers of queer and questioning.

Let me be crystal clear: my use of + isn't meant to shortchange any member of our Community; on the contrary I personally started using the + several years ago as I was understanding how our family was awesomely broadening the ways in which we were self-identifying. So, if you are part of the + please know my use of the LGBTQ+ acronym isn't meant to ignore you or your experience, but more to include the many facets of our Community. Plus, as an added bonus, I lived in Paris for a spell and + is pronounced *plew* in French, so when you say LGBTQ+ and the + is pronounced *plew*, it sounds just so awesome, IMHO (*el-gee-bee-tee-que-plew!*).

I recently read an article in *The Atlantic* where author Jonathan Rauch argues that we should just drop all the letters and use *Q* for *queer*, or to simply represent all of us "sexual minorities" as one collective term and drop the siloed letters (Rauch, 2019). I thought long and hard about that, but—at least for now—opted for LGBTQ+. But, if we as a Community do move toward a different term, I'm very open to using my Microsoft Word's "find-replace" feature in the next edition of this book.

## What About That Uninclusive Subtitle, Steve?

Creating the subtitle, "Strategies for the LGBTQ+ Leader to be the King or Queen of their Jungle" was more of a challenge than I initially realized. I went back and forth on how to create a subtitle that specifically shared who the book was for (that's you, my awesome reader!), what the reader would get out of the book (mad skillz and strategies), and still be engaging as well as supportive of the main title, *Pride Leadership*. After I'd been sharing the book title on social media, I had one person provide me with their feedback: "I have issues with your subtitle: it's really too binary and not totally inclusive." He went on to share that—from his point of view—there's potentially two ways you can wrongly interpret my subtitle:

- That our gender-fluid friends aren't being included, because the title identifies the monarch-ruling binary of a king and a queen; and ...
- The Queen noun is being made as an afterthought to the King (male conscious inclusion and female secondary or unconscious inclusion).

First: I ABSOLUTELY LOVED that someone had the comfort with our friendship to call me out on this; and his perspective is definitely one way to look at this subtitle. When I came up with the title *Pride Leadership*, I wanted to speak to our LBGTQ+ Community, and the pride part seemed pretty darn fitting. This then led me to the whole lions-are-rulers-of-the-jungle train of thought (which also connects with the notion of leadership), and the popular "King of the Jungle" tie-in seemed copacetic. And—to try and be gender inclusive—I added Queen, but then realized the double entendre of queen-the-female-ruler versus "hey gurl, heeeeeey" queen and liked it. So, to me, I was not trying to disenfranchise any member of our Community nor prefer one gender binary over another. No offense meant!

Also, I'm a big fan of the TV show *The Magicians* (and side promo: if you've not seen it, it's really pretty fantastic—like *Harry Potter* set in grad school, with very adult themes and a LOT of inclusiveness from our Community's perspective). In this show, one of the main characters, Margo, became the winning write-in candidate for an election of the highest office in the magical land of Fillory (which makes one of the episode's titles, "Fillory Clinton," that much more cleverer). To the people of Fillory, the title for the highest ruler is "High King," and they don't bat an eye* about calling their new ruler High King Margo. And frankly, that's the world I want to live in: if you feel better being considered the King of Your Jungle, have at it. And by all means, if you want to be the Queen: gurl, it's all yours. Pick the one you like the most, or just know that—by going through this book—you can be Ruler of Your Jungle just as easily! (*And if you are a fan of the show, excuse the Margo and bat an eye pun!)

## To Gay or Not to Gay

So full disclosure: I'm a white, cisgendered gay man. I'm writing this book through my own personal reference point, experience, and lens. While I very much will be as inclusive in my story as I can be, it ultimately is from my experience and observations. I'll attempt to use LGBTQ+ as best as I can (see page xxxi), but for the sake of not being too repetitive, I may on occasion substitute that acronym for "gay" or "homo" or something else. Please know this is in an attempt to not only mix it up, but also to vary the narrative based on my experience—it is not meant to disenfranchise any other facet of our Community. Just go with it ... if you knew me (which I hope you get to know me a bit while reading this book), you'll know that I'm wickedly inclusive and open, and very conscientious of others' feelings as they relate to what I say and how I say it (hence the chapters on empathy and effective communication).

## *Steve's Magpie Approach to Inclusive Language*

There's one thing you need to know about me: I'm a linguistic magpie. "Huh? What the heck does that mean?" you may be asking. Like the story of the magpie bird that steals shiny objects for their nests (alas, this is a myth, BTW), I've always unconsciously picked up various phrases and words from those around me along my life's journey. I worked for a cruise line for several years and was around many Australians, so now I say "gone pear-shaped" a lot (meaning things started out swell and then went to heck). I was fortunate enough to live in Paris for a spell and thus my use of the *plew* pronunciation noted above (and I still say *weefee*, not Wi-Fi. *Vive la France!*). Living in Florida and traveling a lot, I love the influence my Latinx chosen family has on my language (I use "no buenos" in my conversation). I tend to sprinkle these adopted phrases and words—from other cultures, communities, and the people who are part of my world—into my everyday speech.

So, if there's a phrase, word, or concept that seems to be "misplaced" from your perspective by this white, cisgender, gay fortysomething, know that I'm not trying to steal or appropriate the language of any other group, community, or generation. I'm honoring the impact they have had on my experience, perspective, and language. I'm an inclusive person who is openly influenced by the wonderful cornucopia of people I'm lucky to have in my life, so please be OK if my language ventures beyond your definition of what someone of my stated demographics "should" say. That's actually part of the perspective-broadening message of this book and part of being an inclusive leader overall (and we'll talk about how we should broaden the definition of *diversity* in a bit).

## Business versus Organization versus Workplace versus Jungle

I sometimes use the term *business*, but know that I mean that in the broad context of a group working together for a common cause or goal. It could be in reference to a not-for-profit organization you're working with, your for-profit employer, a religious group, academia, or even a volunteer organization. But to me the term *workplace* is the most encompassing, because I interpret it as the place where you work/you are paid to do a job, or you are volunteering your time and energy to do work on behalf of a cause. So again, in the spirit of being inclusive, I'll use workplace but sometimes will veer toward work or company or organization. Interpret it in your context as best as you can.

And that *jungle* descriptor of the workplace: yeah; I think it's a good descriptor. It is indeed a jungle out there. It doesn't necessarily mean that your workplace is savage and overgrown, but the fact that—like a jungle—anything can happen. There's pitfalls, there's other entities/animals, there's beauty and awe, and my hope is that I help you figure out a way to tame that wild frontier through the strategies shared in this book.

With all that setting our stage, let's get this Pride Leadership party started!

· · · · · · · · · · · · · · · · · · · · · · · · · · · · · · · · · · · · · · · · · · · ·

# LET'S GET THIS PRIDE LEADERSHIP PARTY STARTED!

*"Having strong leadership skills is about having strong people skills. The best leaders realize that saying 'effective leadership' is synonymous to saying, 'working with people effectively.'"*
– Dr. Steve Yacovelli
The Gay Leadership Dude

Proactive Communication • Relationship-Building • Integrity, Authenticity, & Courage • Developing Culture • Empathy

## Why the Topic of Leadership Anyway?

**Before you start** ... did you skip the Preface, especially the part where I talked about why I use LGBTQ+? If so, git on' back there, matey ... that's some important stuff. Go ahead ... I'll wait.

OK, back to it. As I shared in the beginning, I've been in the leadership development space for most of my career and even pursued some schoolin' on the topic. When I set out to write a book on leadership two questions popped up in my little noggin:

1. What is *leadership* and how's it different than *management?*
2. *Leadership* is a really broad term. Which leadership concepts should I focus on?

To understand what leadership means to me, let's start with why we say *leadership* versus *management.* Just to be crystal clear: management and leadership are both essential to the success of anyone within the workplace jungle, and honestly, these two terms/concepts are strongly connected and cannot be separated. We are not talking about two people here: you have to be both—a good manager and a good leader—to be successful. It's not enough just to manage your department, team, or area, to make decisions and to develop good plans and scenarios. You have to implement these decisions and plans (that's all management stuff). And, as you implement these plans you will interact with your co-workers, team members, bosses, and customers. You have to convince them that your plans are the right path; you have to convince them to cooperate and to strive for a common goal (that's the leadershippy stuff).

In short: *management* is more concerned with systems, processes, and tasks while *leadership* is always about the people.

Think about your work jungle. Chances are you became a leader in your workplace because you had a certain subject matter expertise. Let's say I'm an accountant (trust me I'm not; but go with me for a sec). I have a degree in accounting. After graduation I got a job as an accountant, and I get so good at playing with my debits and credits that they promote me to Head of Accountants. I was promoted to leadership because I'm such a rock star accountant; I'm great at the task of accounting.

But now my focus shifts: I'm in charge of the accounting *people* now. But there's a really good chance that I didn't necessarily study leading people at university; I focused my energies on accounting and the numbers. And now I'm out of my comfort zone of accounting. I'm now dealing with people, their problems, and their pesky emotions on a daily level. "I didn't sign up for this! I'm a numbers person!"

This is a lot of the leaders I've worked with over the years: SMEs (subject matter experts—or pronounced *smees*) who are so good at their respective areas of expertise that they get promoted into leadership, and they're not sure how to deal with the people factor in their roles. What can happen at this point is frustrating for the new leader. They may revert to what they know (the task) and potentially fall into micromanaging their people because that's what they know. No bueno.

## Drone Perspective

The good news is that you're already on the path to avoid this scenario by picking up this book. And that self-awareness is what will separate you from others within your workplace jungle: the desire to not only see there's room to grow, but taking the steps to do something about that. Bravo!

One of the best strategies leaders can leverage is having that self-awareness. In my leadership workshops we do a lot of self-reflection on our own leadership behavior as it relates to the topic at hand. For example, when discussing "sharing effective feedback" we go into reflecting on how we currently give feedback to others (if at all!) and ask ourselves if it's the right way to do that. That self-reflection muscle isn't always flexed in our 21$^{st}$-century workplace jungle, and taking the time to stop, breathe, and have a think about what we did—and how we can do it better—is key to your growth as an LGBTQ+ Leader.

For some of us, it's hard to "get out of our own head" and objectively look at our behavior. One strategy is through being mindful. *Mindfulness* is "the act of deliberately noticing new things, being present, and considering new perspectives" (Newlon, 2016, para. 4). This is not some "granola crunchy" yogi term, but the idea that through the practice of mindfulness and self-reflection we become more aware of what we are doing, saying, feeling, and acting in any given situation. Mindfulness has been proven to not just help you identify your own actions (especially those related to your unconscious biases and actions), but also to help increase productivity, increase morale, and provide overall health benefits (we'll dive deeper into mindfulness and some good strategies to help with it a later in our convo).

Some folks refer to this as having a helicopter perspective, like you're getting into a helicopter, zooming up, and seeing above the situation on how you're behaving, acting, etc. Frankly, I find that a little old school, so I use the term *drone perspective* because it's the same deal but: (1) drones are cooler and (2) drones are accessible and you can use cameras to see the high-level perspective.

With a drone, you're able to hover above the situation and see the real-time footage through your phone or an app. Self-reflection and mindfulness is like suddenly seeing through the drone what's happening around you; or what you are doing, how you are acting, and how others in the situation are reacting, too. Good, effective LGBTQ+ Leaders can get out of their heads and into that drone to get a read on the situation, learn from that data, and continue or adjust their actions and words to create a more effective situation.

## Why are LGBTQ+ Folks "Good" at Leadership?

I've been leadershippin' (consulting in the leadership development and executive coaching space) for a heap of years (read: I'm old), and I have noticed certain trends over time on what makes a leader, well, awesome. Things like being authentic, having empathy for those who they work with, being courageous in tackling the tough situations, effectively communicating, etc. are all topics that—over the course of twenty-five-ish years—keep surfacing as the "must haves" for leaders to be successful at leading (and—coincidentally—those are topics in this book, but more on that in a few).

And, I've understood that I was a gay dude since about the same time as I entered into my communications profession. I've also noticed—in general terms—there's certain traits that LGBTQ+ people tend to be pretty good at* (*not stereotyping but a trend I observed). So, I theorized (or, as Carrie Bradshaw would say, "I couldn't help but wonder …"): …are LGBTQ+ people really, really good at certain leadership traits?"

After picking around the interwebs, I came across an awesome book, *The G Quotient* by Kirk Snyder. We'll go deep-diving into Kirk's book in a bit (Chapter 2), but overall his research supported my theory that, yes, peeps in our Community have been shown to be good at certain leadership areas. WOOHOO!

But WHY are LGBTQ+ "good" at these certain leadership competencies or skills? I think it has to do with our collective experience as "the other." Whether we're out or not, we have known—consciously or unconsciously—that we're different than the majority (and of course in the most fabulous way). But that feeling of being an outsider—and often an invisible minority—leads one to manage various social situations and interactions differently than an "out" or more obvious minority.

So, over time, I believe our conscious and/or unconscious selves start to understand how to maneuver these interactions: looking at others' level of empathy and following suit, gauging someone's "realness" or authenticity and deciding if we should match it. Through years of social engagement, we've been able to flex these human interaction muscles to help us fit in (and frankly—on an unconscious level—be safe in the group with which we're engaging). So, as an LGBTQ+ person, we've had a lot of practice at understanding how to best engage with other humans, communicate with them, and understand how they're feeling on an emotional level. Generally, that just so happens to be how awesome leaders are, well, awesome. Oh, and doesn't that skill describe our definition of leadership?

## Why These Specific Leadership Topics?

As noted earlier, leadership is a really broad topic; so how did I narrow it down to six specific leadership competencies which we'll focus on in this book? In my experience and what I've observed in the 21ˢᵗ-century workplace jungle is that—while so many different leadership competencies can contribute to overall leadership effectiveness—the six I picked here really keep bubbling up as the crème-de-la-crème competencies that lead to success:

1. Having Authenticity
2. Leadership Courage
3. Leveraging Empathy
4. Effective Communication
5. Building Relationships
6. Shaping Culture

I initially came up with about twenty-six different leadership competency areas. And—venturing a guess—assumed most busy professionals wouldn't have months on end to dredge through my leadership tomb (and nor did I have seven years to write it!). So, with the help of an awesome friend/thinking partner who's also a professional in the leadership and organizational space, we put each of these twenty-six competencies on Post-Its® and took a look. And through some analysis, reflecting on our respective experience, thinking about what our clients have said and seen in the workplace, and looking at the latest books on various leadership topics, we narrowed it all down to six key areas (thanks, Wes!).

What's interesting about the six competency areas we'll be discussing is that they are really intertwined. For example: the thread of "understanding our own emotions and that of others" is woven throughout our conversation. Likewise, managing our own conscious and unconscious biases is, too, a common thread that can impact our own leadership success. So, while we're tackling these six leadership competencies chapter by chapter, they really wonderfully interconnect to make up the whole leadership you.

I'll be frank (even though my name is Steve). It was tough to decide which concepts went where, and so you'll see me take a nod to previous or upcoming topics. For example: having courage is a topic unto itself (it has its own chapter for Pete's sake ... wait: who's Pete? I thought we were taking about Frank? Ahh, I digress). But when we have the conversation about building relationships (Chapter 8) we also touch upon having the courage to step out of our own comfort zone to meet strangers and/or others who may not be like ourselves. So, we're not repeating repeating ourselves ourselves, but again it's how these topics are awesomely intertwined with one another.

While we'll be focusing on each of these concepts as one part, they really make up the whole PRIDE success for you as an LGBTQ+ Leader.

## Howsthatnow? How Adults Learn

As noted earlier, as we keep that drone perspective in mind, let's fly up to take a bigger picture and talk about how adults (really humans overall) learn stuff. One of the best leadership skills—aside from what we share in this book—is the ability to self-diagnose how we're doing in any one area or competency. Part of your challenge in reading this book is to get out of your own space and get into that drone perspective. One of the analytical tools or strategies is to understand how adults learn.

Think about a blank page with four boxes: one at 12 on the clock, one at 3:00, one at 6:00, and one at 9:00. Now think about a skill you know inside and out. Let's say it's driving a car (assuming that you do indeed drive a car). As a toddler, you may have sat in the driver's seat and pretended to drive, sounded the horn, and turned the wheel or used a toy like ones for toddlers that you sit on your lap that looks like a dashboard. You had no idea how to drive and didn't know what you didn't know. That's the stage learning professionals would classify your skill of driving a car as *unconscious incompetence* ... you don't know how to do the skill (incompetence) and you really don't know what it takes to even begin to do it anyway (unconscious) (Curtiss & Warren, 1973). These words—*unconscious/incompetence*—would be written in the 12:00 box.

Flash forward a few years ... that toddler with the lap dashboard is now maybe nine or ten. We can assume they (you) had been in a car and maybe driven some sort of vehicle like a toy car or even a tractor; something with wheels, a motor, brakes, and a steering wheel. This child has a clue as to what it takes to drive a vehicle, but if I took that kid, plopped them into my car, and said (in true Californian speak), "Take the 101 to the 405, Segundo Boulevard, past Oxnard, through Ventura, and stop at this address, pick up a package for me, and then take Sepulveda to the 405 down to Ventura*" do you think they could do that? Very highly unlikely. (*LA friends: don't make fun of me as I'm sure none of those roads connect ... but you get the idea). So, while the child may understand what it generally takes to drive a car successfully, they really can't perform that skill. Our psychologist friends would classify the skill of driving a car for this ten-year-old as *conscious/incompetence*, they're aware of what it takes to drive but still can't do it. We'd write this in our 3:00 box.

Time marches on for the kid, and they're maybe sixteen, seventeen, or eighteen. They are now a newly minted driver, they have taken their first driving lessons, they're very aware of the pedals, the gear lever, indicators, brake, clutch, accelerator, watching out for the other traffic, and all having to go in the right order (all while texting! Just kidding). They may bunny hop, stall, crunch the gears. Suddenly, they're keenly aware of what they don't know about driving a car. We'd classify their skill of driving as having *conscious/competence*, they can do it (drive) but really have to think about it. These are the words—*conscious/competence*—we'd write in our 6:00 box.

Now let's talk about you and your skill of driving a car (again assuming you do drive). It's Friday; you've had a wicked long work week. You make your way to your car, get in, fiddle with the radio, start the ignition, and all of the sudden you're in your driveway or garage and you ask yourself, "How the heck did I get here? I don't really remember driving home!" You have no real memory of actually driving to get home, nor did you really have to think about driving and adjusting the radio, or the temperature, or any other moves you did on the way home. This is where we'd say your skill of driving a car is in the unconscious/competence arena: you can do the task without thinking about it. It's automatic (no car pun intended). This would be in our 9:00 box.

Can you go from our 9:00 *unconscious/competence* to 12:00 *unconscious/incompetence*? Sure. Every time I get in a rental car, I'm back to our 12:00 box. Why? Because I don't sit around thinking what it's like to drive a Hyundai Sonata rental car; but when I get into one, the knobs and control items are in different spots than I'm used to with my car at home. But, by the time I leave the parking garage, I'm back to that *unconscious/competence* level of driving. Going through the Development Cycle (as this is known) doesn't have to take a lifetime, especially when we base the skills off of something we already know (existing schema, as our psychology friends call it).

Next, let's draw a diagonal line up the clock so that 12:00 and 9:00 are on one side of the diagonal line and 3:00 and 6:00 are on the other. Indulge me for a second: grab a piece of paper and a writing implement of your choice. Now, on said paper sign your name. How did that feel? You'd probably think of words like, *easy*, *automatic*, and/or *fast*. Your skill of signing your name is in that 9:00 part: it's part of who you are.

Please switch hands and sign your name with your nondominant hand on that same piece of paper. How did that feel? You're probably thinking things like it was *slow*, *awkward*, clumsy, and/or *I really had to think about it*. Exactly: this is the 3:00 and 6:00 spot, and it's what we in the human development world call the Learning Zone. When skills aren't automatic, it might be slow and awkward to do them; that just means you're working to improve until the skill is so ingrained in you that it moves beyond your diagonal line to the automatic area.

Now let's apply this idea to your leadership competence. As we go through our concepts in this book, I'll challenge you to get into that drone perspective and see—in relationship to the topic—where are you on our four-squared Development Cycle? Conscious/competence (you have to think about it)? Unconscious/competence, (oh, Steve, I got this! It's automatic!)? Starting here will help you begin to not only be self-reflective and aware of your own leadership behavior, but it will also let you start to see where you can focus your energy to make improvements in your LGBTQ+ leadership self.

# Drone Perspective: Reflective ?'s

*"To know thyself is the beginning of wisdom."*
– Socrates, Greek philosopher, inventor, smart dude,
and most likely engaged in some sort of M2M
activity in his day (469–399 B.C.E.)

As we go through our conversation, I'm going to encourage you to practice getting into that drone and reflecting on your leadership skills as it relates to the topic at hand. So, here's a start:

1) What do you want to get out of reading this book? What's one goal—as of right now—that you want to walk away with?

_____

_____

_____

_____

2) When it comes to your leadership skill overall, where would you classify that competence? Conscious/competence? Unconscious/competence? Why?

_____

_____

_____

_____

3) When you think about an awesome leader, who (living or deceased, famous or only famous to you) comes to mind? Write their name down below.

_____

_____

_____

_____

Now, *why* did you think of them? List five to ten adjectives (descriptor words) about what makes them an awesome leader in your world?

1. _____     6. _____

2. _____     7. _____

3. _____     8. _____

4. _____     9. _____

5. _____     10. _____

....................................................

# UNDERSTANDING
# THE "G" QUOTIENT

*"While there's little empirical research out there as to why LGBTQ+ people can be better leaders in the workplace, Kirk Snyder's work with gay executives is one of the best—and telling—data points to look at."*
— Dr. Steve Yacovelli
The Gay Leadership Dude

P̲roactive Communication • R̲elationship-Building • I̲ntegrity, Authenticity, & Courage • D̲eveloping Culture • E̲mpathy

## Why the Pit Stop to Another Book's Ideas, Steve?

When I set out to write this book, like a nerd, I did some research as to what already existed in the "leadership and LGBTQ+" space.

Guess what I found? There is very little academic research out there that focuses on the effectiveness of LGBTQ+ folks from a leadership perspective, aside from one book: *The G Quotient* by Kirk Snyder (2006).

So, buckle up for a book review on Snyder's key findings and think about them in relationship to your own leadership style (and go buy Kirk's book ... it's really a good read).

## The G Quotient Book Summary

Let's start with a story. In 2006, veteran journalist and speaker Marc Gunther wrote an article for *Fortune* titled, "Queer Inc.: How Corporate America Fell in Love with Gays and Lesbians" (Gunther, 2006). In his article, he discussed the ways in which corporations from defense contractors like Raytheon to retail giants like Walmart were not just accepting gay and lesbian employees; they were recruiting, embracing, and supporting them with everything from healthcare benefits to company inclusion in the National Gay and Lesbian Chamber of Commerce (NGLCC). As Gunther explained, in a heartening turnaround from the days when being gay meant concealing the bulk of one's life from co-workers and bosses, in many ways, "homosexuality, once a career-killing secret, has become enough of a competitive advantage in some circles that certification is needed to deter straight people from passing as gay." (Steve's side note: How that certification occurs I'm not so sure ... but I digress).

Why the change in corporate attitudes? One reason is simply a matter of numbers; with growth and the retirement of older staff, companies have an overwhelming need for new employees to fill the ranks, which makes discrimination of any kind wickedly counterproductive. Companies have also seen what to them is a terrifying trend. Starting over a decade ago and continuing today, polls revealed that employee engagement, job satisfaction, and morale are on a steep decline, while turnover is rapidly increasing, even as recruiting new talent is becoming more and more difficult (Snyder, 2006).

The other force behind this change is the realization that outstanding (not merely competent) leadership can make a seismic difference in workforce morale, retention, and productivity. And, as he discusses in his book, over the course of his five-year study, Snyder (2006) finds that the seven principles to which the white-collar gay males he interviewed adhere in their leadership roles—*inclusion, creativity, adaptability, connectivity, communication, intuition,* and *collaboration*—are what makes the difference between relatively capable leaders and those who are outstanding and who can make a real difference (BTW, we'll address Snyder's skewed sample of gay white-collar dudes in a bit). Those principles comprise what Snyder calls G Quotient Leadership, and importantly, in contrast to straight individuals, are developed as gay men make their way through lives that may and, most probably do, include obstacles to their success. According to Snyder, it's the lessons learned via that process that "contributed to the leadership belief system of gay executives that is being successfully applied in workplaces," everywhere (Snyder, 2006, p. xxi).

The need for the rest of us to understand those principles is the *why* of Snyder's book. How does this tie into our *Pride Leadership* book right now? As noted before, the six leadership competencies that we'll focus on in this book are based on two things:

1. What I've seen in the workplace jungle with my clients on what really drives leadership success, and
2. What I believe are the key traits that we LGBTQ+ Leaders process naturally.

Snyder's research—currently the only of its kind out there—awesomely supports that these six leadership competencies are "the ones" for us to focus on. At the end of each chapter where we focus on one of our six aspects of Pride Leadership, I'll point out how the competency has a link (or links) with Snyder's G Quotient. So, before we get into our Pride Leadership stuff, it's important to review Snyder's seven principles that make up his G Quotient. I do highly recommend taking a look at his overall book, as it's a really interesting read.

## G Quotient Principle 1: Inclusion

In the course of his research, Snyder (2006) surveyed executives from Fortune 500 companies, the government, academia, and small businesses about the elements they considered to be fundamental to their success. *Inclusion* was mentioned as the "overarching principle that guides gay executives in inspiring employees to become fully engaged in their work and committed to excellence as *equal participants* in the organization" (Snyder, 2006, p. 3). The emphasis was placed by Snyder and it should be kept in mind that, in this context, the focus of inclusion is on sameness, i.e., every employee receiving an equal degree of support to allow them to succeed.

As Mitchell Gold and Bob Williams, co-founders of The Mitchell Gold Company told Snyder when discussing their motivation to create their organization, "in a practical sense, it's actually one of the benefits of being gay; you learn to respect the fact that all human beings are important" (Snyder, 2006, p. 5). The issue of inclusion and its importance was cited again and again in Snyder's study. When other participants were asked how frequently they found that "diverse populations result in diverse talents and skills, all of which are important for the success of my organization or business," the response of 68.1% of gay male executives was "always" (Snyder, 2006, p. 179). Plus, 75% didn't "believe that my organization or business can reach full potential without the input and participation of all employees" (Snyder, 2006, p. 174).

## G Quotient Principle 2: Creativity

The second principle in Snyder's G Quotient is *creativity*. You might think that creativity is confined to a limited number of lucky people and is something expressed in art, music, theater, or such. However, Snyder takes a different view, particularly in terms of organizations. He says that creativity is "leadership that facilitates an environment designed to engage and extract imagination" (Snyder, 2006, p. 21). It's not enough to just foster creative thought; those ideas must lead to an innovative process, product, etc. that would allow for the realization of creativity. And, taking it one (or several) steps forward, organizations must be able to combine both creativity and innovation to achieve profitability.

In his book, Snyder says that much of this can take place during brainstorming sessions, which are an integral part of employee/executive interaction. Forty-seven percent of gay executives surveyed responded "always" when asked if their contacts with others facilitated their success and that of their organizations, while 88% reported that they always believed in the importance of recognizing and making use of their employees' talents, including their creativity (Snyder, 2006, p. 176).

Snyder says that if an organization is to continually move ahead, it requires the creativity found in G Quotient environments. He breaks this down into three coexisting yet different components:

1. Concepts, original ideas that are the product of imagination that will develop or improve upon products, services, and processes;

2. Possibilities, what can be imagined as the potential of the way in which those ideas can form the foundation for future success; and

3. People, who serve as the source for the implementation of those concepts and possibilities.

An understanding of these elements, as well as their relationship to each other, is crucial for achieving the goals of an organization.

Snyder asks, "What role must leadership assume in [fostering creativity]?" It's their facilitation of team member creativity that provides those whom they supervise with "the encouragement, freedom, and guidance to look at ideas in fresh, new ways" (Snyder, 2006, p. 23). Ralph Hexter, former president of Hampshire College in Amherst, Massachusetts, and one of the earliest non-closeted gay presidents in higher education, said that giving people permission to envision the ways their own abilities will make a positive difference will make their commitment to the work required reach new heights. That is certainly one of the hallmarks of an environment in which the G Quotient is in full effect.

## G Quotient Principle 3: Adaptability

Snyder's third principle was about being able to adapt. In a world that works the way it's meant to, what would result from the creativity and innovation identified in Principle 2? That would be change, which, of course, requires a sometimes-large degree of adaptability. According to Snyder, *adaptability* is representative of "the willingness and capacity of executives to make organizational modifications deemed necessary as a result of change" (Snyder, 2006, p. 35). Looking at the negative end of the spectrum, fewer than 10% of gay executives who were asked if their organizations always spent too much time adapting to nonessential changes answered with a solid "yup" (just over 35% responded, "never"). In contrast, at 67.2%, they showed strong support for the statement that they enjoyed "keeping my organization or business on the move and adapting to the times" (Snyder, 2006, p. 178).

That's pretty indicative of environments in which the G Quotient is clearly in evidence—to where both managers and team members take adaptability as one of their behavioral goals. This limits the kind of groupthink that so badly hamstrings many organizations, even as it augments employee engagement as well as their dedication to the highest level of product, service, or educational quality.

In his book, Snyder adds that, at this point, you may be wondering what being adaptable has to do with being a gay executive. David White, a senior manager at Deloitte Consulting in Los Angeles, was asked his thoughts on this very question, specifically, if being gay impacted his success as a representative of change. Looking back at his childhood and adolescence, he replied that, "When you're growing up and figuring out who you are, you learn to adapt to society because you think that you're the one who needs to change." But, over time, the realization came that "living a truthful life shouldn't require you to change, and you begin to adapt to the reality that some people … are going to have a problem with that decision" (Snyder, 2006, p. 41). That, according to White, causes gay people to become comfortable with ambiguity and learn to turn a lack of clear answers into an advantage, staying in the moment, maintaining a fresh perspective and the agility to move in any direction that suits the situation.

Snyder says that this doesn't mean people must question everything; instead, in a G Quotient setting, challenging the status quo means finding, choosing, and operationalizing changes that will provide organizations with the most substantial rewards, all of which requires adaptability. There are two elements to being adaptable: (1) there is an aspect that is cognitive; executives must understand employees' mindset when it comes to changes in the workplace and how adaptability will actually help them in their work and (2) it's experiential, which has to do with how they incorporate change into the actual performance of their jobs.

## G Quotient Principle 4: Connectivity

The location of Principle 4—connectivity—has in the G Quotient paradigm is significant in that, in order to be successful, changes inspired and operationalized through the use of adaptability frequently demand bringing novel perspectives and tools to the workplace. This requires an ongoing connection to movements within other companies and the industry of which the organization is a part. And this is equally true for individuals, as was pointed out by James Stofan, executive director of the University of California, who has always "… encouraged my employees … to connect with business and corporate partners and appreciate the opportunities these relationships can bring" (Snyder, 2006, p. 54). For gay executives who utilize the elements of the G Quotient, this is hardly news. When asked if their contacts with those in leadership roles facilitated their own success, just over 39% answered "frequently" while 47% said that was "always the case" (Snyder, 2006, p. 176). And these connections are neither temporary nor simply business/career-related. Being *out*, i.e., allowing the world to see the real and authentic person that you are, can lead to relationships that are built on trust and respect, rather than a façade based on the person others think you are.

Snyder observes that connectivity takes two forms. The first is *external networking*, in which employees, encouraged by the increased autonomy found in a G Quotient environment, connect with external information, individuals, and resources that provide knowledge they didn't have, thus augmenting their ability to start change.

The second is *internal awareness*, defined in Snyder's book as, "an ability to connect various types of realities within the organization so as to maximize effectiveness" (Snyder, 2006, p. 48–49). That, of course, requires that leaders and others also connect with what may exist in terms of their own professional weaknesses. As pointed out by one of the gay executives Snyder interviewed, those who fail to recognize and bolster those shortfalls, "and run their organizations as stand-alone hierarchies will soon be standing alone—in the unemployment line" (Snyder, 2006, p. 48). And it should be noted that, over the course of LGBTQ+ history, the formation of networks and communities has been fundamental to survival, providing at least one space in which LGBTQ+ people could fully emerge from the closet and be their authentic selves.

Needless to say, connectivity allows for the spread of knowledge, knowledge that Snyder characterizes as being tribal in nature. In this context, he defines *tribal knowledge* as the "collective, shared intelligence available to everyone in the organization or working unit" (Snyder, 2006, p. 56). Knowledge that is shared maintains the purposeful, efficient movement of everyone involved, importantly, in the same direction. Communication is key here, which leads Snyder to his fifth principle.

# G Quotient Principle 5: Communication

Why would gay executives tend to excel in the area of communication? Imagine, if you will, throwing a light on your most closely guarded secret, one that you may have held close since early adolescence, in the company of family, friends, or your employer. When, much to your surprise and relief, the sun does not fail to rise the next morning, you may very well realize that open, fully truthful communication is something that you can and should adhere to for the rest of your life. That's the reason communication—in all of its forms—is foundational to the other elements of the G Quotient; one must be able to communicate to include others in the conversation, to express creativity, to make others aware of the need and means of adapting to change, and to remain connected.

Snyder says that authentic and truthful communication is related to defining standards of ethical conduct, representing "an open system of verbal and nonverbal interaction between managers and employees committed to [those] same defining standards" (Snyder, 2006, p. 59). This brings the discussion back to the issue of self-identity and the need to communicate with employees from a platform of credibility that is not only real, but that expresses who one truly is as a person. Snyder adds that's very difficult for closeted individuals and much easier for those who are out.

In G Quotient environments, this works to create a trustful, cohesive culture characterized by organizational candor; Snyder calls this "approaching leadership in one's own skin" (Snyder, 2006, p. 60). Deviating from his previous focus on organizations and academia, Snyder discussed the idea of communication with Jarrett Barrios, a then-democratic Senator from Massachusetts. Barrios had more than one barrier to overcome; for him, "going into politics was breaking all the rules, because I was gay *and* Latino" (Snyder, 2006, p. 61). When discussing communication from his perspective, Barrios pointed out that authenticity when communicating served to increase respect, making candor an element of the ability to persuade so essential to be a successful politician.

Snyder notes that communication is more than just speaking; he says if that's all you're doing, you might as well just talk to yourself. Active listening is the other part of the equation and one in which gay executives consistently engage. If they need to know what does or doesn't work within their organizations, they ask those who are doing the work. That may seem intuitive, but Snyder found that apparently it isn't the norm in many workplaces.

Indeed, manager/employee relationships in G Quotient environments were excellent, with active listening skills getting the credit. Positive organizational effects included strengthening the professional bonds between managers and employees, increases in the "truth factor" found within the environment, and the prevention of what Snyder calls the ivory tower syndrome because managers were in touch with the work processes in their organizations.

Snyder argues that *open* communication results in *direct* communication and far smoother problem-solving also affects the power structure of organizations, making it much more of a level playing field rather than the traditional and more frequently seen hierarchy. As noted by Chad Spitler, Principal of Barclays Global Investors, "there's just no room for hierarchical nonsense when your goal is to succeed as an organization" (Snyder, 2006, p. 70). Snyder found this attitude predominated in his research, with nearly 90% of employees surveyed believing they could disagree with their managers without fear of a pink slip (Snyder, 2006, p. 186).

All of this centers on the confines of the workplace; in this expanding and culturally diverse world, what about the global marketplace? In that marketplace, it was discovered that gay executives had an advantage due to their recognition of the important difference sensitivity and awareness of diverse cultural values—a global

consciousness—can make in their organizations' success. This also requires a degree of reading between the lines, i.e., intuition, the sixth principle of the G Quotient.

## G Quotient Principle 6: Intuition

As part of the G Quotient, Snyder writes that intuition centers on the collection of accurate information via one's indirect—as opposed to direct—senses, giving gay men, as well as other minorities, the ability to "pick up on subtle or unspoken communication cues in order to distinguish between friend and foe" (Snyder, 2006, p. 73). It is intuition that allows gay executives to combine traditional male strengths with what is historically thought of as feminine insight into individuals and situations to achieve success within and for their organizations. When asked if they found themselves able to spot a good deal, even while lacking all of the facts, 35.3% of participants answered "frequently" while 40.5% responded, "always" (Snyder, 2006, p. 180).

Often, *feelings* can be as insightful as facts. According to philosopher and educator John Dewey, feelings "give us our sense of rightness and wrongness, of what to select and emphasis and follow up … among the multitude of inchoate meanings that are presenting themselves" (Snyder, 2006, p. 74). Although intuition is subjective rather than objective in nature, those gay executives utilizing this aspect of the G Quotient in their decision-making processes have a distinct advantage.

Snyder writes that this is not to say intuition negates the need for factual knowledge. That information is used for what professor Fred Korthhagen of Utrecht University in Amsterdam refers to as *reflection*, defined as, "an important human activity in which people recapture their experience, think about it, mull it over, and evaluate it" (Snyder, 2006, p. 78). Korthhagen believes that reflection, along with intuition, are significant and complementary processes that, together, are associated with organizational learning. Unfortunately, some leaders find this concept to be problematic as "intuition is not a machine that can be depreciated on a tax form," and hence has no commercial value (Snyder, 2006, p. 78). In contrast, gay executives do see the worth of intuition and reflection, which together, can be thought of as behaviors based on knowledge that hence serve as a novel yet enduring form of currency in the Digital Age.

## G Quotient Principle 7: Collaboration

Collaboration may be the last principle mentioned in Snyder's book, but it's definitely not the least important. According to his research, Snyder notes that 75% of the gay executives surveyed believed collaboration, i.e., "the input and participation of all employees," to be the cornerstone of the organizational cultures they were striving to build ... a major contributor to their organizations' development and management (Snyder, 2006, p. 174). As such, a vibrant collaborative environment is dependent on "a new ethos of leadership," capitalizing on the full utilization and empowerment of their employees' potential; that, in turn, requires and incorporates all of the G Quotient's other elements—inclusion, creativity, adaptability, connectivity, communication, and intuition (Snyder, 2006, p. 85).

In this principle, Snyder observes that collaboration can impact what he calls the three organizational P's, starting with planning.

*Planning* initiates with the placement of the right resources and the applicable linkage of employees to those resources. This allows *proficiency*, because individuals' talents and skills are maximized by the already-mentioned resources, resulting in *profitability* for the organization.

This clearly indicates that authority must be shared. What's the bridge between being gay and checking one's ego for the betterment of an organization and its employees? When asked about this, Trevor Burgess, executive director at Morgan Stanley, was reminded of the cliché that men frequently refuse to ask for directions, preferring to bumble their way haphazardly to their destination. Burgess said that he, "didn't view asking for advice as being an affront to my masculinity, [but rather] as a strength" (Snyder, 2006, p. 88). He spoke against allowing ego to be a barrier to achieving a client's best outcome. In terms of maintaining a climate conducive to collaboration, Burgess said he believed that gay men judged people more fairly and according to their merits, thus allowing everyone the opportunity to participate in decision making.

## Snyder: Why G Quotient Leadership Works

As Snyder mentions earlier in his book and according to the *Gallup Management Journal*, in the early 2000s, when surveyed, 71% of employees reported being either disengaged or, even worse, actively disengaged from their work. Less than 50% of employees between the ages of 35 and 55 were dissatisfied with their jobs. Why does this matter? Gallup says that this employee disengagement costs the U.S. economy approximately $300 billion a year. That's a hella amount of money needlessly spent.

Plus, those numbers represent a great many career expectations needlessly dashed; it has become clear that a paycheck is no longer enough; working individuals want the perception that they are excelling professionally rather than just doing a job. That can "no longer be achieved without an authentic sense of both personal connection and meaning" in the workplace; employees must be empowered (Snyder, 2006, p. 102). And I—Steve—would agree that this notion still holds true in today's workplace jungle.

Another feature of what Snyder calls the "brand new neighborhood" is diversity, not only among staff but, even more importantly, for corporate bottom lines in the boardroom and in the multicultural markets. "Groupthink" is not profitable; when an environment is essentially homogenous, ideas are neither tested nor challenged. What would be the point if everyone thought the same based on nearly identical life experiences and beliefs? (Steve's side note: We'll focus on this a lot throughout our book).

And managing a diverse workplace requires inclusion and the placement of value on employees. That's certainly the case in G Quotient environments, where "*people* rather than products are what drives companies to become successful and stay successful" (Snyder, 2006, p. 106; and BTW, Snyder added that emphasis).

What about the inevitable mistakes? If, as is far too often the case, managers focus on what employees have done wrong, not only will those employees tend to conceal what's occurred until it has become irreparable, the option to analyze what led to the mistake and decide on a better way to do something, hence advancing the organization, is lost. As Leo Burnett, the man credited with everything from General Mills' Jolly Green Giant to the Pillsbury

Doughboy, said to avoid making mistakes, "… all you have to do is swear off having ideas" (Snyder, 2006, p. 115).

Job ownership "grants employees primary authority over their specific areas of responsibility" within their organizations (Snyder, 2006, p. 115). Failure to ensure that individuals feel their jobs are their own is one of the major reasons many leave those positions. As a woman Snyder interviewed pointed out, even if they stay, employees lacking autonomy come to feel more like robots than accomplished individuals. In fact, while in that position, she felt like a victim of creative and emotional abuse. Had she been working in a G Quotient environment, that feeling never would have occurred.

## Snyder: 10 Things Every Manager Needs to Know

Recognizing that the G Quotient is applicable to most, if not all, organizations while remaining unfamiliar to many managers and executives, Snyder concludes with a list of ten items that will help people understand and utilize the concepts in *The G Quotient*:

1. **G Quotient leadership is both objective and subjective.** … Although these qualities are directly at odds with one another, as Snyder explains, gay executives have achieved a completely integrated and therefore balanced management belief system. To do this using the seven G Quotient principles, they are "objective in their examination of relevant workplace data and subjective in their judgment of that data" (Snyder, 2006, p. 121).

2. **G Quotient leadership focuses on the processes of work rather than the final product.** ... Managers working within the organizational models prevalent during the Industrial Age (and, unfortunately, beyond) focused almost completely on the final product, leaving employees unempowered, as if they were secondary to that product. Groups with G Quotient leadership do just the opposite; their peeps believe themselves to be of primary value. Now, no one's going to confuse a day at the office with a day at the beach, but still, working in an environment where you feel valued must be far better than one in which you're just an interchangeable cog in the proverbial machine.

3. **G Quotient leadership models a systems approach to management.** ... There are actually two systems approaches—*closed*, in which work processes are not impacted by interaction with the workplace's environment, or *open*, in which that environment is significantly affected by interaction. There is a commonality to them; when an organization's leaders take either systems approach, that organization's aim is for everyone to work in harmony to complete a mission held in common by everyone.

G Quotient leaders function within an *open* system, continuously under the influence of their interaction with the workplace environment and making an ongoing assessment of the ways in which all of the moving parts, including employees, the greater organization, customers, and clients also interact with that environment.

4. **G Quotient leadership places value on experiential learning.** ... Scholars and researchers in the field of

experiential learning have provided lengthy explanations for what it is and how it works. Snyder simplifies all of that by saying, as many have before him, "people learn by doing," which entails transforming knowledge into skill via action (Snyder, 2006, p. 125). That requires strong employee engagement, an evaluation process that emphasizes open communication, and buy-in from all of the members of an organization who are involved.

5. **G Quotient leadership focuses on the present.** ... This doesn't mean that the past is ignored. Although, as noted before, the leadership qualities of gay executives were greatly affected by events and people from their past, their commitment is on the present as a way to prepare themselves and their organizations for the future. After analyzing the career health of those who participated in Snyder's research, it became clear that the ability to move on prevents entrapment in the what might have been mentality that can stifle innovation and slow success.

6. **G Quotient leaders are still in the trenches.** ... Snyder very neatly summarized this in the first sentence of this section of his book: "the message that's heard when leaders stand side by side with their employees is one of *equality*" (Snyder, 2006, p. 129; and again, Snyder added the emphasis on that one). Leadership aimed at motivating employees places its focus on remaining part of a team and it's that motivation that causes the organization to excel at meeting its goals.

7. **G Quotient leaders manage inspiration.** ... You may believe that inspiration must arise naturally and that

there's no way to force the emergence of ideas. However, gay executives believe inspiration to be a commodity that can be managed. One way in which they do this is to promote negativity-free environments in which managers seek out the talents of their employees with an eye toward making those talents into actual career strengths. In contrast, managers who highlight what's wrong rather than what's right about their employees lose sources of the inspiration, creativity, and innovation that could have greatly benefited their organizations.

8. **G Quotient leaders focus on positive employee characteristics.** ... This can almost be seen as a Part B to number seven above. In his discussion, Snyder references the emerging school of positive psychology, "devoted to the study of understanding and building on strengths and assets so as to facilitate happiness and success" (Snyder, 2006, p. 133). In terms of G Quotient leaders, those strengths can be seen in creativity, open-mindedness, authenticity, and fairness, both as personal characteristics and as traits they encourage in those they supervise. Rather than criticizing and focusing on employee inadequacies, G Quotient leaders emphasize positive attributes; in response, people will willingly and enthusiastically go the extra mile for those executives and for the organization for which they all work.

9. **G Quotient leaders run their organizations like entrepreneurs.** ... Small businesses can be agile, with that agility allowing them to skillfully maneuver through their industries and the marketplace to attain success. This is no small task in large organizations with a multilevel

decision-making process, which is the reason that gay executives run their organizations more according to the pattern of small businesses. That makes for an environment in which new ideas can be implemented more quickly and gut instincts (discussed at length in Principle #6: Intuition) are utilized as keys to success.

Snyder also found that the creation of an environment centered on the philosophy and spirit seen in effective entrepreneurship "eliminated the need ... to carry the entire weight of the working unit on their own shoulders," because, frequently, among entrepreneurs, everyone is part of the team (Snyder, 2006, p. 135).

10. **G Quotient leaders understand and value themselves.** ... Maintaining an image as someone other than their true selves is a task that openly gay executives have left far in their pasts. In fact, when seeking an executive position, the participants in Kirk Snyder's research looked for environments that would allow them to be themselves. They have great confidence in their own both personal and professional value, which allows them to assume the mantle as organizational leaders.

And, because they are seen as being honest about themselves, they inspire trust in their employees, allowing them to build and sustain an engaged and motivated workforce, a group that is eager to follow them on the road to organizational success. This of course doesn't mean that managers whose lives have followed a different course are less likely to inspire their employees ... all they have to remember is to be themselves, whoever and whatever that might be.

# Steve's Input: Some Challenges with Snyder's Work

To start with: I want to be clear that I'm a fan of the work Snyder did in *The G Quotient*. As a self-described nerdy academic, I appreciate the attempts to measure and quantify what makes an LGBTQ+ person a great Leader. Again, BRAVO, Kirk!

Without going into a lot of detail, I do want to share Snyder's approach to his research process and subjects:

- It was a five-year project (starting in 2000), gathering data from over 3,000 professionals in a variety of organizations in various countries around the world
- The defining of the specific G Quotient principles were influenced by the response of about 775 recruiters and hiring managers (2003–2004)
- The qualitative data collected was from over 1,000 employees reporting to gay executives (2004–2005)
- The ranking survey part of the research was sent to 220 managers (straight women, straight men, lesbians, and gay men who all self-identified) (2005)

But I think there are a few flaws and gaps in this analysis that, if addressed, would make it a bit more representative of the LGBTQ+ leadership Community. My first issue is the sample size of those who took Snyder's final G Quotient Assessment. Two-hundred-twenty folks is a small group to represent the leadership trends for all straight men, straight women, lesbians, and gay men. While it provides some insight into the comparison of these four populations, it's not really representative of the overall population.

Second, it's unclear if and how the final 220 participants completing the G Quotient Assessment shared their demographic information. If—as it's assumed—they only had four choices: (1) straight woman, (2) straight man, (3) lesbian, and (4) gay man, then we're not exactly being very inclusive of all our LGBTQ+ Community, and definitely cannot say how these data apply or represent other facets of the LGBTQ+ Community outside of gay men and lesbians.

Third, a bulk of these data comes from the 1,000-ish employees of gay executives (white collar). I think this data set is a bit limiting, and therefore only provides deeper insight into gay, white-collar executives and not a broader swath of the LGBTQ+ Community as well as how that compares to non-LGBTQ+ leaders.

And finally, I wonder—given the quickly changing makeup of our workplace and the demographics of the current workforce—if the date of this work (starting eighteen years ago) does give it a limited shelf life.

BUT ... as I shared before, this is a good starting point; and frankly, it's really our own starting point. Again, these data I'm sharing are more empirical via observational data in nature, but what I'm seeing in the field today does indeed dovetail with some of the initial findings Snyder has in his work in the early 2000s.

## Being Clear: Straight Leaders are Great, Too!

Before we leave this section I (Steve) want to be absolutely crystal clear on something:

*Straight people can be good leaders, too!*

Snyder's book wasn't saying that gay folks (FYI, using *gay* to represent LGBTQ+ people) are the quintessential leaders and that every business needs to fire all their straight executives and fill in the roles with some LGBTQ+ rock stars. No, not at all. What he is saying—and I'm echoing this here in my book—is that there are certain traits and experiences in our (LGBTQ+) shared experience that contribute to leadership success.

It's not to say that non-LGBTQ+ folks don't have those same traits, but the argument is that our LGBTQ+ people—overall—are more likely to have those leadership success traits more often. So, don't go and tell your straight friends that they stink at leadership; on the contrary, I've had amazing leaders in my world who "chose" to be straight (you know, because it's a choice!).

Yes, the concepts that are presented in this book are indeed extremely applicable to any non-LGBTQ+ Leader to use and apply to their own leadership context. However, I want to speak just to you, my awesome LGBTQ+ Leader, about YOUR leadership greatness.

# Drone Perspective: Reflective ?'s

1) When you reflect on the work we shared by Snyder, what jumps out at you first?

_____

_____

_____

_____

2) Do you agree with his conclusions, based upon the research as well as what we shared in our overview?

_____

_____

_____

_____

3) What are some similar or other Principles you would list as traits LGBTQ+ Leaders tend to have from your own experience or observations?

_____

_____

_____

_____

4) Snyder's book was published in 2006, almost fifteen years ago. Do you think—if we redid his research—we'd have similar or different results? Why or why not?

_____

_____

_____

_____

5) What would you say to your straight colleagues about LGBTQ+ Leaders having potentially stronger leadership skills—as outlined in *The G Quotient* and in this book?

_____

_____

_____

_____

# JUNGLE LOVE:
# PRIDE LEADERSHIP IN ACTION

"I've worked at a hospital in Philadelphia for over ten years. I have always felt comfortable with who I am, and I've never had to come out.

Interestingly enough though, when I started at [the hospital], I absolutely had to defend my diverse background in the arts as an asset to my ability to be in a highly technical position (software developer and aspiring scientist). There is significant value to diversity at the institution across the board that you eventually come to the conclusion as a leader that diversity matters to the mission of the hospital: research, family-centered care, education, advocacy all with the mission to help sick kids and prevent kids from getting sick. Sometimes you have to put your ego aside for this mission, so I don't much think about who *I* am in this case unless I really dig.

What I realize is that I am surrounded by other LGBTQ scientists, physicians, research staff, nurses, programmers, etc. I am more importantly surrounded by people with different backgrounds that contribute to creativity and different ways of looking at seriously complex problems. This is the success in leadership at [the hospital]. The dedication to representation of the diversity in staff that reflects the diversity of the city.

With this unrelenting commitment to diversity, having an arts background and a technically focused professional now makes much more sense. My whole team, in fact, are from all walks of life, multiple countries, and some are artists, engineers, and even singers, but the mission and their talent is what matters. We are better positioned to make breakthroughs for kids with a more diverse staff."

*– Dr. Alex F., Supervisor*
*Hospital in Philadelphia, PA, U.S.A.*

········································

# BEING CONSCIOUSLY INCLUSIVE

*"In all the leadership workshops, conversations, and
'best practice' chats I've had over the past twenty-plus
years, the common thread throughout them all is to
be inclusive and be respectful to others. And, if I really
think about it, my parents taught that to me when I was
a kid. If you start your leadership perspective with an
open mind and try to be inclusive and understanding
of others around you, you'll never fail."*
– Dr. Steve Yacovelli
The Gay Leadership Dude

Proactive Communication • Relationship-Building • Integrity,
Authenticity, & Courage • Developing Culture • Empathy

B EFORE WE GET into our six leadership areas of focus, one
of the threads moving through this book—and your leadership success—is the concept of being inclusive.

What do we mean by *inclusive*? I'll start with a brief story. When I first started working in the diversity and inclusion space (I was working for an employer who, let's just say, the "big cheese" is a rodent), a colleague/now-BFF of mine shared with me the difference between "diversity" and "inclusion:"

> Diversity is being *invited* to the dance,
> and inclusion is being *asked* to dance.

That phrasing has stuck with me for decades: it's not enough to just open the doors, but it's a far different thing to actively seek the expression, opinion, or perspective of others around you who aren't the same. That's powerful stuff, and you're actually seeing the diversity part of the phrase "diversity and inclusion" dropping off of departments and titles in the workplace jungle, as people realize that what you want is for all folks to be at the table sharing, not just in the room.

Apply this to you as an LGBTQ+ Leader: being inclusive is powerful stuff. Not only does it bring about differencing perspectives (typically leading to innovation), but it broadens everyone on your team's perspective (since they're all coming from different backgrounds, experiences, etc.). Smart companies have long understood the power of nonhomogeneous teams: they look at things a lot differently than the same cookie-cutter workforce who—because of their shared experiences and perspective—only see things from one facet or perspective.

Now, before I go any further, some of you may be thinking, "Whoa there, Steve-a-rino, this is just that unconscious bias stuff I've been seeing a lot out there." And yes, that's the place—among others—this chapter plays with. However, I've found that, when referring to unconscious bias, some people think that managing and mitigating our unconscious biases is futile. They think, "Well, if they're unconscious, I can't do anything about them!" And frankly, that's not true, as you will discover later in this chapter. So, I like to use the term *consciously inclusive* because—as a leader—you DO indeed have action you can take to not let your unconscious or hidden biases impact your leadership behavior (and thus derail or stop your leadership success). So, with that in mind, let's move on and explore how you can be a more inclusive leader.

## Tell Me an Inclusive Story, Steve!

*Once Upon a Time* ... (I had to use that, see comment above re: formerly worked for a rodent-led Fortune 100), once upon a time I was teaching one of my leadership programs and we were having the chat about inclusiveness and diverse teams. One of the participants— a senior sales executive—shared that they needed to hire a new field sales person. They received a lot of resumés; many of them from existing sales folks at the competition, but one of the resumés was from a yoga instructor. This sales executive was intrigued.

As they looked at the yogi's CV it was pretty spot-on with the education: undergraduate in chemistry (this was a pharma sales role), a lot of extracurricular activities and many leadership roles, and some sales experience but not the field-sales that the sales executive had been seeing on other resumés (BTW, "CV" means curriculum vitae, what some in the academic circles as well as outside the U.S. call a resumé *#themoreyouknow*). So, they interviewed the top two candidates from the "standard" background of field sales, but also brought in the yoga instructor, as this executive just couldn't shake the feeling that this candidate was so unique.

So, who do you think our sale executive hired? Of course: the yoga instructor with the chemistry background. Her approach and unique perspective made her an ideal (and very successful) sales person. She has continued to be one of the top sales folks in her region.

Why the yoga-pharma-sales-expert story? Because our sale executive was exercising what we call being consciously inclusive in their decision to hire a new sale person; and wasn't biased against hiring the typical sales profile.

## OK, So What's Consciously Inclusive?

Being *consciously inclusive* is when you make a conscious (deliberate) effort to seek out ideas, perspectives, and experience that differ from the majority and/or your own. A consciously inclusive leader—like our sales executive above—strives to ensure the greater team isn't looking at things from the same perspective or are all, say, graduates from the same B school. Being consciously inclusive is making sure you ask everyone to dance.

Think of your Facebook feed: how many of your friends post items that support your perspective? Have you reached out to find divergent or contrary ways to look at the world beyond your own? Did the recent political divide in the U.S. cause you to "unfriend" or just "unfollow" people whose perspective wasn't like yours? Then guess what? You're actually being consciously *exclusive*. And that's not what effective leaders do.

# Defining D&I

We've played with the concept of inclusion, but now I want to take an itty-bitty step back and define the first word in that phrase: diversity.

> In its simplest terms, *diversity* means the many similarities and differences between people.

In any group, we have some things in common. And, we have characteristics, experiences, and ways of thinking that are unique to each of us. We said diversity is the similarities and differences that people have. That's a lot to process, since we're unique and complex beings. One strategy that has been created to organize the various parts of our diversity—what makes each one of us unique human beings—is a framework created by Lee Gardenswartz and Anita Rowe, called The 5 Layers of Diversity (Gardenswartz & Rowe, 2010).

The concept here is that we are made up of so many facets of diversity, but they fall into—from Gardenswartz and Rowe's perspective—one of five internal or external "layers," the first two are internal and the others are related to external factors that make us unique. Let's play.

So, picture five circles, one in the center and getting bigger and bigger just like a bullseye (with no disrespect meant to my male bovine friends). The first, an internal layer, is **PERSONALITY**, or what fundamentally makes you, well, you. This is located in the dead center of our bull..., errr, target (*#beinginclusive*).

This includes an individual's likes and dislikes, values, and beliefs. Personality is shaped early in life and is both influenced by, and influences, the other layers throughout one's lifetime and career choices. Personality is unique for every single human since the beginning of time; no two people can be exactly the same. Even identical twins have unique personalities. And our personality is, at its core, what makes each human a beautiful shiny snowflake of uniqueness that will never be replicated … ever.

The second layer out from the center of our target is **INTERNAL DIMENSIONS**. This area includes aspects of diversity over which we have no control, things like our *race, ethnicity, gender, gender identity, sexual orientation, age* (as much as we wish we could change that), and *physical ability* (although physical ability can change over time due to choices we make to be active or not, or in cases of illness or accidents, or just getting older).

This dimension is the layer that many people immediately think of when speaking about diversity, and from which many divisions between and among people exist and that forms the core of many diversity efforts. These dimensions include the first things we see in other people, such as race or gender, and on which we make many assumptions and base judgments.

It's also where many organizations typically start with their diversity efforts. "We're an awesome company! We have _____ Month!" is what you often hear from organizations as an effort to show how wonderfully inclusive they are. While this is a good start, it's a very limited way to define diversity in the workplace.

The next layer out is what Gardenswartz and Rowe call our **EXTERNAL DIMENSIONS**. These include aspects of our lives that we have some control over, which might change over time (maybe even change daily, as with our appearance), and that usually form the basis for decisions on careers and work styles. They include things like *geographic location, income, personal habits, religion, our physical appearance, recreational habits, educational background, work experience, parental status*, and *marital status*.

This layer often determines, in part, with whom we develop friendships and what we do for work. This layer also tells us much about whom we like to be with and decisions we make in hiring, promotions, etc., at work.

The fourth layer—**ORGANIZATIONAL DIMENSIONS**—looks at our diversity through the lens of the organization with which we are a part. This layer concerns the aspects of culture found in a work setting, or really any group or organization we belong to. These are things like *functional level, work content field, division/department, seniority, work location, union affiliation, legacy organization* (like, where did you work before our current company bought you?), and *management status*. So, for example, my perspective is shaped if I'm in, say, the Marketing Department, versus my experience on the front line.

The final layer or the fifth layer (or the outer-most layer) is **COUNTRY OF OPERATION**; these dimensions include the *economy, values, business etiquette, social structure, laws, languages,* and *political system* of, well, the country with which you're operating (see what I did there?). They all give insight to each individual and the importance country culture plays in how we as unique individuals see the world, and how the world sees us.

Since political and economic systems, national values, social structure, laws, and languages (for example) guide interactions between people, this layer is essential to create our "culture," or our preferred way of doing things. This is why we may get some surprises when—I'll say this as "we" (but forgive me if you're not from the U.S.)—we Americans travel outside the U.S. and find that our "normal" way of doing things is not the same elsewhere (shocker!).

So, to summarize, there's a lot to think about here regarding our definition of diversity, which is why diversity is so complex and not limited to those Internal Dimensions (*race, ethnicity, gender, gender identity, sexual orientation, age, physical ability*). And this complexity can lead us to some potential derailers that get in our way as we talk about diversity in the workplace, and we are all likely to do these as we try to create inclusion.

## So, What's Unconscious Biases?

Just in case you aren't falling asleep just yet, I'm going to lay on some statistical goodness: studies show that résumés with "white" sounding names (like "Greg") were about 50% more likely to get a callback for an interview by potential employers than a more stereotypically African-American sounding names (like "Jamal"), even when the résumés were identical aside from the name (Gerdeman, 2017). In another study, brunette and redhead women's salaries are approximately 7% less than their blonde counterparts (Johnston, 2010). And a third study found that almost 60% of corporate CEOs are over six feet tall; a large disproportion compared to the fact that less than 15% of American men are over this height (Gladwell, 2005). In a popular political television show, one character says, "Washington, Jefferson, Lincoln. Tall men make great presidents" (Somvanshi, 2016).

What do these three facts have in common? They are about unconscious bias, and actions taken because of those unconscious or hidden biases. Which, of course, prevents us from creating a consciously inclusive culture.

First, let's talk about *bias*. What is it? By definition, bias is the predisposition or tendency to see someone or something in a positive or negative light or having favoritism for someone because of who they are. Biases come in two types: those that we are quite aware of (overt or conscious) and those we're not quite aware of (implicit or unconscious). Your conscious biases can get you into a bit of leadership trouble, but I want to focus our energy on the unconscious kind of bias.

*Unconscious bias* is the bias we aren't even aware we have; it's working in the back of our brains. You might also hear the terms *implicit* or *hidden* bias. I know personally I tend to use the hidden phrasing more (my own personal hidden or overt bias for that specific phrase perhaps?). In any case, when you hear these terms used, it's all the same: talking about our attitudes or stereotypes that impact our understanding, actions, and decisions in an unconscious manner.

Quick story: Imagine you're in the middle seat of one of those low-cost airline carriers where you don't get an assigned seat. You're the first to sit down in your row. People start to filter in and there's that little voice that starts to categorize people into "sit next to me!" or "please keep going!" This is your unconscious bias voice making itself known.

Here's another example. Please read the paragraph below carefully:

At any moment in time, your conscious and unconscious minds are working together to sort through all the data your senses are sending them. It's rather incredible how our mind works to be so effcient and effective in managing so much information at such great speeds.

If you missed the spelling error in the last sentence (go ahead and check ... I'll wait!), it is because your unconscious or hidden brain rapidly approximated the correct meaning of *efficient* and moved on to the next word (and with kudos to the great Shankar Vedantam, author of the book, *The Hidden Brain: How Our Unconscious Minds Elect Presidents, Control Markets, Wage Wars, and Save Our Lives* (2010), for giving me the idea for this example).

## Where Do These Unconscious Biases Come From?

Question: when I shared the story about the sales executive looking for a new sales person and they hired the yogi, think about the image of the sales executive that popped into your head while reading that story.

What was their gender? (Did you notice I didn't write any gender pronouns, I used *they* versus *he* or *she*). What was their race? (I didn't identify race anywhere in that story.) So why do you think you saw that executive in your mind's eye as a certain gender and race? Chances are—and I'm making a broad assumption here, but it's based on our Western society—the gender was male and he was white. Why? Because, sadly, we tend to have an unconscious bias that all executives are white dudes. Of course, that's not the reality, but that's the unconscious bias that prevails today. And chances are you, too, painted that same mental picture of the executive white dude in your head.

Unconscious, implicit, or hidden biases have some common characteristics:

- **Implicit biases are pervasive** … Everyone possesses them, even people with avowed commitments to impartiality, such as judges. If you are breathing, you have bias.
- **Implicit and explicit biases are related but distinct mental constructs** … They are not mutually exclusive and may even reinforce each other.
- **The implicit associations we hold do not necessarily align with our declared beliefs** … Or even reflect stances we would explicitly endorse.
- **We generally tend to hold implicit biases that favor our own ingroup** … Though research has shown that we can still hold implicit biases against our ingroup. An ingroup is the group of people you're part of. So—I'll assume, dear reader—one of your ingroups is the LGBTQ+ Community.
- **Implicit biases are malleable** … Our brains are incredibly complex, and the implicit associations that we have formed can be gradually unlearned through a variety of debiasing techniques.

I especially like the last one: that we can indeed unlearn bad or harmful biases we may have, so we don't pull in that all executives are white dudes mentality. We'll talk about that in a bit.

Another quick story: when I first started thinking about unconscious bias many years ago, I initially thought, "Nice, but

I've no biases! I teach diversity and inclusion!" Flash forward: if you've ever seen the musical *Avenue Q* (winner of the 2004 Tony for Best Broadway Musical, FYI), you might be familiar with the song "Everyone's a Little Bit Racist." In this song, several of the characters sing (joyously!) about how they're racist. They sing not about overt or explicit racism but more subversive, unconscious bias that we humans all have. It was that moment when I first heard that song that the concept of hidden or unconscious bias hit my, well, consciousness. I was a little bit racist, or something-ist; but what? I'll tell you how I started to find out my own unconscious biases in a bit, and how you can find yours out, too.

Back on track: where do these unconscious biases come from? They come from our cave-ancestors. Think back to our cave-ancestors for a moment. A big, wooly, saber-toothed thing walks through the front of their cave door. They didn't sit there and think, "Gee, that thing has big teeth, but maybe he's an herbivore …" No, they looked at the beast and did one of two things instinctively: they put up their fisticuffs and went into FIGHT mode, or the blood and oxygen automatically went to their feet and they high-tailed it out the back cave door in FLIGHT mode. Much of this decision-making is automatic and unconscious. Our brains determine whether or not something or someone is safe before we can even begin to consciously make a determination. When the object, animal, or person is assessed to be dangerous, a fight-or-flight response occurs in our amygdala—a part of the brain that processes alarm.

Again, a hidden—or implicit—bias is a preference for or against a person, thing, or group held at an unconscious level. This means we don't even know that our minds are holding onto this bias. In contrast, an overt—or explicit—bias is an attitude or prejudice that one endorses at a conscious level.

Research on unconscious bias reveals that, in spite of the best intentions, most people harbor deep-seated resistance to the "different," whether that difference is defined by such evident factors as race, gender, ethnicity, age, or physical characteristics, or more subtle ones such as background, personality type, or experiences. Bias can also exist in a positive sense. We may favor our family, our community, and people with whom we feel a connection based on shared characteristics or experiences.

These implicit biases are not deliberately or consciously created; they are products of our brain's self-generated definition of normal, acceptable, or positive, and they are shaped by many factors—from past experiences—to our local or cultural environment, to the influence of social community and media. We don't consciously create these definitions of normal or different, good or bad, acceptable or unacceptable. In fact, implicit and explicit biases often diverge; our hidden biases may exist in spite of our genuine desire to be bias-free and in direct contradiction of the attitudes we believe we have.

Flash forward to the 21$^{st}$ century. We're not in danger of saber-toothed thingies coming to our cave door, but we are still programed to react this way. And our understanding of unconscious bias has exploded in the past two decades. Over 1,000 studies in the past ten years alone have conclusively shown that **if you're human, you have bias**, and that it impacts almost every variation of human identity: race, gender, sexual orientation, body size, religion, accent, height, hand dominance, etc. Like our organ the appendix—which served a function in us humans at one point—unconscious bias was necessary for our very survival.

But now—while it still has its place—it can impact our behavior in ways we don't really want it to.

Biology lesson: the human body has about 100 billion neurons (think every nerve ending, every cone in your eyes, each piece of cilia in your ear, etc.) and they all send data to your brain. Neurologists estimate that we are exposed to as many as eleven million pieces of information at any one moment, and by moment we're not talking weeks, days, or minutes, but literally seconds. But our *conscious* brains can only functionally deal with about forty bits of data (Wilson, 2002). Consciously think about that for a second (OK, pun intended). So that gap that needs processing? That's where our unconscious brains kick in, analyzing the 99.999999996% [that's six 9s] of the data that hasn't been processed consciously.

Receive eleven million bits of data ... consciously can process forty. As humans it's perfectly OK for these auto systems to work for the most part. It's essential. It's our intellectual shorthand. But we should take a step back and look at the unconscious bias and decide if it needs to be managed or not. Especially in the workplace jungle and when making decisions as an LGBTQ+ Leader, which involves the people around you, we need to take pause and reflect on how our biases are impacting the decisions we make.

So, the question is not *Do we have bias?* but rather *Which are ours?*

## Top 3 Bias Buckets That Impact How You See Things

A quick trip to Wikipedia lists almost two hundred different biases and cognitive (mind) effects we as humans may be influenced by in our world (Bias, n.d.). I don't want to go down and list them all and tell you, say, why we humans may have a bias or tendency to place disproportionately high value on the things we build or partially build, even if they stink (like IKEA furniture, aptly called the IKEA Effect, (Morton, Mochon, & Ariely, 2011)), or the tendency for some people to overestimate the propensity of negative consequences to happen to them (formally called Pessimism Bias, or as I call it, Eeyore Bias (Shepperd, Carroll, Grace, & Terry, 2002)). Instead, I want to take a look at three big categories of how we use or are influenced by biases:

- **THE PEOPLE: We're influenced by biases that help us create our perceptions or impressions of others** ... For example, *authority bias* is the tendency to give a higher level of accuracy on a topic or opinion to a person in authority (which may be unrelated to the actual content at hand or the authority figure's subject matter expertise). So, I may place more weight on the opinions of my awesome Orlando City Commissioner—"Openly Lesbian City Commissioner Patty Sheehan" (we've decided that's her official title)—on the matter of, say, the federal postal system only because she's in a position of authority in my world.

- **THE DATA: We're influenced by where we get our information** ... For example: *confirmation bias* is the tendency to look for, zero in on, and otherwise understand data in such a way that it confirms a person's assumptions. So, when we find ourselves on Facebook and all our friends have the same opinions about XYZ political situation, we're confirming our own assumptions through a biased look at data that supports our own perspective.

- **THE FUTURE: We're influenced by how we prepare for the future** ... For example, *egocentric bias* is the tendency for some people to think they are more responsible for the success of a joint project/effort than an observer would give them credit for. So, there's that person in your work team who—regardless of their level of involvement—will always say they were the one spearheading the project and its success really is "because of them" (insert eye roll or Nancy Pelosi sarcastic clap here).

# Negative Bias (Sadly) in Action: Microinequities

When our biases impact what we say or what we do, then we're creating an uninclusive environment. Let's look at this idea through the lens of two amazing scientists.

## A Tale of Two Scientists

I want to tell you a story about two Stanford professors: Dr. Joan Roughgarden and Dr. Ben Barres. They were both professors at Stanford. Both are published scientists, researchers, and both are members of the transgender community.

Dr. Barres transitioned in his fifties. In his early life, Barbara Barres remembers subtle inequities she experienced while a student at Massachusetts Institute of Technology (MIT): solving incredibly hard math problems only to have her professor say, "You must have had your boyfriend help you." After Dr. Barres transitioned, he was giving a talk when an audience member (who didn't understand that Barbara and Ben were the same person) said, "Dr. Barres gave a great seminar today, but then, his work is much better than his sister's."

Dr. Roughgarden arrived at Stanford in the early 70s, and she recalls that—as a young professional man—the path to success was pretty much laid out for Jonathan. Early in his career, Jonathan Roughgarden came up with a particularly controversial biological theory having to do with the role of tidal pools on certain marine mammals. It was initially met with a lot of skepticism, but the field listened and took his theory seriously. Eventually, this groundbreaking thinking lead Roughgarden to a lot of notoriety, a tenured position at Stanford, and several books.

Roughgarden transitioned later in life as well—in 1998. Dr. Joan Roughgarden—still a highly respected scientist— felt after transition that her ideas were taken less seriously. Her controversial theory on sexual selection (which debunks Darwin's theory) was met with a lot of negative reaction. But—more telling—was that Roughgarden was in this situation of controversy before with Johnathan's earlier theory. At that time, he was engaged to speak his position, debate, and "sell" his thoughts on why he believed what he did, and it eventually led to success. Now, when Joan would share her thoughts or explain her hypothesis, she said people would be very physically threatening, or speak demeaningly to her (as if they were smarter). While she says her scientific theory could be wrong (hey, that's science!), she is not being *proven* wrong. Instead, she's being told—as a woman—it's a wrong theory and is then dismissed. She says, after her transition, she no longer has the right to be wrong.

## Sadly, Not Anomalous: the Microinequities of Gender

Unfortunately, Drs. Roughgarden and Barres' experiences after transition aren't anomalous … they're fairly common. Kristen Schilt draws on in-depth interviews and observational data to show that while individual transmen (someone born biologically female but transitioned to male) have varied experiences, overall, their stories are a testament to systemic gender inequality. The reactions of co-workers and employers to transmen, Schilt demonstrates, reveal the ways assumptions about innate differences between men and women serve as justification for discrimination.

She finds that some transmen gain acceptance—and even privileges or advantage—by becoming "just one of the guys," that some are coerced into working as women or marginalized for being openly transgender, and that other forms of appearance-based discrimination also influence their opportunities. Showcasing the voices of a frequently overlooked group, *Just One of the Guys?* lays bare the social processes that foster forms of inequality that affect us all (Schilt, 2010).

Schilt did another study with Dr. Matt Wiswall on salaries of 43 transgender people after they made their transitions from male to female or female to male. They found that:

- The M-T-F transwomen reported a *decline* of 12% in their earnings.
- The F-T-M transmen reported an *increase* of 7.5% in their earnings (Schilt, 2010).

For many male-to-female transgender individuals, becoming a woman brings a loss of authority and pay, and often harassment and termination. On the other hand, for many female-to-male transgender individuals, becoming a man brings increases in workplace respect, authority, and, in some cases, earnings.

## Defining Microinequities

The examples above from our trans brothers and sisters illustrate one of the challenges when unconscious bias turns into action. So, based upon perceived disadvantage, people can often experience what are called *microinequities*. These are subtle acts of discrimination that are often covert, unintentional, and hard to prove (similar to the experiences in our earlier "tale of two scientists"), those small acts that don't seem to mean a lot but add up over time. Our unconscious biases are our thoughts/beliefs, but microinequities take those thoughts and turn them into actions, whether that be what we do or what we say. Or, said another way, each time we act on our unconscious biases, we commit an act of microinequality.

This is huge. Typically, the perpetrator will brush off comments saying things like, "You're so sensitive," or "I was only kidding ... lighten up!" but this still leaves the impact on the recipient.

Another example is with simple social introductions: when meeting/greeting someone can include a microinequity: like shaking the hand of the male in the group but not the female. No matter the intention (or simply the unconscious lack), here the inference is that the woman is of lesser value.

We saw with our definition of unconscious bias there's the perception of *same* versus *different*. Our cave-person wiring says that different = bad from a safety perspective, and we need to combat that wiring. Again, when we perceive others as different, it can cause us to act on that uneasy feeling of difference. What's the impact to the recipient of this "tiny" form of aggression? They are typically excluded (or have the feeling of exclusion) thereby eroding their confidence in themselves.

Many studies on young girls and women in the sciences and mathematics professions cite that unconscious bias against their ability can erode self-efficacy, or confidence in one's ability. This is what we refer to as the Pygmalion Effect or Golem Effect, where expectations predict behavior. (*Pygmalion* when the effected behavior is positive; *Golem* when the effected behavior is negative) (Bernstein, 2017). And so, as these microinequities build (bringing this back to the workplace jungle), team members disengage, and don't perform the way in which we need them to in the 21$^{st}$-century workplace.

> In short: microinequities create barriers to performance, engagement, and success.

## Why Microinequities Matter in Our Workplace Jungle

Why does it matter for us to identify and mitigate these microinequities in the workplace? For several reasons actually:

- The victim of the microinequity can't foresee them, stop them, or prevent them from recurring.

- Microinequities are a form of punishment for being different and occur in the context of work without regard to performance or merit.
- Microinequities undermine the effectiveness of the recipient.
- Microinequities lead to the Pygmalion or Golem effect (expectations predict results).
- Microinequities take up workplace time and energy and undermine interpersonal trust and relationships.

Studies have found that over **71% of the workforce has experienced some form of workplace incivility or microinequity** in the last five years. Incivility is evidenced by disrespectful behavior (Zauderer, 2002). What happened to these folks? According to this study:

- 28% lost work time avoiding the instigator of the incivility/microinequity
- 53% lost time worrying about the incident/future interactions
- 37% believed their commitment at work declined
- 22% have decreased their effort at work
- 10% decreased the amount of time that they spent at work
- 12% actually changed jobs to avoid the instigator

Dealing with and mitigating the unconscious bias in action microinequities is important for you as an LGBTQ+ Leader, especially as we strive toward being consciously inclusive. Let's find out how.

# How Our Unconscious Biases Impact Our Leadership Effectiveness

As an LGBTQ+ Leader, you're making decisions all the time: what goals you need to focus on as a team, where to channel your teams' individual skills, how to best communicate what you're doing to those key stakeholders around you, yadda, yadda, yadda. You as the Leader are helping to create the context to be successful.

The challenge comes when—given what we now know about unconscious biases—it's impacting our decisions, well, on the unconscious level (and possibly leading to microinequities in the process). So, we may be saying or doing something that's operating from that unconscious input (like picking your seatmate on our low-cost carrier scenario), and maybe it's not the direction we really consciously want to take, nor are we necessarily creating an inclusive culture along the way.

As an LGBTQ+ Leader our challenge is two-fold:

1. How to identify your own unconscious biases so they aren't undermining your leadership success; and
2. How to de-bias yourself so your leadership actions are made from a conscious perspective as best as you can.

## Mitigating Our Own Unconscious Biases

As we talk about mitigating unconscious bias to help ourselves be better LGBTQ+ Leaders, let's start the conversation with yet another story.

A few years ago, I was sitting in a meeting in a conference room at a client's site. It was a big meeting, and there were people there from all levels within the organization, including a senior executive who was the highest-ranking member at the meeting. As the meeting was just about to start and the voices died down, the senior executive (who—it should be noted—was male) could be heard saying, "… and she was a terrible driver. You know how women drive!"

Cue the John Hughes' 80s movie scene where you hear the record scratch and there's dead silence in the room; that was the feeling in this conference room. Everyone stopped talking and looked at the executive, everyone clearly stunned by what they heard. And then … silence. No one said anything. AWKWARD!

Before we conclude our story, let's talk about how we can channel our efforts in order to mitigate our own unconscious bias and the potential subsequent microinequities we may perpetuate within our workplace jungle.

**STRATEGY #1:** One of the best ways to discover our unconscious biases is through the Implicit Association Test (IAT) created by Project Implicit, a "… non-profit organization and international collaboration between researchers who are interested in implicit social cognition; thoughts and feelings outside of conscious awareness and control" (Project Implicit, 2011, para. 1). These are the folks who pioneered the concept of measuring your unconscious biases. Go to their website (https://implicit.harvard.edu/) and take as many free assessment as you'd like to discover your own unconscious biases. Go on … I double-dog dare you!

**STRATEGY #2:** Think about the people with whom you are closest. Think about who are your five "best mates" or—if geography wasn't an issue—who would you "beam" to your favorite coffee shop or pub to have a drink with? Write their names down below (go on, humor me):

1. _____

2. _____

3. _____

4. _____

5. _____

Now, list their demographics: gender, race, sexual orientation, political affiliation, education, etc.

1. _____

2. _____

3. _____

4. _____

5. _____

Ask yourself: Are they homogeneous (the same) or vastly different?

**STRATEGY #3:** Engage the help of your work BFF/workwife or workhubby to help you identify when you engage in unconscious behavior or have them call you out on your microinequities (for example: set up a secret signal that they show you—like tugging their ear—whenever they see or hear you commit a microinequity). I've found this to be really helpful in a safe way: let them know what you're trying to change and allow them the permission to provide you the feedback. It's amazing how your behavior can change once you simply become aware of the issue.

*BTW: The ending to our conference room John Hughes-record-scratch moment? You'll have to wait til Chapter 7 when we chat about communication!*

## Being Active: from Unconscious to Conscious

While sharing the above concepts with other leaders within my leadership workshops, I often have at least one participant at this point say something like, "Well, if it's unconscious, then I can't do anything about it. Ahh well ... onward with my current behavior!"

BUUUZZZZZ! Insert gameshow buzzer here. "Sorry, wrong answer! Thanks for playing ..." or in this case *not* playing. The first time I had someone say this, the "I can't do anything about it!" attitude really got to me; maybe because the best way to combat the perception of being passive in this situation is really to identify the ways in which we should be active. It's not focusing on *unconscious bias*, but focusing on being *consciously inclusive*.

As we already noted earlier, you can do things to de-bias yourself, and that first step is having awareness of your own unconscious biases. So, the first action you as an LGBTQ+ Leader should take is to identify your specific unconscious biases. While you do your personal work on de-biasing yourself, consider these strategies:

- **THE PEOPLE: To manage the biases we may have that help us create our perceptions or impressions of others** ... Think objectively as to why you have the impressions of people that you may have. How did you form them? From experience, word of mouth, their position in your life? Reflect on why you have trust/love/disdain/revulsion or whatever the right descriptor to those in your world.

- **THE DATA: To manage the biases we may have through the sources of data (information) we're receiving** ... This one is a no-brainer: look at where you're getting your info. Do you stick to one news site or station that may be biased toward one side of the political spectrum or another? Do you seek the perspective of those who don't necessarily see things the same way as you? Vary your data gathering to mitigate those one-sided perspectives.

- **THE FUTURE: To manage the biases we may have about the future based upon our current perspectives** ... Do you tend to look at the glass as half full or half empty? Do you tend to point out when plans won't work because of past experience or your gut reaction? Or do you say, "Well, things are different now, let's see what happens?" Having that open-mindedness is a powerful de-biasing tool, as it allows you to be open to possibilities and not biased. This one may be a little harder to manage and may take the help of someone else to guide you along observing your own behavior.

A lot of these strategies can start through that drone perspective we talked about in Chapter 1. In addition, having that focus on being mindful and mindfulness (also shared in Chapter 1 and even more later in Chapter 10) can really help you bring awareness in the moment, so you can see—and maybe stop—potentially biased comments or actions before they hurt folks around you.

# "Mane" Development Strategies: Leveraging Inclusiveness through "The Pride Six"

The reason I share this focus on being consciously inclusive as an LGBTQ+ Leader is that that's ultimately the underlying focus or outcome of what we'll talk about the rest of this book. When we think about how we're supporting being consciously inclusive:

- Consciously Inclusive Leaders are aware of who they are, and seek to understand the uniqueness of others (Chapter 4: Authenticity)
- Consciously Inclusive Leaders have the courage to be open and honest with all team members, and provide the right messages even if they are hard (Chapter 5: Courage)
- Consciously Inclusive Leaders use empathy and try to understand the emotional perspective of others as a way to build rapport, trust, and understand someone's context (Chapter 6: Empathy)
- Consciously Inclusive Leaders adjust their communication style to include the various types needed in order to connect with their team, who may have different styles or need to hear a message in a different way (Chapter 7: Communication)
- Consciously Inclusive Leaders reach out to others to build relationships, understand their needs, and find ways to build bridges and not walls (Chapter 8: Build Relationships)

- Consciously Inclusive Leaders are adept at helping to shape the overall organizational culture through listening to all perspectives and weaving those into the fabric of the workplace

We'll dive deeper into all of these areas and how becoming more proficient (a.k.a. understanding our own *unconscious/competence* from Chapter 1!) will lead to your leadership success. But the takeaway is that the overwhelming outcome of all this work is that you'll be a more inclusive leader and have a greater impact on those around you.

So, your to-do's from this chapter are delayed til the other ones … so go have a coffee or tea; you've earned it.

# Drone Perspective: Reflective ?'s

1) Who in your world is an inclusive leader?

_____

_____

_____

What are five traits, actions, or characteristics that lead you to think of that person as being inclusive?

1. _____

2. _____

3. _____

4. _____

5. _____

2) On a scale of 1–10 with 10 being "I'm as inclusive as anyone out there!" to 1 being "I'm pretty exclusive, introverted, or solo," where would you be?

1    2    3    4    5    6    7    8    9    10

Why would you rank yourself there?

_____

_____

3) Now re-examine that ranking above. What are three things you'll commit to do to increase that inclusive self-rating?

1. _____

2. _____

3. _____

4) Reflect on the definition of *diversity* and our 5 Layers. What was one item you learned from that topic?

_____

_____

_____

_____

How can you apply that key learning to be a more inclusive leader?

_____

_____

_____

_____

5) Microinequities happen all around us all the time. How will you address them when you see them happen in your workplace jungle? What are some ideas you have to stop microinequities in the moment?

_____

_____

_____

_____

# JUNGLE LOVE:
# PRIDE LEADERSHIP IN ACTION

"As a young, openly bisexual woman working as a financial planner in the days before civil unions, I organized seminars for gay couples at our local bars focusing on how to estate plan as 'unmarried' individuals. It became a hugely popular seminar that got thirty-plus couples a month looking at me and my team as experts.

My manager at the time told me I'd never be successful if I didn't wear a tweed skirt suit from Joseph A. Banks. When I told her that I would not be buying skirts to please her, she went out of her way to have me removed from her sales team.

I ended up working for a competitor sales team and cranked up the seminars for them. What I learned … if it works in sales and hurts nothing but your fragile ego, shut up and let it work."

*– Angel J., Owner*
*Consulting Firm in the U.S.A.*

· · · · · · · · · · · · · · · · · · · · · · · · · · · · · · · · · · · · · · · · · · · · · · · ·

# THE SHINY UNICORN THAT IS YOU: BEING YOUR AUTHENTIC SELF

*"The first—and most powerful thing—any LGBTQ+
Leader can do to be great is to just be themselves.
Authenticity, openness, integrity, candor: these are
all amazing strengths that an LGBTQ+ person has in
large supply. By tapping into that authenticity of who
you are you are already light years ahead of the rest of
the pack in being effective."*
– Dr. Steve Yacovelli
The Gay Leadership Dude

Proactive Communication • Relationship-Building • Integrity,
Authenticity, & Courage • Developing Culture • Empathy

# What Do We Mean by *Authenticity* Anyway?

A few years ago, there was a lot of buzz in the leadership field regarding the phrase *authentic leadership*. Like so many leadership-y things out there, some thought it was more of a flavor-of-the-month kinda deal; that the field would move on to the next shiny, new thing in a short while, like the new fall line at The Banana (or your clothes retailer of choice). Funny thing, though: the concept of authenticity as it relates to leadership seems to actually be gaining more traction over the years, not losing it. But what the heck do we mean by the word *authentic* or *authenticity*?

If you Google the term *authentic*, you get the following:

> ... *of undisputed origin; genuine.* Synonyms: *genuine, real, bona fide, true, veritable; legitimate, lawful, legal, valid* (Authentic, n.d.)

*Harvard Business Review* stated in January 2015, "Authenticity has emerged as the gold standard for leadership" (George, 2016, para. 1). An authentic leader is one who is acting in a leadership capacity from their true selves, they are truthful, and have self-awareness of their skills and abilities; they know what they bring to the table as well as where they lack competence.

Authentic leaders manage from the mind but lead from the heart; meaning they are a good mix of understanding what logically needs to happen but don't make decisions without taking into account the relationship and emotional impact of their leadership actions. They understand their own personal history and experiences and how these have shaped their leadership context and perspective, and therefore, how they lead others. Authentic leaders are genuine.

## Authenticity, Integrity, and "Context"

The funky part about being an authentic leader in the workplace jungle today is that we're often put into situations where we haven't been before, or perhaps working with people who are very different than ourselves. And this puts us in a weird space where we're trying to be authentic (based on our past experiences) but have to venture into uncharted territory. Yikes!

Quick story: When I'm facilitating a leadership workshop, my true authentic self is pretty upbeat, outgoing, extraverted, engaging, and (I think!) fun. Even with serious conversations, I try to leverage humor to make my points. I smile (I have a pretty decent grill, thanks, Dentist!), and I maintain eye contact with my peeps in the room. I am passionate about my topics and—at least in the U.S.—I tend to speak a little fast.

In many European countries, large, toothy smiles are perceived as a sign of stupidity and ignorance, and the stereotype that Americans are loud, boisterous, and "in your face" is pretty prevalent. So, whenever I do workshops in Europe, I dial it back a bit. I'm mindful of the amount of smiling I do. I watch my rate of speech (even giving participants yellow cards—like in soccer/football—so they can tell me when to slow down, as English typically isn't their primary language and they're awesomely translating what I'm saying in their noggins IRT). And, I manage the humor, stories, and analogies I use.

Is this Euro-Steve being unauthentic to his true self? I would argue no; I'm still me, I'm still sharing my perspectives and thoughts on the topic at hand just as I would in a U.S.-based workshop. But I'm managing my authenticity of the Real Steve within my current context. It's still me, just slightly adjusted to my Euro-audience.

An effective LGBTQ+ Leader thinks about their authenticity in relationship to the context of their environment and audience. There's a saying "like likes like," meaning people want to relate to you in some way; that we're drawn to people who are similar to us and people who communicate in a similar fashion (that's why you tend to sit with people you know or have rapport with when you're in those meetings or training classes!).

"Hold on, Steve," you might be thinking, "Here you're saying to mind your context, but you're also saying, be you. Which the hell is it?" Awesome point, and my response is **be you, always**. It's like how you act when you're out on the town with your closest friends versus how you act at home with your great Aunt Mildred; both are still you, but your behavior, communication style, and energy are just different. Authentic leadership is simply adjusting your authentic self, based upon context or the environment and people you are with at the moment. But never, ever, ever—if you want to be an effective LGBTQ+ Leader—never fake who you are because you think it will be better perceived by those with whom you're engaging.

Another thing to consider is how authenticity is so intertwined with your own integrity. When teaching my leadership workshops, the concept of integrity often pops up, and I ask folks to define it (even if it's part of their company's listed Corporate Values). My favorite (and frankly most accurate and conscience definition) is: Integrity is doing the right thing when no one is watching. When

I think about being authentic, I think about preserving my own integrity as a human being. I'd like to think that my personal integrity aligns with being a good person (although not everyone has this same alignment, to be honest). But when I think about my personal context and being Steve's true authentic self, it ultimately bolsters my own personal integrity of me doing what I think is the right thing "...when no one is watching."

Use this as a test: Is being your authentic self—even adjusted to your personal context—aligned with your own definition of integrity? If it's not, what needs to change?

## Authenticity and You as an LGBTQ+ Leader

In the context of being an LGBTQ+ Leader, our idea of authenticity also has an even deeper meaning.

To be an authentic Leader, you need to be true to yourself. This means being out at work and being your true authentic self in the workplace jungle (and beyond). So, if you are in the closet or hiding your authentic self at work: let's have a chat about that. One of the things I've seen in my world working with leaders (and specifically LGBTQ+ Leaders) is that those in the closet aren't as effective as those Leaders who are out and their authentic selves in the workplace. So, think about yourself and your out authenticity. The foundation for being the best leader you can be in this book is to be authentic, and that means not hiding who you truly are.

Look, I respect that there's many reasons people don't share their authentic selves at work and stay in the closet; whether you self-identify as gay, bisexual, lesbian, trans, genderfluid, etc., there's a myriad of stories I've heard why people don't share who they authentically are with their co-workers and bosses. I get it ... at one point early in my career I was there, too.

But I see how much time and energy it takes for people to hide their authenticity. The management of pronouns when talking about your partner or significant other, the dodging of "What did you do this weekend?" responses, wrangling that beard to take to the company holiday party—it's exhausting! But that's the point on why "hidden" LGBTQ+ Leaders aren't as effective as those who are openly authentic and leading as their true selves: you don't have to worry about hiding your truth. Out Leaders can channel their focus on leading, building relationships, and instilling trust with those around them instead of hiding in the closet. And that "outness" is so powerful in identifying your authentic self. If you're out you already had to be true to yourself, and this skill easily transfers to you leading through your authenticity. If you're "in," consider rethinking that strategy, especially if you want to be the most powerful, effective, and, frankly, happy Leader you can be.

## Becoming a More Authentic You

So how do you develop or deepen your authenticity? According to research, the number one secret to understanding your authenticity is having self-awareness (Gatling, Castelli, & Cole, 2013). While there's heaps of ways to develop this (and we'll focus on a ton in this book), here's five areas that may help you do a deep dive into yourself* (*therapist not included):

1. **Explore your past** ... Ask yourself, "How did I get to where I'm at now?" and "What were some of the key

milestones that have shaped who I am today?" We're constantly learning and growing through all our experiences (the good and the bad), but it's important to think about what events and people and influences have moved you to this exact spot.

2. **Reflect on immediate actions and practices** ... It's one thing to think about the major milestones that have impacted who you are as an LGBTQ+ Leader, but it's another to think about what happened to you today, and what you can learn from it. I often say we approach the work jungle with a ready-fire-aim mentality, the speed of our collective worlds is wicked fast. By reflecting on the day's events, we are not only practicing the skill of reflection, but also learning from what's occurred to us so we can either repeat it or avoid it.

3. **Ask those around you for open and honest feedback** ... We all have our own blind spots and unconscious biases (see Chapter 3). But we can ask those folks around us we trust to help us see them. From a work context, I've always been lucky to have one or two workwives or workhusbands at the various jobs I've had over the years. They were my trusted advisors who I could have the tough conversations with, and they would tell me the truth about my performance and help me see the blind spots I had where I could not.

In addition, be sure you are active listening when you receive the feedback from your trusted advisors. While we'll talk about strategies for effective listening later (see Chapter 7), it's good to remember now that feedback isn't just giving the words, it's also listening and receiving the feedback. The saying goes, "Y'all got two ears and one mouth for a reason." As good LGBTQ+ Leaders, we should be listening twice as much as we speak.

4. **Know your own personal values system** ... Being authentic is knowing what drives you to do the things you do. We all have a personal values system, whether it's something we are cognizant of or something that's been operating in our subconscious, and we act through this values lens. Be mindful of your Top Five (or so) values and how often you are feeding these values with the actions, behaviors, and work that you do. (FYI, in the next section we'll explore one way to identify your personal values system if you haven't done so already).

5. **Practice at adjusting your authenticity within varying contexts** ... We identified that being your authentic self is the norm, but being able to adjust the dials in the various situational contexts is important, too (U.S.-Steve versus Euro-Steve). Notice how you instinctively already adjust yourself in different contexts; watch others do it between work, home, and different settings. Be mindful of this and adjust yourself accordingly. Practice adjusting your authenticity in varying situations to become more better-er at this skill, but also remember to never lose who you are.

Let's explore a few of these strategies a little more closely to move us from that conscious/competence to the unconscious/competence state of being.

# Authentic LGBTQ+ Leaders Know Their Strengths ... and Their Areas of Opportunity

As an authentic LGBTQ+ Leader, it's important to know your strengths and weaknesses. Let's explore some potentials for ya ...

### STRENGTH: ID-ing Your Personal Value System

As noted earlier, being authentic means understanding your personal values. As I work with Leaders in a variety of organizations, it amazes me, when I ask a Leader what their top three personal values are, and they come up blank.

But what the heck exactly are values? According to our pals at Merriam-Webster, a value is what you personally feel is important or has relative worth within your life (Value, n.d.). Values help us (consciously and unconsciously) make decisions—both at home and within the workplace jungle; they're the lens with which we think, talk, and act. For example: my top three values are *equity and fairness, creativity,* and *personal relationships* (not necess-celery in that order). I've come to realize over my existence that these three tend to always rise to the top of the list, depending on my life's context. While their order may vary depending on where Steve is now, they're consistently there. So, when Steve acts, there's a good chance one—if not a few—of these values are at work in shaping how he takes action, says something, or thinks about a situation.

Where do your values come from? From your experience, your relationships, or "tribe," (a.k.a how I've experienced my world of finding my like-valued peeps based upon being a yogi at Orlando Power Yoga and how we've created such a great inclusive community) society around you, media and advertising, and many other sources. They are created and shaped over time and, of course, can change in importance as life progresses. For example, some people have something like "meeting goals" or "feeling of accomplishment" as a high value early in their careers; they want to be seen as that rock star in their job. "Family and relationships" may be lower on the list. But, as time progresses, they might pair up with an S.O., and being the rock star accountant falls lower as "intimate relationships" rises higher. Values can change in order, but rarely do our top values completely drop off our virtual list over our lives because of their hardwiring within our unconsciousness.

When I conduct leadership workshops, we do an activity that helps participants start to identify their own values system. I've done this a few ways, but the end result is the same: coming up with your top list of values by finding the words that jive with you. Here's the process:

STEP 1: Using the list below, read the words and—using your gut—place a mark next to the words that resonate with you.

What do I mean by *resonate*? As you read the words quickly, think if they mean something to you. Don't over-analyze or think too hard, just do a gut check and see if the word has meaning in your world. If it does, circle it or mark it in some way.

Don't see a word you'd hope to see on the values list? Write it down and use it! This is YOUR value list, not Steve's, and is just meant to get you thinking about values.

Once you finish going through the list one time, do it again to make sure you didn't miss any words that meant something to you.

**ACTIVITY:** *List of Personal Values*

| | | |
|---|---|---|
| Acceptance | Challenge | Courtesy |
| Accomplishment | Charity | Creation |
| Accountability | Cleanliness | Creativity |
| Accuracy | Clear | Credibility |
| Achievement | Clever | Curiosity |
| Adaptability | Comfort | Decisive |
| Alertness | Commitment | Decisiveness |
| Altruism | Common sense | Dedication |
| Ambition | Communication | Dependability |
| Amusement | Community | Determination |
| Assertiveness | Compassion | Development |
| Attentive | Competence | Devotion |
| Awareness | Concentration | Dignity |
| Balance | Confidence | Discipline |
| Beauty | Connection | Discovery |
| Boldness | Consciousness | Drive |
| Bravery | Consistency | Effectiveness |
| Brilliance | Contentment | Efficiency |
| Calm | Contribution | Empathy |
| Candor | Control | Empower |
| Capable | Conviction | Endurance |
| Careful | Cooperation | Energy |
| Certainty | Courage | Enjoyment |

| | | |
|---|---|---|
| Enthusiasm | Hard work | Love |
| Equality | Harmony | Loyalty |
| Ethical | Health | Mastery |
| Excellence | Honesty | Maturity |
| Experience | Honor | Meaning |
| Exploration | Hope | Moderation |
| Expressive | Humility | Motivation |
| Fairness | Imagination | Openness |
| Family | Improvement | Optimism |
| Famous | Independence | Order |
| Fearless | Individuality | Organization |
| Feelings | Innovation | Originality |
| Ferocious | Inquisitive | Passion |
| Fidelity | Insightful | Patience |
| Focus | Inspiring | Peace |
| Foresight | Integrity | Performance |
| Fortitude | Intelligence | Persistence |
| Freedom | Intensity | Playfulness |
| Friendship | Intuitive | Poise |
| Fun | Irreverent | Potential |
| Generosity | Joy | Power |
| Genius | Justice | Present |
| Giving | Kindness | Productivity |
| Goodness | Knowledge | Professionalism |
| Grace | Lawful | Prosperity |
| Gratitude | Leadership | Purpose |
| Greatness | Learning | Quality |
| Growth | Liberty | Realistic |
| Happiness | Logic | Reason |

| | | |
|---|---|---|
| Recognition | Skill | Tolerance |
| Recreation | Skillfulness Smart | Toughness |
| Reflective | Solitude | Traditional |
| Respect | Spirit | Tranquility |
| Responsibility | Spirituality | Transparency |
| Restraint | Spontaneous | Trust |
| Results-oriented | Stability | Trustworthy |
| Reverence | Status | Truth |
| Rigor | Stewardship | Understanding |
| Risk | Strength | Uniqueness |
| Satisfaction | Structure | Unity |
| Security | Success | Valor |
| Self-reliance | Support | Victory |
| Selfless | Surprise | Vigor |
| Sensitivity | Sustainability | Vision |
| Serenity | Talent | Vitality |
| Service | Teamwork | Wealth |
| Sharing | Temperance | Welcoming |
| Significance | Thankful | Winning |
| Silence | Thorough | Wisdom |
| Simplicity | Thoughtful | Wonder |
| Sincerity | Timeliness | |

**STEP 2:** After you go through the list, you'll probably have about 15 to 30 words that meant something to you. Take these words and write them on a Post-It® note or notecard. Cluster the words that are similar in meaning to you. If there's some words that are interchangeable to you (like for me, *developing* and *growing* are the same), pick the one that

most resonates to you. You'll probably end up with about 7 to 10 clusters.

**STEP 3:** With your word clusters that are left, sort them in order of importance: the one you feel strongest about to the one end of your list and those you feel least strong about on the other.

**STEP 4:** When you feel your list is in your importance order, what do you see? Write down the Top 5 Values you have in the space below:

## MY TOP VALUES (AS OF TODAY):

1. _____

2. _____

3. _____

4. _____

5. _____

# Drone Perspective: Reflective ?'s

1) Are you surprised by your Top 5 Values?

_____

_____

_____

_____

_____

2) Think about what you've done in the past 48 hours—at home and at your workplace jungle. What have you done in your life that supports one (or a few) of your Top 5 Values?

_____

_____

_____

_____

_____

3) Did you do anything in the last 48 hours that didn't somehow align with your personal values? If so, how did that feel to you?

_____

_____

_____

_____

_____

# Your Personal Values and Organizational Alignment

Pretty much every organization has come up with their own set of values; the expectation with which those working within the group are expected to conduct business. It's kinda like your social contract with your employer; and everyone agrees—by taking a job or working within the team—on how to behave.

I've both worked in and worked with organizations that have stated values, usually posted on the break room walls or listed in the annual Performance Review document. For most people, the workplace values align with or at least complement their own personal values, but for some I have seen, two things play out that could derail people's authenticity within the workplace:

1. **When the stated organizational values aren't really what's lived within the organization.** Many years ago, I was working for a small tech company. It was one of my first opportunities to be a leader within a business and I was excited. One of the Values-On-The-Breakroom-Wall was "We honor work/life balance." The definition went on to identify how the business wanted people to work hard, but also not be all-consumed with work and have a balanced personal life. I loved it: that aligned with my personal values.

   In my adult life, I've become a bit of a morning person: I love getting up early, beating traffic, being the first in the office, and enjoying that quiet time before others arrive and start their day around 9:00 AM. And with this job I was pretty much the one first in the office, turning on the coffee and lights usually just after 7:00 AM. So, I would typically leave the office around 4:30 or 5:00 PM, give or take, since I was in the office for about ten hours. After about a month or so, a peer came up to me, pulled me aside, and said, "You're leaving too early. Everyone at our level is really expected to stay until about 6:00 or so, after their boss leaves." Wait a minute, honor work/life balance … but Steve worked ten-plus hour workdays? So, this was a case where the stated corporate values were pretty much bunk.

Punch line: Be mindful to truly understand what values are being lived within your workplace, and if these real values align with yours. You can't be your authentic self if the lived values at work aren't what jives with your personal values. Don't believe the poster on the wall, but see what really happens in the business and if it fits with your authentic self.

2. **When the work you do consistently doesn't "feed" your personal values.** One of the *Drone Perspective: Reflection ?'s* earlier asked you—once you identified your personal values—to think about what you do and see if the tasks you do align or "feed" your personal values. Let's dive deeper into that and see how it leads to your authenticity as an LGBTQ+ Leader.

At work, we have those tasks we do frequently; it's part of our role or our job. But stop and think if that fits within your values system. For example, one of my values is to help people grow and be better. My job as a development professional—someone who wants to improve others and help them be more successful—is 1,000% aligned with my job (I didn't write this book to make oodles of bucks, my friend!). So, when I'm doing my job as a leadership consultant, I am feeding my value of helping others grow and be their better selves, and more successful.

I think of it like the House Points in the *Harry Potter* books (yes, I'm a Potterhead). If you're not familiar, each of the school Houses (separate teams if you will) at Hogwarts (the magical school of the series) can earn points for doing general good deeds, answering questions in class correctly, etc. Subsequently, they can lose points for doing bad things (like break curfew or be late to class). Each student earns or costs points by their behavior for their own House, so it's a collective benefit or hindrance if you don't do your best. For your tasks and feeding your values, I envision the same big vials that fill up with a ping-pong ball as you do something that feeds your values system. Every task or action gives you some virtual commodity. "Ten points for Gryffindor!"

But there are things that I have to do in my world (just like you) that don't necessarily feed Steve's Values. For example, at some point this weekend I'll have to mow my lawn (unless I bribe my hubby to do it). I don't like to mow it, but it has to get done. Does mowing my lawn as a task feed my values? Nope, not at all. So, when I do it, it isn't enjoyable.

Your challenge is to look at what you typically do and see how it aligns or doesn't align with your personal values system. Sure: we all have the mow my lawn items on our list. But if you find that you consistently have way more mow my lawns than not, then this is where you may want to rethink what you're doing. You can't feed your values if the vast majority of the tasks you have to do don't align with them; as a result, you're not being authentic to yourself and as an LGBTQ+ Leader. And at what cost? Yes, some would argue that you don't need to feed your values at work; you can do that outside of the place where you get your paycheck. I would slightly agree. However, you aren't bringing your authentic self to your job if this is how you operate in the world: phoning it in at work and getting your values fix outside. We spend a heckuva lot of time in our workplace jungle; don't you want to be feeding your values with the work that you do?

## AREA OF OPPORTUNITY: Understanding Your Own Unconscious Biases

SIDE NOTE: I'm a glass-half-full kinda guy; and so, when I started working for a certain Fortune 100 employer-whose-boss-is-a-rodent in the early 2000s, we would not talk about *weaknesses* as a leader but *areas of opportunity*, and frankly, this always resonated with me (talk about values alignment). But I use the synonym *areas of opportunity* to mean things that aren't at your best but could be if you worked at them. Some glass-half-empty folks would just call them weaknesses.

As I've worked with leaders over the years, one of the biggest pitfalls I've seen is being hijacked by their own unconscious biases. As we explored these in Chapter 3, unconscious biases are something we all have: if you're human, you're biased. However, it's the leaders who don't make an effort to start to unpack and understand their unconscious biases that can get them into mucho trouble.

In Chapter 3, we covered strategies on how to identify and de-bias yourself, but I want to make sure we tie this into the potential of not engaging in de-biasing yourself as an LGBTQ+ Leader and how it relates to your authenticity. Part of being authentic is identifying and managing the unconscious biases you may have. If we don't begin to uncover our unconscious biases—and allow those microinequities to creep into what we say and what we do as a Leader—we can quickly erode our leadership effectiveness and any trust we've built along the way.

## Your Personal Branding & Being Your Authentic Self

A final thought on being your best LGBTQ+ leadership self as it relates to authenticity is thinking about your own personal brand, especially your online brand.

I've lived in Orlando for over twenty years (and yes, we are WAY more than just theme parks and tourist stuff, BTW), and like many of you, I've celebrated many a Pride each June (and eventually October for us Southerners, as June is way too hot!). Pride is OUR month, and it's our chance to express who we are (our authentic selves!) and what we're passionate about.

I remember my first few Pride celebrations in the days before "MyFace" (my weird, shmushed term meaning *all social media*), we snapped pictures on our fancy cameras-that-were-only-cameras, saved our pennies to do as many events as possible, invited friends from all over to come and play in O-town (that's Orlando, ICYDK) for the weekend, and afterward, enjoyed the memories and the paper photos we made each year, and shared those memories and pics only with those we wanted to share.

Like me, I suspect that you—during your Pride celebrations and beyond—snap a bunch of pics of a lot of people (and you) celebrating, Instagramming or Facebooking parties and festivities celebrating our LGBTQ-ness in your respective town, and basically letting everyone know what we're doing to celebrate the time of year when our Community makes sure people know: "We're here, we're queer" (and, for some, "Where's the beer?").

The challenge is that we have instant documentation of all that we do, and it lives on (seemingly) forever. According to the statistical website Statista (www.statista.com), as of the end of 2018, Facebook has 2.3 *billion* global monthly active users, Twitter boasts more than 321 *million* monthly active users world-wide (as of Q4, 2018), and, by 2020, Instagram is projected to reach 120.3 million monthly active users in the United States alone, up from 104.7 million users in 2018 (Statista.com, n.d.). It's pretty safe to say that the vast majority of Pride celebrators are connected to social media, and most likely in multiple fashions. What you are doing is somewhere being digitally archived for all the world to see.

To be clear: I think that the proliferation of social media is (as my Boston friends say) wicked awesome. In a few clicks I can find out what my friends, family, co-workers, and acquaintances are up to at any given moment. But it also leads to some challenges in how we as LGBTQ+ Leaders balance our authenticity along with presenting the personal and professional brand we want to those in our workplace.

Like it or not, each one of us is an authentic "brand" and our online presence supports that brand, or the perception that people make about us from that data. While of course we want you to be your authentic selves in the world, just be mindful as to the authentic brand you're shaping with your online presence. I have been in the position of being a hiring manager many times recently, and after I have a candidate's name I immediately do three things: (1) check out their LinkedIn profile (if they have one) and also look for people we have in common; (2) do a Facebook search and see both what comes up and—if I find the right candidate—what friends we have in common; and (3) a generic Google search to see what data pops up (specifically in the "images" tab). Why all the Nancy Drew-ing? Because it's silly in this day and age to go into any meeting without doing a few minutes of homework. Our brands are out there; and it's fascinating to find them.

And I'm not the only one doing this: you can assume your bosses, hiring managers, co-workers, and team members are doing this, too. Why does this matter to you as an LGBTQ+ Leader? Because you need to control your digital brand and make sure it's accurately representing your authenticity. Here's a few suggestions from what I've seen "out there:"

1. **Posts thru the Grandmom Test:** Consider anything you post online to go through the Grandmom Test. Would Grandmother/Nana/Mommom be embarrassed by your post on social media? If so, reconsider what it's doing to your personal brand.

   (And yes, I get that some grandmoms are more liberal or conservative than others; the idea here is to challenge your own idea of what's "appropriate" through the lens of someone else. So, if the Mommom analogy doesn't work think about your religious organization or a very conservative friend in Nana's place).

2. **Pics of Skin and Booze:** Similar to the Grandmom Test, be sure not every picture of you posted online is you with a drink in your hand or where you're scantily clad. Sure, a glass of vino here or there or you at the beach frolicking in the surf on occasion is cool. But if you look back and all your pics are toasting (or you're toasted) or there's a heap of skin showing, then have a think what this is saying about your brand. If it's what you want to project, then you're good; if it's not, consider changing.

3. **Topics of Sex, Religion, & Politics:** Be mindful of the reaction of topics you post about on social media. Again— to be crystal clear—I'm not advocating that you censor yourself and limit what you post; I'm simply saying be mindful of the potential reactions you may get and the perception these posts may have on others. I'm an extremely passionate person about equality and fairness, especially as it relates to our LGBTQ+ Community (see values conversation above). So, on social media (Facebook and LinkedIn specifically) I post things about equality that may not be as well perceived by those of a more conservative perspective. But I do these posts in as much of a respectful and positive way as I can. I'm being authentic about the topic, but still shaping the context.

A little more here on posts: when citing a source about posts, try and be as fair in your sources as you can (back to

Chapter 3 and our data bias). Reposting that pic you saw from LiberalLefties.com or ConservativeRightWingers. org may not be the most balanced perspective. Please be authentic and have your position on an issue you feel passionate about, but don't perpetuate fake news or extremely biased perspectives as best as you can.

4. **Manage the Access:** Manage both your LinkedIn account and your personal social media accounts as if everyone is looking. Keep LinkedIn up to date and honest (it's too easy these days to check your work); and you may want to lock down your Facebook and Insta to only those folk who you want to see everything about you (not open to the public) and either don't accept acquaintances or—at least with Facebook—set up a Friends List that severely limits the info that group can see and bucket people into different viewing areas as you see fit.

5. **Control How You Want to Show Your Authenticity:** Leverage social media to shape the authentic self you want people to see. For example, I have a friend whose Facebook posts are about 80% of her doing business-y things: presenting at a client, soliciting stories for an article she's writing, etc. This is how she wishes to present her authenticity: limitedly.

Personally, I see a power in presenting as accessible and human on social media. For every "Steve talking about TopDog Learning Group, LLC (my consulting firm) and what we're doing" pic, there's a balance of "Steve's paddle boarding on a lake" personal stuff. This isn't insincere or contrived; I just try to balance the facets of my authentic self (a.k.a. the context we discussed above) to share a whole view of Steve as part of my authenticity online. It also helps people see the "real" me for when they meet me in person. Regardless, just be mindful of your balance and how you're presenting your online self.

Final thought: whether we like it or not, as an out LGBTQ+ professional, we're representing the greater LGBTQ+ Community; what we do as an individual may impact how people perceive the overall LGBTQ+ Community. So, get back in that drone and ask yourself if you're repping our peeps in the most positive light. No, all gay people aren't the same and shouldn't act that same; that's silly. But we all shape the data that contributes to how people perceive our overall Community. Be mindful of that; you have the power to disrupt misconceptions about us or reinforce them (even if they may not be the most favorable). You—especially you as an LGBTQ+ Leader—are partly in charge of how the world perceives us. Handle that responsibility with thoughtfulness and care.

# Tie to G Quotient

For each of our leadership competencies that make up *Pride Leadership*, I want to quickly tie it back to Snyder's work from *The G Quotient* (Snyder, 2006) just to close our leadership story.

When I look at the concepts of authenticity and being one's authentic self in the workplace jungle, it actually touches upon three of Snyder's seven G Quotient principles:

- **Principle #1: Inclusion** ... Being authentic to yourself is being inclusive of others; being out includes them to know the real you and to include them in your world. Being authentic is allowing yourself to be who you are and to reach that full potential.
- **Principle #3: Adaptability** ... Authenticity touches upon the concept of adapting to your context and balancing being authentic with adjusting yourself to the situation and people those around you so you're most effective.
- **Principle #4: Connectivity** ... When we're authentic in the way we work we are able to better connect with those around us. Our authentic selves are genuine and allow us to engage with people on an honest level. Authentic LGBTQ+ Leaders have the skill to not only connect with those like them but can connect with those who are different because we've been that other, and can respect their perspective.

# "Mane" Development Strategies: Building Your Authenticity

Here are a few activities you can do to increase your own authenticity:

**ACTIVITY #1: Your Personal Value System** ... If you haven't already done so, be sure to go back to the section above and discover your Top 5(ish) Personal Values.

Once you have them, place them somewhere that's prevalent in your world (a sticky note on your computer, in your phone, on a prominent white board in your office, tattoo on your forearm, etc.).

Challenge yourself once a week to reflect on what you did do (tasks and accomplishments; where you focused your energy that week) in relationship to your personal values. Are you feeding them well by the activities and tasks you're doing? If you aren't, how does that feel right now? What can you do to shift your world so that you are indeed feeding those personal values more consistently?

**ACTIVITY #2: Your Resource Wheel (to identify your strengths)** ... On a sheet of paper draw a circle. In that circle divide it into eight equal slices (like you're slicing a pizza ... mmmm ... pizza). In each of the pie slices write one resource that you bring to the proverbial table: a resource is a strength, skill, or ability you strongly have.

As you think about your authenticity and the skills you bring to the table, do others see these skills in you or recognize those strengths within you? If not, how can you share those strengths with them in a respectful manner?

**ACTIVITY #3: Explore your Unconscious Biases through Project Implicit** ... go to Project Implicit's website and take at least three IAT assessments, selecting some combinations that you may already think you have unconscious biases toward and some you think, "Naaaa, I am good here." What do the results show? Do these results surprise you?

Reflect on this quote in regard to unconscious bias:

*"Unconscious bias in organizations is like a current in the ocean. When you swim with it you don't necessarily notice it. But when you have to swim against it is when it becomes all too clear you're swimming against that current."*

– Dr. Steve Yacovelli, that Gay Leadership Dude again.

Think: How does Unconscious Bias relate to your leadership success and you being authentic as an LGBTQ+ Leader?

**ACTIVITY #4: Social Media Audit** ... We shared about being authentic and your own personal brand. Go to two of your social media accounts (assuming you have more than one) and conduct an impartial (unbiased!) audit. Look at your posts, photos, and—via the activity history—your likes. What do you see? Is there a trend in your social media behavior? Does this behavior support the brand you want out there? If not, what can you do to change that perception?

ACTIVITY #5: Authenticity Descriptions ... On a sheet of paper, write down ten adjectives that you'd really like people to use to describe you. Next, find five people and ask them to write down the ten adjectives that they would use to describe you.

Compare your results. Is there a trend? Do you see certain words continually pop up on people's list of descriptor words of you?

# Drone Perspective: Reflective ?'s

1) On a scale of 1–10 with 10 being "I'm a rock star at adjusting my authentic self in the context of the moment" to 1 being "I never adjust my authentic self," where would you be?

   1     2     3     4     5     6     7     8     9     10

   Why would you rank yourself there?

   _____

   _____

   _____

   _____

2) Is that where you'd like to be? If not, how could you adjust your context filter?

   _____

   _____

   _____

   _____

3) Your personal brand—especially in the age of so much digital content—is really a big deal. How do you balance your own authenticity and integrity with your online presence? What are some tactics you will do to ensure your online brand is in line with representing who you really are?

_____

_____

_____

_____

4) Assuming you've come out to someone, how did it feel when you told close family and friends? If you haven't, reflect on what is preventing you from telling people about your authentic self.

_____

_____

_____

_____

5) Think of someone—famous or famous to you—who you'd rate as a 10 on our Authenticity Scale (in Question #1). Who is it?

_____

_____

_____

_____

Why did you list them? What is it about them that makes you give them a 10 in authenticity?

_____

_____

_____

_____

What could you learn from them to help you be a more authentic leader?

_____

_____

_____

_____

# JUNGLE LOVE:
# PRIDE LEADERSHIP IN ACTION

"I came out in my professional career relatively late in life. My boss, the president of the company where I worked, immediately accepted and embraced me. Honestly, that didn't surprise me because she is a pretty terrific person! More importantly, her support was also demonstrated by her actions.

In 2005, Tennessee State Senator Jim Bryson co-sponsored a bill (HB 775) to 'prohibit adoptions by homosexual persons.' Bryson was also the president of a research company that our company contracted on a regular basis. My boss not only sent Bryson a letter condemning his sponsorship of the bill, she also made an unwavering commitment to terminate all business dealings with his company.

For many, this would have been a difficult decision because Bryson's company was a preferred vendor to her company as well as many of her clients. But her courage made the decision easy and I really respected her for that!"

*– Thor F., President*
*Data Analytics Firm, U.S.A.*

. . . . . . . . . . . . . . . . . . . . . . . . . . . . . . . . . . . . . . . . . . . . . . . . . . . . . . .

# ROAR LIKE A LION: HAVING COURAGE

*"Remember in* The Wizard of Oz *how the Cowardly Lion—when he got to see the Wizard—was like, 'What? I already had courage? WTH?' I mean, it was kinda poopy that the Wizard made the poor cat go all the way through that drama, only to say, 'That gift you want? You already got it!' Well, leadership courage is a lot like that; when leaders ask me, 'How can I get more courageous in my leadership?' I share that—like the Lion—you already got this; just tap into it (or click your heels a few times like Dorothy)!"*

– Dr. Steve Yacovelli

The Gay Leadership Dude

Proactive Communication • Relationship-Building • Integrity, Authenticity, & Courage • Developing Culture • Empathy

# Experience: Our Strength or Our Weakness?

When you think about it, we're all students of history (despite what you may have thought in high school).

It's true. I'm not just talking about history lessons in your favorite alma mater, although that can be a part of it. I'm talking about our personal history. We learn from our mistakes (some of us more slowly than others) and we use those experiences to shape how we interact with the world going forward. This is basic human nature, and it's one of the reasons we are (or at least seem to be, at times!) the dominant species on the planet. Our ability to observe, reason, and adapt from our experiences helps us to "make good choices!" (my favorite quote from the movie *Pitch Perfect* (Banks, Brooks, Handelman & Moore, 2012)).

But, what if that's not always true? What if, instead of helping us, our past experiences are holding us back from making good choices, especially in our workplace jungle? Often, when we find a routine that delivers results, it's easier to kick back and repeat that process until the well runs dry; we get comfortable with our own boundaries. And this complacency is probably one of the greatest mistakes we can make, especially as an LGBTQ+ Leader. When we get comfortable, we often get lazy. Sticking to our comfort zones can strip us of the tools we need to remain successful and continue innovating, especially in the 21$^{st}$-century workplace jungle. Even worse, it can turn would-be Leaders into argumentative bosses who lack the ability or desire to take risks.

That's why *courage* is so important in our daily leadership lives. Courage is the antidote to leadership driven by complacency and fear. It's the secret sauce that drives us onto our feet, pushes us forward, and encourages us to take smart (note the word *smart*) risks. It's one of the most important qualities in modern leadership, and our relationship with it goes way, way back.

## What the Whaaaaat Is Courage?

In its most rudimentary form, it's easiest to think of courage as that adrenaline-filled action hero that we see in the movies or when we're home Netflixing and chillin'. And what's kinda funky is that the *idea* of courage is so ingrained in our psyche that we recognize it as soon as we see it. Consider these key movie moments and see if you can spot where courage lives (and full disclosure: these are some of my favorite movies, so I'm very aware of my bias here!):

- In *Star Wars* (1977)—you know, the "real" first *Star Wars*—Luke takes that initial step to begin his journey toward being a Jedi Master after seeing the holographic distress message from Princess Leia (spoiler alert! His sister!) and leaving the safety of his home on Tatooine.
- In *Harry Potter and the Deathly Hallows, Part 2* (2011), Harry must face the final showdown with his nemesis (and killer of his 'rents) Voldemort—even knowing he must die in the battle.
- In *Wonder Woman* (2017), Diana makes the decision that she must leave the safety of her home island of Themyscira to enter the dangerous arena of World War I, knowing the path could lead to destruction and pain.

It's that moment where our heroes step *beyond* that which is expected of them and venture into unknown territory. As viewers, we don't need to have that bravery explained to us: it's clear and present on the screen, and it's something each of us can identify with.

And frankly, that's not an accident. It's a nod to a cultural construct thousands of years in the making where notions of bravery and courage have existed since ancient times. Plato (you know: pre-eminent Greek philosopher and founder of the Academy in Athens, basically the first university in the western world—kinda wicked smart, oh and an alleged homo) considered *courage* one of the four cardinal virtues, along with *prudence, temperance,* and *justice.* In *The Nicomachean Ethics* Aristotle defines courage this way:

> "What sort of fearful things, then, has the courageous man to do with; the greatest, for no man is more able than he is to undergo terrible things; but death is the most terrible of all things; for it is a limit, and it is thought that to the dead there is nothing beyond, good or bad."
> (Aristotle, Browne & Bohn, 1850, p. 71)

OK, while ancient Greek philosophers may not be your cup o' tea, it's worth pointing out that this definition of *courage* is the same thing we're talking about when we're referring to courageous leadership in today's workplace jungle. *Courage* as defined by Merriam-Webster is the **"mental or moral strength to venture, persevere, and withstand danger, fear, or difficulty"** (Courage, n.d.).

In most ancient writing, the terms *dangerous* and *bravery* are most connected with battlefield courage and the willingness to confront danger (and maybe death) at the hands of the enemy.

It's the same thing we see with Luke, Harry, or Diana, but it's not exactly what anyone expects you to do when you show up to your cubicle or workplace ready to tackle the day.

## Courage Today

Let's take a look at a counterpoint to the classics and connect the dots through someone who understands battlefield courage very well.

In his book, *The Culture Code: The Secrets of Highly Successful Groups*, author Daniel Coyle tells the story of Dave Cooper, a nondescript member of one of Seal Team Six, one of the most respected and high-performing teams on the planet (2018). Now retired, neither Cooper nor his colleagues—all of whom give him glowing reviews and high praise—would tell you that he's the smartest or the strongest member of the team. However, what all of his peers will say is that Cooper understands how to build effective teams.

Coyle explains the story like this: after a night in which his team was captured by insurgents and then (miraculously) released, Cooper decided that he needed to help his teams function more effectively despite the traditional rank and file, top-down leadership for which the military is known. Breaking with tradition, Cooper started asking his team to speak up and poke holes in mission strategies. He worked to build team cohesion and separate himself from his military rank in favor of humility and the ability for himself and his team to admit when they screwed up. Cooper's willingness to break rank and even challenge authority during critical, operational moments played a major role in the Bin Laden raid in 2011.

For Cooper, a soldier with extensive battlefield experience, courage isn't defined by whizzing bullets and noble sacrifice: it's something far subtler. "When we talk about courage, we think it's going against an enemy with a machine gun," Cooper says. "The real courage is seeing the truth and speaking the truth to each other. People never want to be the person who says, 'Wait a second, what's really going on here?' But inside the squadron, that is the culture, and that's why we're successful" (Coyle, 2018, p. 145).

There's something that bears repeating: *seeing the truth and speaking it to one another.* Often, strict organization structure complicates this simple and effective strategy. It's stifling. Criticism is transformed into feedback, a tool that is often used as a stick to smack team members and peers into submission through malicious and punitive critique. It's no wonder people seize up when someone initiates a feedback process. (Seriously: someone walks up to you and says, "I have some feedback for you." What's your initial gut reaction? For most folks it's "ewwww" or something negative. We'll talk about effective feedback in Chapter 7.)

Those "policy fences" can smother innovation and creativity. It takes a strong LGBTQ+ Leader to step outside of those norms and build bridges from those fences. That willingness to take risks, to break out of the mold and pursue an alternative path, is what courageous leadership is all about. And guess what? As an LGBTQ+ Leader you've got this ... you're already a courageous person (but more on that in a few).

## Example: The Courage of the Rock Star Entrepreneur

In a piece for *Inc.com*, author Geoffrey James points out that courage is one of the key drivers of entrepreneurship (2018). "And courage is very rare in our world," he writes. "Numerous surveys of the population at large have shown that, above everything else, most people value security. It's sad, really" (James, 2018, para. 6). If you know anything about Maslow and his Hierarchy of Needs, this makes complete sense, as humans we need that safety and security (job security falls in this area, too!) in order to move further up the hierarchy toward self-actualization, or being one's best self.

While it's true that entrepreneurship comes with risk, it's not for everyone. But think of those folks around you who have their own business, or who leave their six-figure salaries to venture out on their own. Think about the farmer or franchisee in your world. What do they have in common? I'd venture a guess it was the courage to take risks for the payoff of a better outcome than where they were.

I'd bet dollars to donuts (mmmm … donuts) that exercising leadership courage is something that would benefit most workplaces in today's competitive landscape. Having courage is speaking your mind. Having courage in the workplace is admitting when you're wrong, or when others may be more right than you. And having courage in the workplace jungle is being authentic—being your authentic self in all that you do, day in and day out.

## Leadership Courage and the LGBTQ+ Leader

If you're not a Navy SEAL or a lightsaber-wielding Jedi or an immortal Amazonian princess, you're in luck! Courageous leadership doesn't require you to be any of those. But—by nature of who you are as an LGBTQ+ person—I'd argue that you already have a whole ton of courage up your sleeve. If you've taken the steps to be your true, authentic self in all aspects of your world, then you've already exercised that special courage that typically goes against the norm. We can channel that power to help you be a more effective leader in the workplace jungle.

You might be asking yourself about the benefits of courageous leadership at work, or you may be weighing the cost/benefit of engaging in courageous behavior in your workplace. We'll cover these in just a minute, but for now, let's take a look at the qualities of courageous leadership and some of the real-world traits that courageous leaders possess (or frankly that *you* already possess, and maybe didn't realize it, you amazing LGBTQ+ Leader).

## Cue Adele: Goin' (Not Rollin') in the Deep

Let's get a little deeper here and, if you're new to the idea of courageous leadership, take a step back and consider the two words separately. In the last section, we defined *courage* as the **"mental or moral strength to venture, persevere, and withstand danger, fear, or difficulty"** (Courage, n.d.). But what about *leadership*?

Mental break. Close your eyes. Wait! Don't do that until you read the next sentence. Reflect on this: What comes to your mind when you imagine a courageous leader? (OK, that eyes closed thing can come in now if you want.)

Perhaps you imagine courage as leadership from the front. The idea of a senior manager or C-Suite exec leading the charge toward goals by driving results through one-on-one customer interactions (while providing great coaching along the way) is an idea that resonates strongly among the employees toward the bottom of the org chart. Alternatively, maybe you see courageous leaders as those who push their team toward success by taking smart risks and implementing new technologies into a corporate structure, all while building a great team through training and back-end support. Neither of these is wrong, but the actions of a courageous leader can be big and grand, or they can be small and itty bitty.

You can find any number of books and articles out there about leading from the front or leading from behind. Regardless of your choice or preference toward leadership, I want to let you in on a little secret:

*Courageous leadership has nothing to do with whether you lead from the front or the back.*

Regardless of your leadership style, making room for courage will change the way you approach your obligations to your bosses, your team members, and your customers. Courage isn't what you paint on the outside of a house—it's what you pour into the foundation. That's where it should be: embedded so deeply in the core of your decision-making that you don't even know it's there.

That's the idea behind courage. It's deep. It's ingrained. It's with you down to the bedrock, down to the bones. It doesn't have to be something you're born with; it's something you can and should practice, daily, until it's second nature in every business decision you make (unconscious/competence again).

And, as an LGBTQ+ Leader, it's already in your foundation.

## Reflect on How You've Already Been Courageous

As an out LGBQ+ professional, you've done one of the most coura-geous things someone can do: come out as your authentic self (that is assuming you have come out of course; see my note in Chapter 4: Authenticity). For so many of us, that was probably one of the most challenging things to do: tell your closest friends, family, co-workers, and those around you in your world who you actually, authentically are, and manage the potential fallout. Well done!

Now, apply that to you as a present-day LGBTQ+ Leader. You got this courage thing. Each day—as you live your authentic self— being a minority in our society lends itself to having a certain level of courage to be you (especially depending on where you live and the community with which you are living, or what organization you work in, or even what field you are in as a professional).

Just think for a moment on the past week you've had: where have you exercised courage about being your authentic self? Was it holding your significant other's hand in public? Wearing what you felt most comfortable in to work, regarding of silly gender assumptions or dressing how a man/woman is "supposed" to dress? What about just being you as butch or nelly or whatever as you are? THAT'S true courage: being *you*. And that's the type of thing that—as you look at what makes a leader an excellent leader— you got already, my amazing LGBTQ+ Leader: being authentic is indeed being courageous.

## But WWWHHHYYY? Look In to Lead Out

In his book *Start with Why*, Simon Sinek presents the idea that the most successful companies and businesspeople aren't always the most well-funded or the most popular (2011). Often times, they're the companies that most understand *why* they're doing what they're doing in the first place. He writes:

> WHY: Very few people or companies can clearly articulate WHY they do WHAT they do. When I say WHY, I don't mean to make money—that's a result. By WHY, I mean what is your purpose, cause, or belief? WHY does your company exist? WHY do you get out of bed every morning? And WHY should anyone care? (Sinek, 2011, p. 28).

The question of *why* isn't only paramount to great results—it's essential to courageous leadership. If you don't know *why* you're making the decisions you're making, *why* you're leading the group you're leading, or *why* your team members work for your organization instead of someone else, that's a great starting point for introspection (drone leadership again).

The first step toward courage is to challenge some of those off-limit concepts, those ideas or processes within your workplace jungle where people's initial reaction is, "We can't change that because …". It's hard, it's messy, and it can be terrifying. At the end of the day, though, it's a foundational step toward courageous leadership and the success that follows.

This also speaks to breaking the yes-person mentality. You know: those folks in the team meeting who just agree with the senior executive in the room without really challenging the "why are we doing this?" perspective. Challenging the why—in a respectful and nonconfrontational manner—is a powerful way to show your value, but it takes courage to question the norm.

Courageous leadership isn't something that happens overnight. Courage itself can be a great catalyst for change both on a personal and professional level, but it has to start in a place much deeper than the surface (and we'll explore shaping your organizational change in Chapter 9).

# The Top 3 Challenges of Leadership Courage

When we think about being courageous in the workplace jungle, there are a lot of factors that can prevent us from being our most courageous selves. Time and again, these are the top three that tend to come up for leaders—especially LGBTQ+ Leaders:

## 1. The Challenge of Fear

If you were to ask around, you'd very likely find that a lack of courage and abundance of complacency comes down to one simple thing: fear. When we think about this in the business context it can be broken down into two subtypes of fear:

A. **Fear of (Perceived or Actual) Failure:** We all have our fears, both at work and at home. Maybe that fear manifests itself in something like perfectionism, where the idea of submitting anything less than perfect could alter the opinion of a boss or trusted ally. Some of my good friends are control freaks; they can't let it go (where's Elsa when you need her?). They're terrified that if they can't control every aspect of a project, it will fall to pieces while they watch hopelessly from the sidelines—and get blamed.

B. **Fear of Feeling Like an Outsider:** Maybe this fear comes from an even more personal place, where challenging the status quo will make you feel like an other or an outsider within your own workplace. As LGBTQ+ people, we've most likely had that feeling of being the outsider in the past (or maybe in the present). It's not fun. It's alienating and, for some of us, it's a feeling we don't want to ever feel again. So, in a work context, this desire to avoid the feeling of being the other leads us to be compliant, even if in our core we know the idea at hand really needs to be challenged for the good of the organization.

In both cases, fear doesn't cause paralysis: it causes stagnation.

Maybe hiding behind the fear of failure or the fear of feeling like the other has worked for you in the past. Heck, they might have even propelled you to success within your workplace jungle. Once we achieve success, it makes sense that we'd try the same tactic again—and again—and again until it becomes second nature.

It's like Pavlov and his pup. If you're not familiar with Ivan Pavlov, he's considered the father of behaviorism in psychology circles. Dr. Pavlov was a Russian physiologist who had a dog. He noticed that, when he fed his pooch, the dog salivated. Then, he started ringing a bell as he fed Fido. Of course, the dog continued to salivate. He then just rang the bell and the dog continued to salivate, even without seeing the food (don't worry: he eventually fed the pooch). So, he deduced that dogs (and humans) can be conditioned to respond to certain stimuli (McLeod, 2018).

This happens to us all the time within the workplace jungle, even to us lions and not dogs. We are conditioned to act a certain way based upon the stimuli around us. If, for example, we get accolades for maintaining the status quo and being that yes-person without asking the why, we won't change our behavior. And here's where the problem lies: if we want to be the most effective LGBTQ+ Leader out there, we want to have the courage to break out of those Pavlovian condition-responses and look at things objectively.

## 2. The Challenge of Assumptions (or Filling in The Blanks)

Quick story: it's 1976 (when I was personally −20 years old). Imagine we're looking at the surface of the planet Mars. Before touching down on the Martian surface in search of extraterrestrial life, we see the real Viking 1 orbit the Red Planet in search of a landing site for its sister probe: Viking 2. One of the images the spacecraft sent back caused quite a stir when NASA released it to the public: the likeness of a face, nearly two miles from end to end, seemed to be staring up at the probe.

Since then, the famous Face on Mars has become a cultural icon. It touched off conspiracy theories about ancient civilizations and ancient Martian wonders. To some, it wasn't a trick of the light: it was hard evidence of something else. The mystery surrounding the face wouldn't be resolved until eighteen years later, when the Mars Global Surveyor passed over the same region and captured ten photos of the same landform, and higher resolution in image capturing helped show that the original image of the "face" was simply a play on shadows and light, similar to New Hampshire's Man in the Mountain. Alas—as far as we know—Marvin the Martian (and his kin) didn't create the giant face Viking 1 saw. Despite this shiny, new evidence, some people still don't consider the matter settled; they're convinced that someONE (or ones) carved the face on the Martian surface.

Our non-Matt Damon Martian story illustrates something key to our biology that you've probably heard mentioned elsewhere: our brains are powerful survival tools, but many of the things that we've learned over the course of thousands of years aren't conducive to the type of society we've built for ourselves. As humans, we often fill in the gaps when we're presented with a situation where we don't know all the data. It's easy for us to connect the dots between one problem and the next, even when the two aren't related, without taking the time to examine our own approach. It's how we humans are wired.

When we think of this in the context of courage, we're either avoiding truly understanding the here and now, or we're scared (back to fear again!) to dive deeper into the truth of the situation. Having leadership courage means lifting up those rocks and seeing what's underneath; lack of courage is making assumptions about the situation without knowing all the information.

## 3. The Challenge of Being Locked into Current Behaviors

Let's talk about change for a minute. I'll tell you something you probably already know: **Most people don't like change.**

I know what people say in meetings and in employee reviews ("Change is awesome!"). I've seen it on quarterly documents and those inspirational posters from the 90s with the waves majestically rolling in the ocean ("The Only Constant is Change!"). On a fundamental level, change is a really fab idea: it's fresh and new, it expands horizons, it allows us to be innovative and to have new experiences. In the workplace jungle context, we initiate change so that our organization can grow and prosper. But the hard truth? The vast majority of people hate change.

Why? Well, on one hand (at the unconscious level) humans don't like to change because it hits a part of our brain that likes safety and security. As our cave-ancestors survived and grew as a species; they (like us) were wired to be fearful of changes. Engaging in something new could lead to a dangerous situation. Now, flash forward to today: we're still wired like this in changing situations. When most people engage in change, it leads to an unsettling feeling of vulnerability (you read more on our cave-selves in Chapter 3).

On the other hand, our conscious selves (for most folks anyway) don't like change because it's hard. We tend to get used to situations and know how to act and adjust to them, even if the situation isn't ideal. You might have heard the old adage: "the devil you know versus the devil you don't," meaning that we as humans tend to be OK with even bad situations/bosses/friends/relationships/etc. because we know where we stand in this context. Some humans don't like change so much that they'd sooner stay in a bad situation because it's not new to them than make a move to newness.

So, whether unconscious or conscious, for most folks, change is hard! Don't believe me? Let me ask you two questions:

1. When is the last time you changed anything at all about your morning routine? Anything? What time you get up, the order in which you do things every morning, the route you take to your workplace?

2. When is the last time you made a change that wasn't made out of necessity? I'm not talking about big events, like getting married or new pet ownership where you *had to* change your routine. Instead, I'm talking about those experimental times when you decided to shuffle things around and see how they turned out.

Every morning, people all over the world are scrambling out the door at the very last second to get to their workplace on time. For the most part, that rush is unnecessary: they're hitting snooze on their alarm three extra times before climbing out of bed and scrambling to punch a clock. Why? Because change is hard. We don't want to get up earlier. We don't want to go to bed earlier. We don't want to alter the way we do things. We don't want to make a change. We will if we have to, but if there's nothing forcing us to do it, we find an excuse to put it off.

One of the most important and fundamental things to recognize about most people is that we're creatures of habit, and habits are made of up of a set of behaviors. Those things are hard to change, especially after we're stuck in that rut. Don't think you have patterns? Get a dog. I have two awesome canine kids, and I swear one—my sweet canine daughter Ella—is in the puppy gifted program. She's so smart. For our morning walks, she watched the pattern I unconsciously created before we are at the point of getting out the door. First it was "Oh! He put my leash on me ... YAY! Walk!" to about five steps before where I'd (1) grab my iPhone headset, (2) put on my shoes, (3) get the poop bags, (4) put on a jacket, (5) put on her harness, and THEN (6) put on her leash. I was inadvertently creating these patterns every morning that eventually Ella picked up on and knew what the end outcomes would be: sniffing on a walk.

In *The Coaching Habit*, author Michael Bungay Stanier notes, "It's hard to change your behavior, and it takes courage to have a go at doing something differently, and resilience to keep at it when it doesn't work perfectly the first time (which it won't)" (Stanier, 2016, p. 25; and BTW, we play quite a bit with organizational change in Chapter 9).

## BONUS: Sidesteppin' da Fear

Let's wrap this chapter up by pointing out something that's not obvious at first glance. When you see heroes in those action flicks or you think of battlefield courage, something often gets lost in translation between what we see on the outside and what those leaders—especially when they're real people—are feeling on the inside. Often times, leaders are afraid even when they take a stand. This is especially true when the stakes are high.

Courage isn't the absence of fear: it's the ability to confront it, stand your ground, and hold firm in your belief that what you're doing—and why you're doing it—is right. The fear will still be there. Trust me, it's not going anywhere—but courageous leadership has nothing to do with erasing fear. It has everything to do with addressing it.

In *The ONE Thing*, author Gary Keller mentions that there are some things you should fear:

> Don't fear big. Fear mediocrity. Fear waste. Fear the lack of living to your fullest. When we fear big, we either consciously or subconsciously work against it. We either run toward lesser outcomes and opportunities or we simply run away from the big ones. If courage isn't the absence of fear, but moving past it, then thinking big isn't the absence of doubts, but moving past them. Only living big will let you experience your true life and work potential (Keller & Papasan, 2012, p. 89).

If you let it, fear can rule your life. Courageous leadership is about taking a step in the opposite direction and pushing past those boundaries you've set up for yourself.

## Becoming a (More) Courageous LGBTQ+ Leader

Up to this point, we've talked a lot about courage and leadership and the common pitfalls to both: fear and complacency. Let's look at specific steps you can take to become a more courageous LGBTQ+ Leader and what a healthy dose of courage might look like in your organization.

It's important to remember that courageous leadership isn't a self-centered process. True leadership is selfless. It's not about you, it's about the people you lead (and, recall leadership doesn't necessarily mean direct reports, you can be an individual contributor within your workplace jungle and still be a leader). As Dr. Brené Brown (BTW, she's a rock star) points out in her amazing book, *Dare to Lead*:

> There is incredible relief and power in naming and normalizing fear and uncertainty. We have to find the courage to look back at the people who are looking at us for leadership and say, "This is difficult. There are no simple answers. There is pain and fear that would be easy to unload on others—but that would be unfair and out of our integrity. We will walk through this in a way that makes us feel proud. It will be hard, but we will do it together" (Brown, 2018, p. 69).

Courageous leadership isn't an easy road. It requires patience, selflessness, trust, and vulnerability on your part. I know that might sound like a big ask, but when you're comfortable with who you are and you focus on building others, all of those things feel like second nature.

## Traits of Courage

In an article for *Forbes*, Authentic Leadership Alliance CEO Susan Tardanico pointed out ten traits of courageous leaders (2013):

1.  **Confront reality head-on.** Face the reality of where your organization is—don't view it through an "Everything is

Awesome!" *LEGO® Movie* fantasy. You can't make efforts to improve your organization if you don't own up to the reality.

2. **Seek feedback and listen.** We are our worst enemy at times; because we view the world through our own lens. Seek feedback from others to get their view. It's hard to listen to sometimes, but it can uncover those blind spots we may have (Steve's side note: We talk a lot about active listening in Chapter 7).

3. **Say what needs to be said.** Be real and engage in authentic conversation; as icky as it can feel. Having these critical convos is the only way true change and improvement can happen. It also means saying what needs to be said even if it's against the majority or might not be the most popular idea in your team.

4. **Encourage push-back.** As an LGBTQ+ Leader, you don't have to be a know-it-all; admitting to not knowing isn't a weakness but actually a strength. Encourage your people to ask the "why are we doing this?" question often. And encourage divergent perspectives.

5. **Take action on performance issues.** Don't shy away from confrontation with team members, peers, and even bosses. While it's tough for many to do, ignoring them and hoping they will go away actually makes things worse. Take timely action to mitigate people issues (around performance, attitude, etc.) before it impacts the rest of the team.

6. **Communicate openly and frequently.** In the Leadership World, you can't over-communicate. Even when you don't have all the answers, continue the dialogue and conversation with your team members. "I don't know" isn't a bad

phrase to use; but be sure to find the answer. And don't take the knowledge is power idea to mean the power is all for you, dear LGBTQ+ Leader, share (Cher?) it with the team so everyone is in the know.

7. **Lead change.** We'll talk a lot about change in Chapter 9, but Tardanico (2013) notes that keeping the status quo can be deadly to any organization; that change is inevitable. Get in front of the change and prepare your team for it. Actively engage in thinking about change and have the courage to embrace the ambiguity or unknown head-on with your team.

8. **Make decisions and move forward.** Don't succumb to analysis paralysis, meaning when you make decisions do so thoughtfully, but don't second-guess after those decisions are made. Fear can cause you to get stuck, while courage propels you forward and—even if the decision was not the best in hindsight—pick up the pieces, learn from it, and move on.

9. **Give credit to others.** An effective and courageous LGBTQ+ Leader shares the spotlight; they give credit where credit is due and they don't hog all the attention. Acknowledging the efforts of others won't put you out of a job, but actually strengthen your "street cred" within the organization.

10. **Hold people (and yourself) accountable.** Trust. Trust that people will do what they say they will do. Have courage and faith that they will come to you if they need help. Don't micromanage, but hold team members (and you,

dear LGBTQ+ Leader!) accountable for what happens (or doesn't happen). Model appropriate accountability when the time comes.

Take a minute to review that list. What strikes me most are the verbs she used to describe the actions a courageous leader should take: *confront, seek, say, encourage, take, communicate, lead, make, give, hold.* These aren't meek verbs; they're power words designed to drive results and create and foster change. They're bold, brave, and, well, courageous. Most importantly, those single words are clear and defining actions that you'd expect from a courageous leader.

If you take that analysis a step further, you might notice none of those phrases involve a single person. They're collaborative. They each involve an action you have to take in order to create change and empower others. They are about relationships and working with others, another leadership skill we'll talk about in Chapter 8.

## Courage is Straight Talk (Well, so to Speak)

As we think about the idea of courageous leadership, one thing that jumps out at me is the directness of it. Most people will tell you that they'd prefer a direct answer to their questions and concerns rather than playing corporate politics, being afraid to cause confrontation, or be a Debbie Downer or a naysayer—even if that's the way you feel. But that's exactly what we do. Many organizations have built entire policies and procedures around helping people communicate what they want to say without actually helping them say it! Sometimes, it's disguised as feedback in the form of an anonymous employee survey. Other times, it might be a comment card or suggestion box.

In her book *Radical Candor: Be a Kick-Ass Boss Without Losing Your Humanity*, author and CEO Kim Scott tells the story of an employee she calls "Bob" (Scott, 2017). Describing him as "one of those instantly likable people who makes going to work a pleasure," Scott outlines in detail her main problem with him. "His work," she writes, "was terrible."

However, instead of telling Bob that his work was pretty poopy, Scott accepted his work and couldn't find a way to address the problem with him directly. She worried that he might break down and told herself that she could fix it herself. It's the end result of the story that really sticks with me:

> As I faced the prospect of losing my team, I realized I couldn't put it off any longer. I invited Bob to have coffee with me. He expected to have a nice chat, but instead, after a few false starts, I fired him. Now we were both huddled miserably over our muffins and lattes. After an excruciating silence, Bob pushed his chair back, metal screeching on marble, and looked me straight in the eye. "Why didn't you tell me?" (Scott, 2017, p. xi).

If you feel like Scott in similar situations, it's time to re-evaluate your stance on courage, especially when it comes to those more difficult conversations. Don't wait for the problem to balloon out of proportion; confront that reality now, take action on those issues, and say what needs to be said. You're not doing yourself or the Bobs of the world any favors by keeping that information to yourself. Have the courage to speak the truth, even if it's icky and hard to do. But as long as you're doing with respect and from a good-hearted place, you can't go wrong as a courageous LGBTQ+ Leader.

## Courage is a Process ... Not a Destination

Before the brilliant Leonardo da Vinci was known as the quintessential Renaissance Man, he had to learn how to paint, analyze, and study the world around him. The great athlete and activist Billie Jean King wasn't born the most amazing of tennis players, but she started learning, on Day 1, how to hold her racquet. Legendary singer Johnny Mathis didn't start his career with admission into the Grammy Hall of Fame, but had to sing in bars and nightclubs before achieving global success. We see those individuals as titans of success in their respective fields, but often we don't realize how much work it took to get there.

And here's the thing I want to point out about courageous leadership: Like everything else, **it's a process.**

Steve Tobak, an executive coach and managing partner at Invisor Consulting, writes in an article for *Inc.com*, "Where does courage come from? You're not born with it. You develop it through experience" (Tobak, 2013, para. 15). I believe that's the most important takeaway that you can learn from courageous leadership. **It takes courage to practice becoming a courageous leader.** I practice yoga, and one of the things that struck me as really cool was how my instructors all talked about *practicing* yoga. They say, as you continue to practice your yoga, it's not a competition to be the best yogi, but for you to continue to get better yourself. Your practice is just that: YOUR practice. Make the most of it and know that—some days—your practice will be stronger than others. But as long as you keep practicing, you'll always keep moving forward in your skills.

## Final Thinks on Courage

As noted above, growing your LGBTQ+ leadership courage isn't an overnight experience, but something you need to practice and cultivate. Here's some actionable items to help you either get started on your path to a more courageous LGBTQ+ leadership style or become even more of a rock star:

1. **Start with the why.** Take a minute each day and ask yourself why you do things the way you do (this ties to our thoughts on being authentic in Chapter 3). Whether you're getting ready for work or communicating with a colleague, take a minute and consider whether your current strategy and the current leadership tools you're using are the best ones for the job.

2. **Don't assume.** As humans, we're prone to pattern recognition. We like to connect the dots and fill in gaps in our information. We make faces out of Martian hills when we do that. Instead of assuming that a colleague or team member is acting a certain way for a perceived reason, ask them out for coffee and dig into those questions with

them. Don't wait until it's too late and leave a co-worker asking why you kicked them to the curb.

3. **Don't try to bury your fear when you choose courage over complacency.** Butterflies in the stomach and goosebumps on the skin might be uncomfortable, but they shouldn't stop you from taking necessary steps. Acknowledge the discomfort, sidestep it, and get on with the business of the day.

4. **Remember: at its core, leadership is about empowering others.** Courageous leadership isn't mean, vindictive, or self-aggrandizing. By speaking clearly and saying what needs to be said—and holding yourself and others accountable—you're giving your team the tools and clarity they need to excel in their roles.

5. **Find your weakness, pull an Elsa, and just let it go.** Are you a control freak? Practice having the courage to delegate tasks. Do you find yourself frustrated by a particular individual or team focus goals? Don't shy away from those rough patches. Dig in. Get your hands dirty. Lead by example where you can and take the first step toward making things right.

Lastly, and this bears repeating (hehe: I said "bears"), remember that **courage is a process**. It doesn't happen overnight. But with proper dedication and an earnest commitment, it's something every LGBT+ Leader is capable of, just like practicing yoga. So namaste, bitches.

# Tie to G Quotient

For each of our leadership competencies that make up *Pride Leadership*, I want to quickly tie it back to Snyder's work from *The G Quotient* (Snyder, 2006) just to close our leadership story.

When I look at the concepts of courage we identified here and how it relates to your effectiveness as an LGBTQ+ Leader, it really touches upon three of Snyder's seven G Quotient principles:

- **Principle #1: Inclusion** … Having the courage to be inclusive is not always easy for a Leader; we are human, and we often like to be with people similar to us (our pack or, in a lion's case, our pride). But by exercising our courage to be more inclusive, we bring new perspectives, new insights, and new dimensions with those whom uncourageous Leaders may have ignored.

- **Principle #5: Communication** … If you're "doing" communication correctly as a Leader, you're approaching it as sharing the right message at the right time to the right people. To do this, an LGBTQ+ Leader has to sometimes share that key message—whether it's feedback, performance results, or simply organizational bad news—with those who need the message. This can be hard, and an effective LGBTQ+ Leader summons their courage when it's time to deliver those "tough messages."

- **Principle #6: Intuition** … Snyder's concept of intuition is the ability to pick up on those subtle clues that provide added information to your Leadership mix. A courageous leader often leverages their intuition while engaging with others to help understand how they're reacting to the context. Whether it's with engagement or discomfort, there are cues we as LGBTQ+ Leaders can leverage to manage the messages and the fear we may have and that of others around us.

# "Mane" Development Strategies: Building Your Leadership Courage

Here are a few activities you can do to increase your own leadership courage:

**ACTIVITY #1: Simply Try a New Activity** … Studies on building individual resilience and courage show that simply engaging in a new activity can help "rewire your brain" to be open to new (and previously unknown) experiences.

So, try that new hobby that looks interesting, maybe a new sport or athletic activity (sky diving, anyone?). Or maybe it's going to a meeting, social club, or religious organization of a demographic with which you're not associated.

All these things help us see situations differently, put us (safely) outside our comfort zone, and broaden our experiences.

**ACTIVITY #2: Delegate a Task to Someone** … If you ask any Leader, one of the scariest things to do is delegate a task (we discussed this above). But delegation not only is a great way to leverage team resources and/or develop others, it's a great way for you as an LGBTQ+ Leader to get comfortable with giving away responsibility (overcome that fear).

Be sure to follow delegation best practices, such as clearly identifying the task to delegate, establishing check-in times for the person responsible, and defining what success looks like for the task and what autonomy the delegate will have. And then practice letting go!

ACTIVITY #3: "Courageous" Movie Night ... Using what we shared about defining *courage*, watch a movie where you feel the main character(s) were acting in a courageous way (and no, *Wonder Woman* and that kind of hero movie doesn't count!).

What was it about the characters that resonated with you and courageous leadership? What are some of the skills and traits you can borrow from these characters to enhance your own leadership courage?

ACTIVITY #4: Business Process Audit ... Look at your work processes and find one that could be better. Ask yourself, "Why are we doing it this way?" if it's not working as you think it should?

Gather a team together to solicit input on how the process could be better. What are some of the tools, communication strategies, and resources needed to improve the process?

Share these with your senior leaders and see if they will help find these resources to make this new plan a reality (and you'll be exercising your courage along the way, too!).

ACTIVITY #5: Confront one of the Biggest Fears in Western Society ... While we'll cover this in Chapter 7 (Communication), one of the biggest fears people have is speaking in public. So, confront that fear (and develop your speaking skillz) by putting yourself into the spotlight.

Find opportunities for you to flex your public speaking muscles. Maybe it's opportunities within your workplace jungle at that next All Hands Meeting or Department Retreat, maybe it's at an industry conference, or perhaps outside of work at a civic group, volunteer organization, or place of worship: seek out opportunities to put you on stage and in the spotlight (and oh: this also helps with that communication skill from Chapter 7, too!).

# Drone Perspective: Reflective ?'s

1) On a scale of 1–10 with 10 being "I'm a rock star at leveraging my leadership courage" to 1 being "I'm pretty Cowardly Lion at the beginning of *The Wizard of Oz*," where would you rate yourself?

1    2    3    4    5    6    7    8    9    10

Why would you rate yourself there?

_____

_____

_____

_____

2) In your workplace jungle, what are you *most* afraid of?

_____

_____

_____

_____

How can or will you address this workplace fear?

_____

_____

_____

_____

3) Courage and vulnerability go hand-in-hand. When was the last time you showed vulnerability in your workplace?

_____

_____

_____

_____

What happened?

_____

_____

_____

What can you learn from that past experience?

_____

_____

_____

_____

4) How do you have the courage to engage in Radical Candor, or having those open and honest (and often hard) conversations?

_____

_____

_____

_____

What's easiest for you in these situations? What's hardest?

_____

_____

_____

_____

5) How do you plan to continually practice your leadership courage? What are three steps you can take to make it part of your everyday leadership world?

_____

_____

_____

_____

# JUNGLE LOVE:
# PRIDE LEADERSHIP IN ACTION

"As an infantry soldier, it's easy to assume that we are all tough and mean. After all, we train to fight our nation's wars. I have been a soldier in the infantry for twenty years. I was America's first transgender infantry soldier. While we do spend time learning to shoot and to fight, we also get the chance to do so much more. As parents, children, and spouses ourselves, when we go to a foreign country, we see ourselves and our families in those around us.

In 2003, my squad was on patrol in Kabul, Afghanistan. It was July, and it was hot. With body armor, helmets, rifles, and packs in the heat of the Afghan sun, my soldiers and I were sweating as we walked through the streets of the city. We must have looked tired because a man with a roadside stand came up to us as we walked. Our translator told us that the man would like to give us some sodas. I explained that we didn't have any money with us to pay for it. The Afghan man told us, 'These are for you. You are here making our country safe for my wife and children. I want you to have them.' No soda has ever tasted so good.

We continued our patrol and saw children playing in the field of a farm. They ran up to us as we walked asking us, 'What's that?' and pointing at our various bits and bobbles. While keeping vigilant we also talked with the children. When we returned to base we had talked about our experience. They reminded us of our own children."

*– Patricia K., U.S. Army veteran and Owner*
*Public Speaking & Consulting Firm*

## CHAPTER SIX

# YIELDING THE MAGIC FAIRY WAND (OR SWORD) OF EMPATHY

*"Having empathy and managing emotions are vastly under-represented in our modern workplace. The focus on the numbers, return on investment, and fiscal results is overshadowing our need to also balance this against how we're doing business, and how people feel about working for and with us. As the workplace demographics shifts, organizations—and smart leaders—best be looking at how to up their collective emotional intelligence or lose out in retaining the best talent and best customers."*

– Dr. Steve Yacovelli
The Gay Leadership Dude

Proactive Communication • Relationship-Building • Integrity, Authenticity, & Courage • Developing Culture • Empathy

# The Power of the Elephant

Before we dive into the concept of empathy, I want to share a concept from a most amazing book (seriously one of my favorites) written by brothers Chip and Dan Heath called *Switch*. In the book, they describe what psychologists know as two systems working away in our human brains:

1. the rational (or logical) system ... and
2. the emotional system (Heath & Heath, 2010).

Dr. Jonathan Haidt (a psychologist at New York University) came up with a great analogy for these two systems. He said to think of your brain as a person riding atop an Elephant. The Rider represents the rational, logical system that's the part of us that plans and problem-solves. The Rider might do some analyzing and decide, "Hey I want to go that way!" but it's the Elephant—representing our emotional system—that provides the power for the journey.

The Rider can try to lead the Elephant or drag the Elephant, and the Elephant can go along and be like, "OK, I'll go that way, Rider." But if these two ever disagree, who would you bet on to win the argument? (FYI, the Elephant has about a six-ton weight advantage). And it's exactly that power imbalance that makes adopting new behaviors very hard, and ultimately the emotional-self can overpower the logical-self if it wants.

Think about yourself: have you ever made New Year's resolutions to, say, get fit, eat healthier, cut back on the booze, or consistently exercise? How'd that work for ya? Chances are—like so many people—the Rider said, "Ya know, it would be really smart of me to knock off the Snickers® Bars and get to the gym," but that Elephant says, at 6:00 AM when that alarm goes off, "Oh come on, it's cold out. You're snuggly in bed. This feels so good. Just stay; you can work out tomorrow." Elephant is the winner winner, chicken dinner. And unless we really focus and appeal to our Elephant, that emotional side will be the prevailing force.

## Logic = Workplace World; Emotion = Personal World ... Not

"There's a lot of talk in this country about the federal deficit. But I think we should talk more about our empathy deficit—the ability to put ourselves in someone else's shoes; to see the world through those who are different from us ..." ~ President Barack Obama (Northwestern University, 2006).

OK, with our Rider and Elephant in our back pocket, let's focus on the chapter topic at hand: empathy. We throw the word *empathy* around a lot, but what actually does it mean? While there's a plethora of perspectives on the concept, we'll turn again to our dictionary peeps at Merriam-Webster to start, who define empathy as:

The action of understanding, being aware of, being sensitive to, and vicariously experiencing the feelings, thoughts, and experience of another of either the past or present without having the feelings, thoughts, and experience fully communicated in an objectively explicit manner (Empathy, n.d.).

Huh? Said another way, having empathy is when you can put yourself into the other person's context and see what's going on from their perspective; you can put yourself in their place to get a feeling of their emotions and experience, and respond accordingly. It's not an easy thing for some to do, but I suspect you—as an LGBTQ+ Leader—have a bit more experience in putting yourself in someone else's shoes (pumps?) than most.

I've worked with a lot of leaders over the years, and I've seen many fall into the "I'm the most smartest, so I'm in charge!" mentality (hellooooo, Rider!). They focus on having the subject matter expertise, the logical side of the equation, and completely ignore the human or emotional side of things. (To heck with you, Elephant!) This eventually bites them in the behind as humans are pesky, emotional creatures, and emotions don't stop at the front door of our workplace (much to the chagrin of many a manager).

## Why Can LGBTQ+ Folks Be Able to Put on Other People's Pumps Anyway?

Think about your life: for many of us we often hid our authentic selves, either because we weren't too sure what our authentic self actually was at the time, or our environment or context didn't seem as welcoming as we'd hope, preventing us from showing our true selves. Regardless, we trained ourselves (unconsciously or consciously) to adjust and fit into the prevailing context. For example, I didn't come out until I had graduated undergrad (circa 1994).

In college, I was the quintessential overachiever: president of my fraternity, involved in a bunch of clubs, honor roll, yadda yadda yadda. On an unconscious level, I was very good at maneuvering the social norms and understanding the emotions of those around me. In hindsight, this was a safety mechanism to help see who I needed to keep my guard up with or let it down for folks to see the (almost) authentic Steve.

Think about your experience. Have you been able to get a read on people, get a sense on their openness to and acceptance of you? What about having feelings for others who are marginalized, disenfranchised, or being treated unfairly because of who they are? Yes, these are situations where we—as LGBTQ+ people—have exercised our empathetic muscles. While I'm not saying our straight friends don't do this, we as LGBTQ+ people have had a lot of opportunity to exercise these skills just given who we are and our context in today's society.

Be careful not to confuse empathy with either compassion or sympathy. Compassion and sympathy are really about your feelings for someone: you see someone in pain, for example, and you "feel" for them. Compassion puts that feeling into action, where sympathy is just feeling for the person in their situation. Remember empathy is bigger than that. In fact, psychologists actually define three different—but complimentary—types or facets of empathy:

- **Cognitive empathy** … This is where we—using our logical side—can put ourselves in the other person's situation or proverbial shoes. We may have "been there" or we can at least imagine the challenge or the job or whatever the emotion of that certain citation. So here we're simply understanding the other person's situation or context.

- **Emotional (or social) empathy** ... This is where we are actually feeling—with emotions—what the other person is going through. It's like their emotional state is contagious and you are sensing their perspective. So here, we're not just understanding, but we're responding to the other person's situation through appropriate emotional response on our side.

- **Empathetic concern** ... This is where we feel compelled to help the person who's in an emotional state. If you're a parent (canine, feline, human, or otherwise), that feeling you have when you see your boo needing help and you feel compelled to help; that's your empathetic concern springing to life (Goleman, 2006).

As an LGBTQ+ Leader, you've most likely exercised these three areas of empathy to be successful in your world. What we want to do is channel that awesomeness into being an effective leader, but let's face it: it's a skill that goes well, well beyond the workplace jungle.

## The 3 E's: Elephants, Emotions, and Empathy (Oh My!)

When we think about being an empathetic LGBTQ+ Leader, while we leverage a little logic (yay, Rider!), we are largely talking about emotions (*bonjour*, Elephant!). Effective leaders understand this fact and don't underestimate emotions with influencing and leading their people. But let's get into our time machine and understand how the modern workplace has wanted to separate these two ideas.

Since the ancient Greeks, Western culture has long separated reason from emotion, setting emotions aside from logic has long been assumed to aid in clarity of thinking. For example; when 20th-century psychologists began to write about intelligence, they focused on areas such as memory and problem-solving. Heck, even as a kid, I was assessed by my (what I now understand to be) logical brain (think IQ tests, placement exams, etc.), without a real thought (no pun intended) to how we humans function from an emotional perspective (Cherniss, & Goleman, 2001).

Today, scientists recognize that our cognition is intimately tied up with our emotions. Research now shows that emotions play an integral role in our thought process; our mind isn't just remembering facts and logical stuff but a complex interconnectedness of rational and emotional. So much so, in fact, that some now believe that we cannot make decisions based on logic alone; even the most logical decision is routed in our emotions.

Yet much of our higher educational system is focused on the acquisition of knowledge, and development of emotion is secondary (for example: the role of Student Affairs and nonacademic activities are usually considered secondary services to the "service" of teaching and lecturing, and not accounting for the social learning and intelligence that occurs from outside-the-classroom learning). Traditionally, in the business world leaders have emphasized terms such as *return on investment* and *shareholder value*, and not emotional impact on employees or customers. Managers have always recognized the importance of psychology as the foundation underlying human behavior, but only in the past few years has *emotional intelligence* cropped up in business context—and even now the term is used with some hesitation.

As we hear more about emotional intelligence, some leaders are beginning to accept that there may be something to it, although others see it as, at best, a soft skill or, at worst, a fad. But we smart LGBTQ+ Leaders know that understanding emotions in the workplace can be the difference between success (rock star!) and mediocrity (meh … thanks for trying) in most cases.

## Minding our *E*'s & *Q*'s: Understanding EQ

But the times: they are a-changin'! The 21st-century workforce understands that there's an awesome shift in the importance of emotional intelligence versus cognitive intelligence at work. One famous study of over 2,500 hiring managers found that 71% of them preferred potential team members with higher *emotional quotient* (or EQ, meaning "emotional quotient," like "intelligence quotient," or Snyder's work in *The G Quotient* from Chapter 2) versus higher intelligence quotient (or IQ). Why? They mentioned things such as:

- High EQ candidates are better at remaining calm under stress
- High EQ candidates listen more than they speak, and
- High EQ candidates take criticism well and own up to their mistakes and—most importantly—learn from them (Grasz, 2011).

The term *emotional intelligence* is really your ability to identify, make sense of, and manage your feelings and emotions as well as those of others (both in and out of the workplace). Dr. Daniel

Goleman, author of a lot of books, articles, and studies on emotional intelligence, divides the concept into two distinct areas, with supportive areas within each:

AREA #1: Personal Competence—Focus on Self ... Here Goleman is saying that—in order to be emotionally intelligent—one needs to first look within and understand their own emotions. This makes up three distinct but complimentary areas:

- **Self-Awareness:** This is where we recognize and understand our own strengths and weaknesses, our own emotional ups and downs, and the impact our emotional state has on those around us. This area includes having not just emotional self-awareness, but having an accurate self-assessment of one's emotions. It also includes self-confidence; the self-aware individual isn't derailed by critics but reflects on and learns from their experiences and adapts accordingly.
- **Self-Regulation:** This is where we exercise restraint with regard to emotional situations. We pause and think before we express how we feel in a mature, thoughtful manner. Emotionally intelligent people don't let their emotions control their reactions to the world (looking at you, road rager!). Here we're defining concepts such as self-control, trustworthiness, conscientiousness, one's emotional adaptability, and innovativeness.
- **Self-Motivation:** This is where we have our achievement drive, our commitment to tasks and people, our initiative or the ability to reach personal goals, and optimism or

finding positives in a situation to motivate oneself, even in the face of adversity (you know; the glass-half-full thing).

**AREA #2: Social Competence—Focus on Others** ... Here Goleman is saying that—once the self's connection to emotions is understood and managed—one can focus energy on managing the engagement of the emotions of others, their moods, and their motives. This makes up two distinct but complimentary areas:

- **Social Awareness:** This is the ability to correctly read the emotions of other people and their emotional needs and concerns, and understand what is really going on— on an emotional level.
- **Social Skills:** This is where we take our social awareness and apply it to the "real world" and real people; we exercise our skills in areas such as desirable responses in others, supporting their emotional state, reading nonverbal cues, and responding appropriately in situations where emotions are involved (and that's pretty much every human interaction).

Said another way: emotional intelligence is a measure of one's street smarts or social radar regarding emotions, or the ability to read social cues and then to respond to them in a way that demonstrates an understanding of others' perspectives.

Let's talk about what EQ is not. It's not what you know; that's your IQ. EQ is not your personality, which for the most part is also pretty stable for your life; psychologists note that your personality doesn't change much. But your emotional intelligence can change. Emotional intelligence is not about being touchy feely, being nice, or just letting your emotions all hang out for all to see. It is about being aware of your feelings and those of others. It's about being mindful of your own emotions, how your emotional state can influence and impact others, and relating to others' emotional states in a productive manner. And it's definitely not about being emotional, but it is about being smart with your emotions.

Recall our definition from dictionary peeps at Merriam-Webster:

*... understanding, being aware of, being sensitive to, and vicariously experiencing the feelings, thoughts, and experience of another ...*

As an LGBTQ+ Leader, we strive to leverage empathy to best relate to, understand, and engage with those around us. And when you look at the concepts of emotional intelligence, it's really—at its core—empathy. The magic wand of empathy is an extremely powerful tool for us to use in our leadership world ... and well beyond.

## Balancing Our Emotions, Empathy, and Control

Emotions are messy, icky, and often unpredictable. Yet—as we know from our Rider and our Elephant—they can wonderfully overpower, move, shape, and form relationships and perceptions better than logic or facts or figures. We humans operate on that emotional level. Yet the workplace jungle (as we've covered) prefers that logical side to our emo side.

The key to emotions in the workplace jungle is balance. For ourselves as LGBTQ+ Leaders, we want our team to see us as humans (Chapters 3), as authentic (Chapter 4), and as having vulnerability (Chapter 5). Showing emotions within the workplace allows all of these wonderful leadership attributes to shine through.

One of the challenges with emotions—at work or at home—is that they're contagious. Think about it: you walk into work, in a peppy little mood after a good commute, and then you walk into that meeting. Everyone is Debbie Downer or Monday Moaner. The sky (at least from their perspective) is falling. Suddenly you see your own mood shift, you start to lose your pep step. Now you're the one who's saying things and that trombone—*whomp whomp*—is playing in the background. Emotions are contagious from others around you (humans are pack animals!), but you also have the opportunity to infect others with your emotional state (or at least try).

There's been heaps of studies about the power of positivity and how your emotional state can impact those around you. Your job as an LGBTQ+ Leader is to be mindful of your own emotional state and that of others. Strategies like a personal Emotional Temperature Check or one for your whole team can help bring a top-of-mind approach to understanding the emotions of others around you (see "Mane" Development Strategies: EQ-ing Yourself to the $N^{th}$ Level at the end of this chapter).

Maybe it's not them: it's you. You walk into work and you're bringing the emotional Tumi from home, the drama from your commute to work, or the reaction you have when the nice productive day you've planned goes to heck in a handbasket from a series of 9-1-1 fires. You're stressed; and now you're emotionally hijacked. Your emotions have taken over and you're working totally from an emotional place. That Elephant is in CONTROL! What do you do?

Stop. Take a deep breath. Think about what you are feeling and why. A study done years ago identified the top negative emotions felt in the workplace:

1. frustration or irritation;
2. worry or nervousness;
3. anger or aggravation;
4. dislike; and
5. disappointment or unhappiness.

How can we manage or control these emotions when we feel them in the workplace, to not only make ourselves feel better but to also minimize the impact these emotions have on others around us? (Fisher, 1997)

If you're feeling frustrated or irritated, think about what's causing the root of that frustration. We tend to feel this way when we're in a situation where we don't have control and/or we aren't making headway like we feel we should. One of the best things to do here is analyze what is working in the situation. Or—as you'll see is a strategy for many of these—identify one thing occurring in the situation that is good or positive (this can help shift the focus from the negative to the positive).

Feeling worried or nervous in your workplace? Consider removing yourself from others who can perpetuate or "swirl" the worried feelings to expand them (see "emotions are contagious" from earlier!) Worry tends to come from the feeling of the unknown, so focus your energy on what is known or what can be influenced in the situation. Focusing on what you can do versus what may or may not happen helps squelch that out-of-control feeling.

When we feel angry or aggravated in the jungle workplace, we can do a poop-ton of damage: not necessarily physical (although I did have a co-worker who used to throw office supplies while angry), but emotional damage to those around us. We can really do harm to our business relationships. This one can be tough: it takes a lot of reliance on our drone perspective to feel when we are getting angry. What are the typical signs you exhibit when you feel really mad? Note them and be aware when they rear their ugly heads. This is where breathing exercises, taking five deep, diaphragmatic breaths (deep breaths from your abdomen) can immediately lower your blood pressure and calm you down. Sometimes it's just best to remove yourself from the space so that you don't harm those around you, too.

The feeling of dislike can be pretty prevalent in the workplace jungle: especially toward people. Whether they are uninclusive peeps, people with vastly different personalities that we just can't seem to connect with, or people who just don't want to make the effort to connect with you, having people you dislike in the workplace is common. When you experience this, practice two simple rules. First, be respectful of them … meaning set aside your ego and try your best to be open. Leverage that empathy and imagine what it's like for that person. Second, if the person is being aggressive or uncooperative, don't simply take it, but be prepared to leverage key workplace phrases or tools to combat their negativity. For example: Once I had a client who would be really negative about others within the workplace (like, on the verge of being racist). It was annoying and it cut to the core of my personal values. But the company I was doing work with had a corporate value of valuing differences and being inclusive. So, when Annoying Alan would say some nasty comment, I'd be prepared to make a rebuttal like, "Wow, Alan, that statement doesn't seem to represent the XYZ Corporate Value of being inclusive, does it?" (Note: This is one of the strategies we'll learn in our next chapter on inclusive communication skills). Stand up for what's right but be respectful.

Disappointment or unhappiness is our final negative feeling we may have in the workplace jungle. Of all the bad feelings you may have at work, this one has the biggest hit on prolonged productivity: you lose energy, desire, and the willingness to take risks or try new things. To manage this, simply stop—and again, look for the good in the situation. Didn't get that promotion? Well, poop. Instead of focusing on the feeling of disappointment, reflect on the good that came out of the situation—what's the silver lining? While this seems easier said than done, it can go far in shifting your perspective to the positive (see Activity #7 under "Mane" Development Strategies for more help here).

Being hit by other people's emotional baggage can derail our success. But—more importantly—as an LGBTQ+ Leader, being mindful of our own emotional state and how it's impacting those around us is paramount. Being too emotional can create problems: it impedes our objectiveness and judgment, it can cause our "rational selves" to go away from the conversation, or—as my good friend and workwife used to say—it can "emotionally hijack" your rational self so that no logical thought comes into play in that heat of the moment.

We don't want to be a robot in the workplace and lack emotions, but we also don't want to be that overly emotional stressball, blubberer, or Oscar the Grouch in our workplace jungle. Gain perspective on why you're emotionally acting as the Elephant, and how you can leverage that Rider to steer that emotional Elephant in a positive direction.

## Amping Up Your Team's EQ

If emotional intelligence and leveraging empathy are such powerful ruby slippers of a leadership tool, Steve, how can we amp up these mad skillz? Glad you asked, Mr/Ms/Mx Leader!

While we'll focus on increasing our own personal EQ later in the chapter, let's focus our collective leadership awesomeness on how we can help our teams and others within our worlds become more empathetic and emotionally aware. Here's a few tactics to help:

1. **Incorporate Emo Checks Into the Team Mix** ... The goal for this exercise is a combination of self-awareness as well as allowing others around you to know where you're at from an emotional/mood perspective. It can be done on a simple index card. At the bottom write a scale from one to ten, with one being, "My stress is low!" to ten being, "Help! I'm a stressball!" Have this visual indicator in a common place for the team members to both identify their own emotional state and their personal perception of the overall team. Use this as a conversation starter in team meetings: "I see most of you thought last week was really stressful. Why is that?" This not only helps you as an

LGBTQ+ Leader get a gauge on the team's overall emotional status, but it also helps them start to have collective self-awareness of their own emotional states.

2. **Use a "Listen-To-Respond" Buzzer** ... In Chapter 7 we'll talk a lot about effective communication, especially effective listening. One of the concepts we talk about is how we tend to listen to respond to someone versus really listen to what they have to say. Share these concepts and— during team meetings—encourage others to identify when someone on the team is responding and not listening to understand. Make it fun by using a board game buzzer (my personal favorite is the buzzer from the game Taboo). Doing this not only brings the behavior to top-of-mind but creates fun and trust as well.

3. **Define "Emotional Rules of Engagement"** ... Every team should have ground rules on how they will work together, how they will communicate in meetings, etc. This includes an understanding on how to engage when angered, upset, or stressed by a co-worker. It's best to identify the "how we will work through in a stressful situation" than expect people—in the emotional grip during said situation—to manage effectively. This not only lays out expectations of engagement, but also allows for logic to come into play before emotions (not a bad idea in stressful interactions).

4. **Define the Team's Collective Emotional Strengths and "Areas of Opportunity"** ... An often-used workplace analytical tool is the famed "S.W.O.T. Analysis," where you identify your **S**trengths, **W**eaknesses **O**pportunities, and

Threats in any given work situation (for example you often see this conducted from a marketing perspective). Why not use the S.W.O.T. method to look at your team's overall emotional health? Do you have, say, trust already—which would translate into a huge strength? Have your team be the ones to populate the S.W.O.T. and see what bubbles up. This not only gets you the emotional data you can use as an LGBTQ+ Leader but gets the team to be self-aware of their own emotional stance.

5. **List What Are the Team Motivators** … Similar to the S.W.O.T. Analysis above, have your team identify what motivates them. In this exercise, have each person write on a Post-It® Note one thing that motivates them (each person on the team having their own color Post-It® is helpful, too). After a few minutes, have them present to the rest of the group. As the LGBTQ+ Leader, start to group like-items together to see trends among team members. Once all Post-Its® are on the wall ask participants what they see? Then—on a white board or flip chart—list what the team needs to accomplish (could be very detailed or high-level). Once this list is done, ask the team to determine a game plan so that the work the team is doing aligns with someone's areas of motivation. This not only helps the team do some self-reflection on what motivates them, but also helps align the work to those who will get the most out of it (of course if I'm motivated to do a task, I tend to enjoy doing it and also do it rather well). Take note of what motivates each person for future task assignments, too.

6. **Create Stress Relief Space** ... As you move to help your team be more emotionally aware, understand that you're creating the space for them to share their emotions. One of the most "taboo" emotions for people to share in the workplace is stress or distress. So, create a space that is safe and judgment-free for people to vent these emotions. For example, while I was working for a small marketing company, we often had wonderful clients call and "share their perspective" on things (read: bitch us out for no reason but to use us as a verbal punching bag). So, one of my smart leaders took a small underutilized storage closet and turned it into the De-Stress Room. Inside was a comfy chair, a jump rope, tissues, and a punching bag. She had the room padded with that noise-deafening foam (like in recording studios) to muffle the sounds. We were encouraged to vent as needed in that space. This worked not just as a space to truly vent but it went far as a symbol from our leadership team that, "Yes, this job can be stressful, and you need this space without judgment." Create some safe space in your workplace for people to feel free to vent judgment-free.

7. **Practice "Glass Half-Full" Mentality** ... This one can be really hard for some team members, as it's hitting the root of what challenges some people from enjoying life: looking at the glass as half empty. Studies show time and again that those who can find the most positive aspects— even in the poopiest of situations—tend to be more successful, emotionally well-adjusted, and frankly better to be

around than those who are consistently seeing the negative. Challenge your team to look at the brighter side of situations (see the #2—Buzzer idea, above). For you as the Leader, model the way by frequently asking (after those negative comments are shared), "Thanks for sharing, but what's one good thing that came out of that situation?" to help team members look for those silver linings.

Building the team's collective emotional intelligence of course increases their collective empathy, but also builds team identity and culture (we'll talk more about this in Chapter 9) and—most importantly—builds trust among members as well as with you, their fearless LGBTQ+ Leader.

# Tie to G Quotient

For each of our leadership competencies that make up *Pride Leadership*, I want to quickly tie it back to Snyder's work from *The G Quotient* (Snyder, 2006) just to close our leadership story.

When I look at the concepts of empathy and emotional intelligence we've shared here and how they relate to your effectiveness as an LGBTQ+ Leader, they touch upon three of Snyder's seven G Quotient principles:

- **Principle #3: Adaptability** ... LGBTQ+ Leaders must be adaptable to the emotional state of those around them. Being emotionally intelligent isn't just about managing your own emotions, but how you should manage your emotions in relationship to those in your workplace. Effective LGBTQ+ Leaders can adjust and adapt their empathy to the needs of their team members.
- **Principle #4: Connectivity** ... Emotions are about connection. Think of storytelling: we connect with stories because of our emotional attachment to the themes, the characters, etc. Smart LGBTQ+ Leaders understand that emotions are a conduit to connect people with places and with team members with work goals and objectives. It's not manipulative, but rather tapping into how we humans connect to one another through the heart, as well as the head.
- **Principle #6: Intuition** ... Small social cues, body language, tone; they're some of the many ways in which

LGBTQ+ Leaders gather data to engage with team members and others around them in the workplace. Snyder notes that feelings—to the LGBTQ+ Leader— can be just as insightful and telling as facts. Much of our intuitiveness as Leaders comes from the cues we've learned to read over the course of our lives, and we can leverage this experience in the workplace to be more effective leaders.

# "Mane" Development Strategies: EQ-ing Yourself to the Nth Level

Here are several activities you can do to increase your own empathy and emotional intelligence:

ACTIVITY #1: Analyze Your Own "Danger Radar" ... A good way to learn what triggers your *flight* or *fight*, response is through some self-analysis (back in that drone again!). For the next day or two, notice yourself as you get angry, frustrated, afraid, or defensive. Ask yourself what other feelings you have at the same time. When do you find yourself wanting to *fight*? to *flee*? What physical sensations do you have—in your palms, your gut, your neck/back/shoulders? As we analyze these data and bring it to a heightened sense of awareness, we're able to see these signs as they pop up in the future and manage them a little bit better.

ACTIVITY #2: Measure with Your "Stress-O-Meter" ... This activity is very similar to the one described earlier for teams, but this one is just for you, dear LGBTQ+ Leader. The goal for this exercise is also self-awareness, but also allowing others around you to know where you're at from an emotional/mood perspective. As with the team version of this activity, it can be done on a simple index card. At the bottom write a scale from one to ten, with one being, "My stress is low!" to ten being, "Help! I'm a stressball!". Set a timer to go off every 90 to 120 minutes; at that time identify on your meter where you feel at that moment. Don't do anything to manage the stress right now—just notice. Reflect on why you are ranking your stress-o-meter at that setting. Feel free to share with others (posting it outside your office or cubical in the workplace) to let others know where you're at stress-wise at that moment.

ACTIVITY #3: Play "Netflix Sans Sound" ... This tactic is to help us flex those understanding others' emotions muscles. While you're at lunch, in the mall, or in an airport, simply watch people around you (where you can't hear their words) and see if you can guess what's going on inside. This helps you become more attune to their emotions, especially emotional signals being sent nonverbally. This strategy is more fun when you have someone playing along—each of you observe the same scene, then compare notes on what you think each person was feeling.

ACTIVITY #4: Create Names for Your Emotions ... Imagine: you're in a restaurant for a romantic dinner with your significant other; it's a pricey place, but hey: it's a special occasion. You sit down (you're hungry, it's 8:00 PM after all) and then from a few tables over you hear it: the crying baby. And it's not just making noise, it's wailing. Ever happen to you? The tactic here is to—after taking a deep breath—identify the emotions you're feeling right now. Anger? Frustration? Disappointment? Now name the amalgamation (or combo) of all those feelings in this given situation. This is a true Steve scenario (I love kids, just not in restaurants at 8:00 PM when they should be in bed and I'm about to spend $50 on an entree for me and my hubby). *Babynightyells*? *Dinnerinterruptus*? *Screamnailschalkboard*? Psychologists call this an exercise in emotional granularity, which helps refine your emotional intelligence. It's like switching from standard TV to HiDef: the image is the same but the details, specificity, and understanding get a lot more refined.

**ACTIVITY #5: Leverage Your Workspouse** ... Sometimes we need help with our own self-awareness, and that's where the help of our workwife or workhusband comes in. We've shared before the benefit of having that trusted person in your workplace be the sounding board and extra eyes to help coach your desired behavior. Leverage them to, say, identify your emotional state during that staff meeting. Compare what you thought was your emotional state. Are they aligned? Did your workspouse see things differently? Use their perspective to broaden your own self-awareness of how others are interpreting your emotional state.

**ACTIVITY #6: Start a Motivation Journal** ... One of the facets of self-awareness in emotional intelligence is understanding what drives you to do things. Spend just a few minutes a day reflecting and writing down your thoughts on what moved you into action during the previous day. What do you find? A sense of accomplishment? Accolades from co-workers? Knowing you helped someone who needed it? By truly identifying what moves us into action, we can start to seek out opportunities that support that feeling, as well as be mindful as to why certain tasks don't "jive" with us (most likely they aren't feeding our values or hitting an area that drives us to begin with).

ACTIVITY #7: Start a What-Went-Well Journal ... Keeping with the documentation track, consider starting a What-Went-Well journal. Each night write down the five things that went well during the day—could be big things (landed that big client!) to small things (the cafeteria had liver for lunch!). Some nights it will be easy to rattle off five, while other nights you'll struggle to get just one. What you're doing is reprogramming your mind to look for the positive things in your world each day, especially on those really, really hard days. Studies show within two to three months it will actually change your perception to be more positive.

ACTIVITY #8: Practice Mindful Meditation ... We'll dive deep into the wells of mindfulness a little later (Chapter 10), but know that the concepts of being mindful and mindful meditation are a great way to bring about self-awareness on anything going on in your own body (without judgment), including your own emotions.

# Drone Perspective: Reflective ?'s

1) On a scale of 1 to 10 with 10 being "I'm wicked good at managing my emotions in the workplace" to 1 being "I'm pretty emotional all over the place at work" where would you rate yourself?

1    2    3    4    5    6    7    8    9    10

Why would you rate yourself there?

_____

_____

_____

_____

2) Sticking with our scale, where would you rate your focus on having a positive outlook on the world? Are you closer to 10 being "The world is amazing and everything is AWESOME!!!" or to 1 being "Life just stinks. Everything is sad."

1    2    3    4    5    6    7    8    9    10

Why would you rate yourself there?

_____

_____

_____

_____

Is that where you want to be?

_____

_____

_____

_____

3)  Looking at our two areas of Emotional Intelligence, are you stronger at *Personal Competence* or *Social Competence?*

_____

_____

_____

_____

Why would you say that?

_____

_____

_____

_____

Is this where you want to be?

_____

_____

_____

_____

4) Do you find yourself often getting "emotionally hijacked" in your workplace jungle, especially around the five negative emotions we identified (*frustration or irritation, worry or nervousness, anger or aggravation, dislike,* and *disappointment or unhappiness*)?

_____

_____

_____

_____

Is there a pattern? Which of these do you tend to experience more often?

_____

_____

_____

_____

Why do you think that is?

_____

_____

_____

_____

5) Think of a time when you saw someone engage in "bad" emotional behavior in your workplace jungle. What happened?

_____

_____

_____

What lasting impact did that person's outburst or negative feelings have on those around them?

_____

_____

_____

_____

What can you learn from their mistake?

_____

_____

_____

_____

# JUNGLE LOVE:
# PRIDE LEADERSHIP IN ACTION

"During my tenure as a regional manager with a home furnishing retailer, we had major changes in top leadership. One in particular was extremely influential in reshaping how I lead my team. Her name was Sharon and she was the Executive Vice President of all stores for North America, reporting directly to our CEO. She did so much to redirect the trajectory of our company that it would be nearly impossible to sum up in this one story. What I will share with you is how her leadership impacted me personally.

She was the first executive to personally make time to fearlessly listen to concerns and ask probing questions that made both you and her think about how to lead differently and more effectively. She made it very apparent that she was in this with you. For example, during every corporate tour, she was the only executive to hold round table discussions with multiple subordinates, in which she truly fostered open discussions about our people's daily struggles and what role senior leadership could take in correcting them. She took responsibility, without blaming anyone, for any and all concerns that were uncovered.

This showed me how someone so powerful could stay in touch with the front lines, bolstering morale, while still challenging each person on their personal contribution to the overall results. She listened, she took ownership for the problems, and she very consistently, very publicly praised individual successes. People felt heard, they felt supported, they felt valued. Many of our most successful corporate solutions and strategies arose from these round tables: people spoke up and she listened.

She once said to me, 'Lead with questions and truly listen.' It was in that listening that I learned what true leadership and change management looks like."

*— Mark D., Regional Manager,*
*Major Home Furnishing Retailer, U.S.A.*

. . . . . . . . . . . . . . . . . . . . . . . . . . . . . . . . . . . . . . . . . . . . . . . . .

# BEING KRYSTAL (CARRINGTON) CLEAR: FABULOUS COMMUNICATION

*"When we look at the most-used tool in an LGBTQ+
Leader's tool belt, it's the power of effective
communication. Whether it's aligning goals and work
effort, to understanding how team members are
feeling, to sharing the needs of the team to higher ups,
effective communication not only gets things done
but—when done well—it builds rapport and instills
trust with those around you. And that's powerful stuff
for any leader."*
– Dr. Steve Yacovelli
The Gay Leadership Dude

Proactive Communication • Relationship-Building • Integrity,
Authenticity, & Courage • Developing Culture • Empathy

# Startin' to Talk Goodly

Have you ever wondered about what you said or didn't say? What you should have said or shouldn't have said? What you thought you said or wished you had said? What you heard or didn't hear?

Duh, of course you have. We all have let words fly from our pie holes or let our fingers do too much of the talking on that keyboard that we wished we could take back, modify, or forget it ever happened. We communicate on a daily basis (it's kinda what us humans do), but we don't always do so in such a way that we say what we mean to say and mean, or what we mean to say is actually what was understood.

And, if you ask any leadership guru what are the top five skills an effective leader has, I'd bet dollars to donuts (mmmm ... donuts again) that they'd all say, "Awesome communication skills!" are in their top five. Effective communication is not a lost art; it's just that with the many modes of communication tools available at our disposal, it can be very easy, embarrassing, and often unforgiving when someone accidentally responds to an email or text without proofreading or thinking before hitting SEND. There are numerous examples of communicating selective, sensitive, and even highly secure information via the wrong method, at the wrong time, or even to the wrong person(s) (hello REPLY ALL!), resulting in the dreaded need to have to defend the message and do cleanup, which could easily derail your leadership effectiveness and your credibility and trust.

What's important is for LGBTQ+ Leaders to have the *courage* to learn to communicate effectively and to make it a priority (see what I did there? If not, revisit Chapter 5, my friend).

# Why are LGTBQ+ Folks Good at Communicating?

If you skim ahead at some of the noted best practices, what do you see? (Spoiler Alert!) Things like being open and honest, using active listening, connecting with those we're speaking to, and thinking about your communication style in relationship to others' perspective; these are things that we as LGBTQ+ people naturally tend to do. Sa-weet!

Go back to what Snyder found in his research for *The G Quotient* (summarized in Chapter 2). As LGBTQ+ people who—it's assumed—came out in our respective ways, we communicated a big honkin' deal about our authentic selves at one time in our lives to those around us. And—as Snyder noted—that experience showed us that overall, the sky didn't fall, life went on, and sharing our authenticity reinforced for many of us that being open and honest with our communication and our message is the right thing to do. We realized the value of truthful communication, and that experience carries over to us in our professional world and the messages we need to communicate within the workplace jungle. We tend to be OK with the hard conversations because, frankly, we've had some doozies in our life and survived.

In addition, as we tend to be better at leveraging empathy and putting ourselves in the position of how the "other" feels, we've had the practice of adapting our communication style so that it best resonates with those with whom we're engaging. We're inclusive by nature and want to hear the perspectives of those around us just as we want others to hear our perspective (see Chapters 3 and 6). Non-verbal cues, language choice, and possibly what's not being said are all helpful indicators that LGBTQ+ people naturally pick up on during their communication interactions with others. As LGTBQ+ Leaders, these are invaluable traits.

The challenge comes when we are communicating with those who aren't as inclusive as we are and close off those communication pathways of openness and honesty. LGBTQ+ Leaders (us) just need to keep our patience in check if and when we engage in communication experiences with those who are less inclusive and open as we are (or would like to be).

## Comm Together: How to Be a More Effective Communicator

Being an effective communicator is indeed your "secret sauce" for being a rock star LGBTQ+ Leader. But how do you "up your game" for comm success? Experts at *Inc. Magazine* shared several best practices for you to be a most awesome (and effective) communicator (Young Entrepreneur Council, 2015). These dozen-ish practices are worth including in your repertoire of how to improve your LGBTQ+ leadership comm style.

### It's All About You, Awesome Communicator

One of the three buckets or themes that the folks at *Inc.* share is focusing your communication energies on you as an individual communicator. So, for example, take a breath and have an open mind and ask before you speak (which sounds kinda of silly, but hear me out). Just because you hear about something doesn't mean that you have all the facts to speak about XYZ topic. To arm yourself to communicate effectively, consider asking questions, having honest and open conversations, avoiding prejudgments, and listening before you draw conclusions or address complex situations.

In addition, make sure you're relatable in your communication style. Nothing helps successful LGBTQ+ Leaders connect with team members and others in the organization more than being someone others can relate to and enjoy engaging with in meaningful small talk. As a Leader, when you let your guard down and show you're human, you give others permission to relax and feel they can relate—and potentially trust you (and yes, we've mentioned the whole "be human" thing several times within our book so far, especially Chapter 2 on *inclusion* and Chapter 6 on *empathy.*)

One of the most amazing communication tools that not everyone can use is having a good sense of humor. Even when situations may be uncomfortable or dreadfully serious, humor can be used effectively to ease minds, be memorable, and still communicate what needs to be said. Of course, not all humor is appropriate or acceptable, and frankly not all folks are lucky enough to be able to yield the gift of humor (kinda like Thor's mighty hammer: only some are worthy to yield it). If you're not typically a funny person, leverage the comm tool of humor with extreme care, Shecky Greene (and if you don't know that comedian, wouldn't it be cool if you had a little computer in your pocket that you could ask?).

We think we instinctively know how to listen; we don't have to think about it. However, the concept of *active listening* is an important part of the effective communication process. In basic communication you have a **sender** (the speaker; the one sending the **message**) and a **receiver**, the one who's not speaking and *should* be paying attention and listening. But active listening engages the receiver in a, well, more active role than just sitting and listening; they use nonverbal cues to show to the **sender** they are engaged, they nod their heads, say things like "ahhh-haas" and such, and ask the right questions for clarity. These are all signals the **receiver** sends back to the **sender** to show their interest, respect, and care. Above all, active listening helps you be sure that you understand what's being said so that you can respond appropriately.

Famed leadership guru Stephen Covey says, "Most people do not listen with the intent to understand; they listen with the intent to reply. They're either speaking or preparing to speak" (Covey, 1989, p. 239). Be sure to listen to understand, not just to respond (more on active listening a little later).

## Shaping Our Storytelling Like Tori Spelling

Once you think through you as the sender/receiver, the next communication bucket or area of focus is (for you the sender of the message) to think about how to effectively create your message or, as I like to say, story. To communicate effectively, you have to ensure your thoughts are clear, concise, coherent, and can be followed and remembered. One of the best storytelling strategies to help make your message "stick" and be clear is the use of repetition. Repetition helps you highlight, review, and emphasize your key points or themes for your audience—think Martin Luther King's "I Have A Dream" speech, one of the most well-known uses of repetition (Duarte, 2010). If you are using multimedia, take advantage of color and design to showcase your key points so those who are taking notes can capture them quickly, and repeat those same key points to bring closure. It's OK to repeat repeat yourself yourself.

In short: tell 'em what you're going to tell them, tell them, then tell 'em what you told them.

Another excellent communication strategy is the use of analogies. Analogies are like short stories with a point (see what I did there?), and great communicators use them effectively to convey more challenging stories and information. Analogies can help leaders answer questions, convey information, understand the organization's vision, and even assist with feedback on performance evaluations.

Finally, leverage the power of *finding your voice*. When we say, finding your voice, it's not necessarily about message delivery but message *creation*. When crafting your messages, if you want to effectively communicate and engage with your team, be yourself (back to that authenticity thing from Chapter 4). Don't be afraid to let the people around you see that you're a human with both emotions and logic (Chapter 6's Elephant and Rider). It doesn't mean that you disregard being professional, but that you have respect for yourself as a person and for those with whom you are speaking.

## Professionally & Passionately Process the Process, Please

The final bucket of effective communication strategies is not about you or your message, but more so about how you're engaging in the communication process in general. For example, when you receive a message, be sure to respond in a timely manner. No matter how good of a communicator you are (looking at YOU, LGBTQ+ rock star!), if you don't respond in a timely manner, that's a put off. Effective communicators value their time and that of others; timely responses become part of your reputation and street cred, not responding in a timely manner can put a *ding* in your rep.

Also, LGBTQ+ Leaders who communicate effectively know that when they're present in the moment for the conversation, dialogue, or exchange of information, they give and get trust and respect. Present communicators show they realize that that moment or experience is unique and will not happen in the same way again, so they eliminate distractions and pay attention to what they are doing right then. Oh, and present communicators ignore their phones when they are talking to people, too.

Great communicators know that, in order to communicate what they want to get across to others, they have to be flexible and ready to adjust their message, their words, their delivery, or even their medium for maximum effectiveness. Awesome LGBTQ+ leaders are nimble in their communication execution. That doesn't mean they aren't authentic (see our chapter on authenticity), but—like our dialing of ourselves in the context of the situation (remember U.S.-Steve and Euro-Steve?), effective LGBTQ+ communicators "turn the dials" on their authenticity to best meet the needs of their audience.

Beyond adjusting your delivery style to meet your audience, when we can, take the time to prepare the communication or the delivery means in ways that meet the needs of how people like to be communicated to, especially with important information such as rules, processes, and procedures. Effective communication can be considered *compassionate communication* because it takes into account that not everyone responds to messages the same or through the same channels in the exact same way; taking the time to determine how your peeps like to be communicated to is a wickedly simple and worthwhile investment. So, for example, if someone prefers receiving basic data via email or text, use that to share the info. But, some folks like that same time exchange, a phone call, webchat, or walk to their jungle nest may be better.

To that point, an effective LGBTQ+ communicator is consistently thinking about their audience. They know that their audience truly matters and strive to ensure they are in a good space to receive the message at hand. You don't need to ever be condescending to your team members (like, speaking to them like they're in kindergarten), but it can be effective if you can speak their language or at least use more common, casual terms that help to bring calm and comfort to the situation (especially the emotionally charged ones). When you do something that shows people that you are just like them, you communicate more effectively.

While listening and communicating, remember the written word and good visuals not only tell your story better but also are great for the future. It makes sense that you don't want to miscommunicate information, so to ensure that you communicate accurately and effectively, take brief notes of takeaways or key points from those jungle workplace convos. If you have some written notes (even if they're on your phone of tablet), you may need them and can access them quickly. Use that fancy phone of yours and take photos of flip charts or white board drawings to jog your memory. Sometimes the mind forgets, but it doesn't mean that you'll be forgiven if you forget something that's really significant.

As an LGBTQ+ Leader and effective communicator, remember that you're always "on." What does this mean? Simply put, it means that you are always prepared, on time, and on point. Effective LGBTQ+ communicators *stay* ready, so they don't have to *get* ready. And remember: your team and the peeps around you are always watching, so being "on" helps you to always be ready to respond (see personal branding in Chapter 4).

One final note here: there's a reason why there's a heckuva lot more tips for the communication process versus the "you" and the "story;" that's because people aren't just taking your message through the words you pick, but how you say them and communicate to them. There's a lot more data that is given to a recipient of a message than just the words you choose; so be very cognizant of how you're delivering your message, and how you follow up on that message after the fact. Which leads us to our next communication concept ...

## Whatdidwesay?!? Effective Listening Practices

Quick question: if you rearrange the letters of the word *listen* do you know what else you can spell? Yes, you can indeed spell words like *stilen*, *tislen*, and *nilste* (I have no clue what these words mean, if anything), but you CAN indeed spell the word *silent*. We mentioned active listening already, but I feel it's a topic that gets overlooked (underlistened?) in the effective leadership space and really think its power is underutilized.

Effective listening can show respect and that you are paying attention to your speaker, it gives your undivided attention and intentionally focuses on the storyteller. When attending workplace meetings, LGBTQ+ Leaders should be sure to model appropriate listening best practices, such as putting down the phone, not engaging in side conversations, or appearing disinterested or bored with the conversation at hand (and yes; people can tell by your nonverbal communication that you're bored; you're not that good, pa-pa-pa-Poker Face). Encouraging effective listening contributes to effective communication because sometimes the reason why communication is ineffective is simply due to the failure to listen. As the saying goes you do have two ears and one mouth for a reason; you should be listening twice as much as you speak.

## Sporty Spice: Leveraging Active Listening

Let's ignore that last bit of advice in that last sentence and go back to other ways in which we as humans listen—not with their ears. Have you ever noticed someone's body language and thought to yourself that they are either listening and paying attention, or they aren't? Your body language sends wickedly clear messages to people that you're paying attention, or not.

This is what we call *active listening*. It's the process of not just listening with our ears, but with our whole body. Leaning in, looking at the speaker, and, when appropriate, paraphrasing what you're hearing to make sure you're understanding their intent correctly, are all elements of active listening. Let's focus on the body language part. As an effective LGBTQ+ Leader you'll want to demonstrate that you are listening by ensuring that your body language is relaxed and shows that you are open, positive, and receptive. LGBTQ+ Leaders should ensure that when they are communicating they pay particular attention to their body language so that they don't miscommunicate something. (Oh, and if you are using a phone to, say, take notes: tell those around you that that's what you're doing. Seriously, it will manage their bias or expectations so they won't silently judge you while you're typing away while they speak).

Also, if you flip it around to where you're the speaker, body language can be a way for Leaders to effectively gauge how people in the audience may be receiving information. Respond appropriately to questions or comments or else risk being judged as someone who doesn't listen well.

OK, let's address that active listening paraphrasing thingy. Paraphrasing involves a restatement of the information given by the speaker and demonstrates to the speaker that you're both listening to them and actually understanding what they are saying. To improve your listening skills, try inserting paraphrasing statements such as:

- "I'm not sure I'm with you, but what I'm hearing is ..."
- "If I'm hearing you correctly ..."
- "So, from your perspective you see ..."
- "Listening to you, it seems as if ..."
- "So, as you see it, the thing you feel is most important is ..."
- "To me it's almost like you're saying ..."

## Another Way to Use the Term "Questioning"

Another effective way to acknowledge that you are listening is to use open-ended questions. Open-ended questions (OEQ's) help start a dialogue versus that one-sided conversation. OEQ's not only show that you're listening ('cause you're asking the right question at the right time and not that "umm hmmm" response that we sometimes give our significant other while "listening" to them ... I know you!). Give some of these OEQ's a shot:

- "Help me understand how you got to that perspective …"
- "What alternatives have you thought about … ?"
- "What do you mean by … ?"
- "What could some of the consequences be … ?"
- "What other possibilities are there… ?"
- "What were the considerations that led up to this … ?"
- "Why is this element the most important aspect?"
- "Where might this rule not necessarily hold true?"
- "How else could this situation be explained?"

### Listening Is Thru Our Own Personal Shiny Lens of Reality

Finally, when listening, be sure you are hearing not just the speaker's perspective but also remembering that we all have our own communication context with which we're sharing our story; we all have our own shiny lens of reality that filters our stories. While you should be paying attention to the speaker at hand, understand that they're presenting *their* perspective of the situation. Suspend your judgment until you've had the opportunity to hear the whole story, ask questions, and seek to truly understand. Assume good intent, but also feel free to seek out other perspectives if possible, to understand the full complexity of the situation.

# Your Delivery Method: Catching More Flies with Honey

As a LGBTQ+ Leader, you've probably heard, "It's not *what* you say, but *how* you say it." That's not just referring to the words you use to craft your message, the tone of your voice, and how you deliver your message, but it's also on the *delivery method* you pick (or are forced to use!) to share your story. The beauty of effective communication is not that it sounds good and makes you look like a rock star, but that it helps to avoid misunderstandings, creates a positive, peaceful work culture, and frankly helps you get stuff done ... if you use the *right* medium with the *right* delivery of that medium.

Let's explore some simple—yet effective—thoughts on how to leverage the different communication tools in our workplace jungle with the ease of swingin' on a vine.

**NOTE:** We'll be using the terms *synchronous* and *asynchronous* as it relates to our communication situations. So synchronous means at the same time, like we're communicating IRT with the receivers of our message. Asynchronous means—you guessed it—communication when we aren't somehow live and in person. So, my asynchronous friend, read on.

## Synchronous: Meetin' and Greetin'

Let's start with everyone's favorite communication method in the workplace jungle; *the meeting* (cue that sad trombone *waa-waa-waa* Debbie Downer sound here). Actually, meetings can be an awesome way to quickly share ideas and concepts (verbally or otherwise), discuss topics with the team, and build rapport and trust because you're in the same physical space as the others (we'll talk about blended methods below).

Effective face-to-face meetings have an agenda—even if it's a few bullet points—as well as an overarching purpose. Be sure to send that agenda BEFORE the meeting; there's nothing worse than showing up for a meeting and not being prepared because the LGBTQ+ Leader didn't share the agenda or just put "Meeting!" in the Outlook invite. Also, don't be that co-worker who calls meetings for every flippin' reason and invites God and Country to it (typically this is due to a lack of trust on the meeting-caller's part in either their ability to make decisions or their ability to do the work). Be respectful of people's time in face-to-face meetings and you will get a lot more out of them.

**Steve's Pro Tip:** If you want a meeting to be really short, remove the chairs in the room. Seriously, I used to do this when I worked as a consultant with a "Big Blue" company (whose initials correspond with HAL from *2001: A Space Odyssey*). If you've identified an agenda and what needs to be accomplished (and you honestly thought about the length of time it would take to meet said agenda and it's not that long) remove the chairs. People become very succinct when forced to stand* (*be mindful of those with differing abilities and check to ensure that if anyone does want to sit—due to physical reasons—that a chair is available for them. Thanks, HR Steve!).

## Synchronous: Formal Prezzies

Let's say you're still doing a face-to-face, but now it's your face to many, many others in a larger space. Don't fret (although *glossophobia* or the fear of public speaking is one of Gallup's most common fears), because as an effective LGBTQ+ communicator you got this (Newcomer, 2017). While there's a ton we could share here about effective public speaking (that's my next book most likely), the biggest things that you need to remember: overcome that glossophobia, that fear of standing up in front of folks and sharing your story (back to Chapter 5 on courage and hitting that fear head-on).

Why do some people get nervous when they speak in public? It actually goes back to our cave-wiring from our cave-ancestors again (we talked about some of this in Chapter 3 with unconscious bias). As you may recall, back in the cave-day, when our cave-relatives were in their cozy cave and a big, wooly, saber-toothed beast came to their cave door, they didn't sit and debate on what it wanted; they reacted—through their unconscious bias—with either the fight or flight approach. We humans are wired to react this way (or, some would argue, there's also the freeze mode, with inaction). If our cave-ancestors reacted from a fight perspective, the blood and oxygen flowed to their upper extremities—hands, arms—so they were ready to have the energy they need to fight that wooly beast. On the other hand, if they reacted from the flight position, the blood and oxygen flowed to the lower extremities—legs and feet. So, our cave-ancestors could run out the back cave door to safety.

Flash forward to you, dear LGBTQ+ Leader, standing at that podium in front of your division at the All Hands meeting in the 21$^{st}$ century. You're still wired in this fight-or-flight way when faced with perceived danger or a fearful situation, and your blood and much-needed oxygen leaves our head and core and moves to the arms or feet. This is when you can actually see or hear the presenter get physically nervous: they potentially have shortness of breath, dry mouth, fidgeting fingers, moving legs, or a lack of concentration because there's no oxygen in their heads to help them think of what they want to say next (maybe making them say "umm" or "ahh" to fill in the gaps to get them thinking). Darn cave-wiring!

OK, now it's you back up at that podium, eyeballs from the audience staring back at you and waiting for your amazing wisdom. Here's seven quick tips to combat those nervous butterflies in the stomach (and maybe elsewhere):

1. **Smile** ... Believe it or not, smiling has physiological positive effects on the brain and the body. Now don't Cheshire Cat it (grinning ear to ear in a serial-killer-sorta-way), but naturally smile to release dopamine, endorphins and serotonin (good brain stuff) to calm your nerves before you speak.

2. **Make friends** ... Because you'll have made the space of your speech or training session "your own" (see point #7), before you're scheduled to start, stand at the back of the room and greet people as they come in. Shake their hands, look them in the eye, introduce yourself, and connect. Then, while you're up front giving your spiel, you'll see these friendly faces in the audience. This trick goes very far in calming your nerves, as you psychologically have "allies" in the audience that you've connected to earlier.

3. **Establish eye contact** ... Connecting with your audience is key to speaking and getting your message across; it's also great to calm the nerves. Establish eye contact with the audience (but not in a staring-contest way). If the room is large enough you can actually look at people's foreheads if eye contact makes you nervous. (Oh, and be mindful of the context of culture; not all cultures handle eye contact the same way).

4. **Muscle tense and release** ... A handy (pun intended) trick before the speech: shrug your shoulder up, hold for a

few seconds, then release. Make fists for five seconds while your arms are folded up toward your shoulders; throw them down to get the blood and oxygen moving around your arms. Pretend your toes are in the sand and the beach and squish your toes together and release. These are quick and easy ways in which to combat the nervous energy going to the hands or the feet.

5. **Breathe** … Seems simple, but nervous speakers forget to breath. Taking three very deep breaths from the diaphragm (deep from the stomach, not shallow upper lung kinda breaths) can lower your heart rate quickly. If you're a yogi or know diaphragmatic breathing techniques from activities like singing or sports, insert them here!

6. **Positive Self-Talk** … OK, as open as you may be to all of this, this concept is where Leaders give me pushback. "Steve," they whine, "You want me to look in a mirror and give myself a pep talk?" Yup, that's it. While this may sound odd to some, psychologically it works to focus the mind and envision success. Studies have shown time and again what we visualize is what tends to transpire (it's called self-efficacy). See—and tell—yourself you will succeed, and it will work (and it will wrangle those stomach butterflies quite a bit*. (*30 Rock fans: Don't pull a Jack Donaghy and give yourself that pep talk … in the bathroom … with your mic turned on #themoreyouknow).

7. **"Owning the Room"** … One of the best pieces of advice I received as I started my speaking career was to—if possible—get into the physical space where you're going to give your speech or run your training event before the

actual event. This not only helps you visualize your success in that space (see #5, above), but also allows you to make the space your own through adjusting what needs to change for your talk. I absolutely hate podiums, and it shocks me how many of my clients have hard-wired podiums with computer stands at the front of the room. I frequently change things around (sorry, clients!) so the space is mine and I'm most comfortable to give my best.

## Synchronous: Uno-a-Unos

Not a lot to say here about one-on-one conversations, other than have a reason for the chat (when it comes to the workplace). Need to align goals? Share sensitive information? Just shoot the breeze (and thus build rapport and trust)? All good reasons to have a private chat.

One thing to consider goes back to our Pavlov and his pup story from Chapter 5. As you may recall, my canine daughter Ella is amazing at knowing when it's walk time based upon my behavior: five steps before we grab the leash, she knows it's walk time by observing my behavior. Your team members are like Ella: they know your behaviors and where this is going. For example: If you only have one-on-ones with your peeps to give them bad news, guess what happens when a team member sees that calendar invite pop up for us to meet one-on-one. ANXIETY! DREAD! And that's on you, as you've conditioned them to think that way. Same goes if you are in an open office situation and you only schedule one-on-ones for that private huddle room, but any other feedback you share openly for all to hear.

So, just be mindful of the patterns of behavior you have, especially with things like one-on-one meetings. Mix it up, meet to say, "Awesome job!" (you should be doing that anyway, LGBTQ+ rock star).

## Synchronous: Smile Perdy—Webinars & Video Chat

Webinars and video chats are a wonderful way to cross distance with team members (and family alike!). But be mindful that the medium (the webcam) doesn't destroy the message you're trying to send.

Think of your webcam space as a production studio (because it actually is). What does your lighting look like? Too dark? Too light? What's the angle of your camera (if you're using the laptop embedded webcam and your laptop isn't on a stand or raised up: please just stop—we don't want to look up your nose or at your chin for the conversation, just like I don't want to sit on the floor and look up at you in a face-to-face meeting!). What are you wearing? Is that shirt too loud, is the print distracting?

Think about your space around you. What's behind you on camera? A bookcase with distracting art? A window (so the lighting looks like you're an angelic silhouette to your audience)? I can't tell you how many times people were inadvertently wearing "hats" (lamps behind them that looked like some royal family fascinator on their noggins) on webinars I've attended.

Using webcams and video is great, but—like any other story delivery method—it can be wickedly distracting. Be mindful of the setup you have and how you use the tools, and if you need to be sure to practice.

## Synchronous: Telephonin' (Cue Gaga and Beyonce, You Little Monster)

While the telephone/conference call is something we've been using for quite some time, there are still things to be mindful of so that our message/story is clearly heard. First, for a one-on-one call, revisit the items we shared in the previous section about effective storytelling (especially the one about being present). It's easier to get sidetracked on the phone than in person (your fellow communicator can't see what you're doing), but guess what? They can hear it. It's obvious when you are checking email or distracted, and that erodes you being present and building rapport with the other person.

For conference calls: be sure everyone is engaged in the call. Like one-on-one phone chats, it's very easy for a participant to be distracted or totally disengaged from the call. As an effective LGBTQ+ Leader—even if you're not leading the meeting—ask phone participants for their perspective on things. Not only does this send a message that you're expecting them to pay attention (just like high school and the teacher calling on you!), but more importantly, it's opening the way for them to interject their thoughts. This is especially important for our introverted friends on conference calls who often check out because for them it's exhausting to try and jump in over those extraverts who are babbling.

Also, for some people, the echo of a conference call on speaker phone is very hard to hear. Some is due to the technology (FYI, most conference call systems auto turn off the speaker unless it hears a sound; so, if there is constant noise it will shut off until it hears a sound, and it often causes a lag in the mic). Some is due to people's hearing (for me: I have canine hearing, but for some reason,

I struggle to filter through all the noise on a conference call). Be sure people use their mute buttons appropriately, or if there's communication issues consider using the addition of another method like webchat (where there's typically virtual white boards and a chat window).

## Synchronous: Margarita Messages—Turning on the Comm Blender

Often, in our $21^{st}$-century jungle of a workplace, we aren't just using one synchronous (people meeting at the same time) method—no, ma'am, we're mixin' it up. Some peeps in the conference room, some dialed in on the phone, others on the interwebs via VoiP or maybe with a webcam turned on; it's awesomely inexpensive for teams across regions or countries to meet in the virtual space to get stuff done.

The challenge comes when the leader of the meeting (assuming that's you, LGBTQ+ rock star) isn't super savvy with setting up these blended situations for success or doesn't know how to best blend the use of all of these together.

Basic rule of thumb: using technology for teaching and learning is meant to get as close to the experience as a face-to-face (F2F) meeting experience as possible (this is what a doctorate in instructional technology gets ya: good Pro Tips for distance communication AND student loan indebtedness!). Seriously, your job as the LGBTQ+ Leader is to bridge the gaps for the participants to have as equal of a communication experience as possible. So, manage the in-room people to be mindful of those side conversations (since they add extra noise to the space). Encourage distance participants to speak up, maybe even calling on them specifically to share their thoughts on the topic at hand. Maybe it's assigning someone to be the "Engagement Ambassador" to help you ensure everyone feels like their voice is literally being heard in the meeting.

Don't have a bias toward those in the physical space versus those dialing in on alternative communication methods. This sends a signal (unconscious) that those in the physical space are more important to the conversation than those joining virtually. It's being an inclusive communicator, but in a different way: ensuring all voices and ideas—no matter where they're coming from—are being heard.

## Asynchronous: Email and Text (not Sexting ... You're at Work! HR!!)

For asynchronous message-sending (email or text) your job is to be succinct. Seventeen-paragraph email? Maybe that's a message better shared in person and followed up with stuff in writing. Need to acknowledge receipt of a message? The REPLY ALL to say, "OK!" is probably not a good use of everyone's inbox or time.

With asynchronous communication, your challenge—as an effective LGBTQ+ communicator—is to try and interpret the tone of the message from your recipient's perspective. This is key (and often overlooked): we use things like email and text often because we prefer it, or it's easier for us, or it's quick and simple. However, this type of communication really assumes tone (which is a big part of communication) is understood by sender and receiver. For example, I absolutely despise when people reply to my text with a simple, "K." I know this might not be the tone they meant, but—for whatever unconscious bias reason—I interpret this as being short-toned; the sender couldn't be bothered to find the O to complete the word *OK*? I'm not worth that extra 0.25 seconds effort? Just be mindful of how your tone is being interpreted in asynchronous communication, and maybe ask the recipient what tone they received from the message. Are they in sync?

### Regardless of the Medium, Be "Swet as Tea" (that's How We Say "Sweet" in the South)

There is an old saying that you can catch more flies with honey than you do with vinegar because the flies are attracted to the sweetness. So, it makes sense to create a receptive atmosphere for communicating—regardless of the delivery method. Speak articulately and use the appropriate tone of voice with your team, face-to-face or via distance. And, again regardless of media delivery, be appreciative and realize that you get to be an LGBTQ+ Leader. Let those you're communicating with know you value and respect their time and engagement in the conversation—synchronously or asynchronously.

## Inclusive Communication: Playing with MOP+SAM

In Chapter 3 (Being an Inclusive Leader) I started a story about when I was in a conference room and the senior executive said the "… you know how women drivers are!" comment and we had our John Hughes' record-scratch moment? Well it's time to wrap up that story.

That moment—when no one said anything after the exec's poopy comments on women drivers—is what we call *silent collusion*. Silent collusion is the practice of neither supporting nor defending the rights of others to be fully included in the workplace (Aguilar, 2006). Silent collusion basically says that, if those of us in the space where the uninclusive comment is said or the exclusionary action is being done remain silent and don't act, then we are tacitly endorsing the comment or behavior.

To finish our story from Chapter 3 … after what seemed like an eternity, a young man—who had actually just started with the organization not that long ago—muttered just loud enough for everyone to hear, "DAMN!" in a very-obvious way that he didn't support what the executive said. At that moment, the executive realized what he said and did some serious back-peddling. But, from that simple "DAMN!" from the young man, it was very obvious he didn't support the stereotype on the proverbial table. (And the executive? He quickly did a lot of apologies and back-peddling, as this simple "DAMN!" jarred him out of his unconscious bias and he went into damage-control mode.)

As an LGBTQ+ Leader, we strive to create an inclusive environment, and that includes stopping uninclusive situations like the one above, even if it's uncomfortable or icky (see Chapter 5 on courage). And one of the strategies we can use is with the help of a dog named Sam. Sam is what's called a Hungarian Puli Mop, or Mop Dog for short. You've seen pups like Sam before: he seriously looks like—if I attached a stick on his back—I could scrub my floors with his puppy butt (don't believe me? Google "mop dog" to see Sam's kin).

Sam's going to help us remember The 6 Ways We Can Beat Silent Collusion in our Jungle Workplace … using his name and the slang name of his breed (mop [dog] + Sam = the six ways we can combat silent collusion ... MOP+SAM (pronounced *mop sam* ... don't pronounce the +). SIDE NOTE: OK, this is silly, but I've been using this as a way for people to remember what they can do to combat silent collusion and it works. So, trust me and, well, Sam.

**M—Me** ... The first *M* in MOP+SAM stands for *me*. Ask yourself, "Is the uninclusive statement something that impacts me personally?" If so, you can address the person from your own feelings and perspective (after all, your perception is your reality). Then you can speak to the comment from the first person. For example (referring to our story from above), "As a woman, Bob (Bob is now the name of our executive), I find that statement to be inaccurate. I feel I'm a very good driver." The good thing about this strategy is that it focuses on you as a person, not the stereotype Bob engaged in. The challenge is that it could be perceived as confrontational in nature, so some people may immediately be put on the defensive.

**O—Out** ... The next strategy, according to our friend Sam, is *O*, which in MOP+SAM stands for *out*. While the comment may not be about *me*, you can call OUT any absolutes, stereotypes, or gross generalizations you may hear someone say in order to beat silent collusion. "So, Bob, you've driven with every woman in the world?" could be one way to address the stereotype being said. The good thing here is, if Bob is operating on his unconscious bias, it may bring his microinequity to his consciousness, allowing him to see how he's turned his bias against women drivers into a hurtful statement. The challenging thing here—like our ME strategy—is that it could come off as confrontational to Bob. If Bob's unconscious bias toward women drivers is deeply held, he could quickly fall into a defensive stance.

**P—Point ...** The next MOP+SAM strategy is *P*, which stands for *point*. After the statement is said, point to a specific example that refutes the statement being said. "Well actually, Bob, I think we would both agree that Juanita—who drove us to lunch yesterday—is an awesome driver who happens to be female." The benefit of this strategy is that it illustrates an example that the person saying the microinequity can relate to, and immediately provides evidence to contradict their statement. The challenge is that the rebuttal can come across as something like, "Well, she's the exception, not the norm," and provides a way for the owner of the biased statement to brush away the microinequity they stated.

**S—Say ...** Sam the pup says that the next strategy is *S*, which stands for *say*. When we use *say*, we mean saying a nonword that at least indicates you don't agree with what's being said. Responses like "Woah!" "Damn!" "Whaaaat?" or "Huh?" are some you can try here. But find one that fits with you and your personality; don't force something. The benefit of this response is that it's not very confrontational, but sends the message that you don't necessarily agree with the statement said. You break the *silence* in the silent collusion. The challenge is that it's nothing more than acknowledging that you personally don't agree with the statement being said. It doesn't go far in addressing the statement. In addition, if you say a nonword that is not in line with how you speak or your personality, the comment could come across as insincere.

**A—Ask ...** This MOP+SAM strategy is *A*, which stands for *ask*. This one is rather simple: ask the person exactly what they meant by their comment. Ask a question directly such as, "Bob, what exactly did you mean by that statement?" The benefit is—like some other strategies—it directly addresses the statement and may allow the microaggressor to break out of their unconscious bias statement and hear it for what it is. It is also more of a neutral statement; whenever you are asking for clarification—in a neutral tone—you cannot be accused of being aggressive or adversarial. The challenge is with the tone in which the statement is given. It would be easy for emotions to get the better of the deliverer (that's you!) and ask the same question in an accusatory tone. Be careful here; the words are fine but it's the tone that matters.

**M—Move ...** Our final strategy in MOP+SAM is the second *M*, which stands for *move*. As a last resort, if you cannot or don't feel comfortable speaking up, then physically remove yourself from the situation/conversation. The benefit is that your nonverbal movement will speak volumes that you don't agree with what's being said. The challenge is that—like our SAY strategy—it's nothing more than acknowledging that you personally don't agree with the statement being said; it doesn't go far in addressing the statement.

As an effective LGBTQ+ communicator, we aren't only trying to get our message across, but looking for ways to help shape our culture to be more inclusive. We'll explore a lot more of this in Chapter 9.

# Tie to G Quotient

Again, for each of our leadership competencies that make up *Pride Leadership*, I want to quickly tie it back to Snyder's work from *The G Quotient* (Snyder, 2006) just to close our leadership story.

When I look at the concept of effective communication and how it connects to your LGBTQ+ awesomeness, it touches upon three of Snyder's G Quotient principles:

- **Principle #5: Communication** ... This one is a no-(know?) brainer: Snyder's definition of communication perfectly fits with our ideal associated with effective communication. From courageous communication to open and direct strategies that make an LGBTQ+ Leader effective from Snyder's research, so, too do we align in our thoughts on communication as it relates to leadership success.
- **Principle #1: Inclusion** ... To be an effective communicator is to be an inclusive one. LTBGQ+ Leaders by nature of who they are, are positioned to be inclusive in how they communicate, as it's how they tend to act and engage with others. Inclusive in not only demographics, but in preferred methods of communication and story strategies all ties in with being an inclusive communicator.
- **Principle #2: Creativity** ... From adjusting our story to better meet the needs of the receiver to innovative uses of various delivery methods to best tell our story, LGBTQ+ Leaders leverage their natural creative instincts to not only communicate effectively, but to craft messages and stories that stick with the receiver.

# "Mane" Development Strategies: Cultivating Our Krystal-Clear Communications

Here are several activities you can do to increase your own communication excellence, dear LGBTQ+ Leader:

**ACTIVITY #1: Practice Playing with MOP+SAM ...** We covered the concepts of inclusive communication and mitigating the whole silent collusion situation in the workplace jungle (MOP+SAM!). As an effective LGBTQ+ Leader, how can you make this part if your overall organizational culture (yes, we're getting ahead of ourselves and there's some good strategies we can use from Chapter 9 so stay tuned!).

How can you at least get your team to embrace and use the MOP+SAM method to be more inclusive in your jungle workplace?

**ACTIVITY #2: Improv Storytelling ...** This activity requires a workwife/workhubby to play. The idea here is to improve the crafting of your stories and messages through the use of improv. First, find a public area with your BFF: could be a mall, outside near a cafe, an airport (if you're traveling)—anywhere where there's a lot of people coming and going. Then the first person picks someone "interesting" (in quotes, as that's up to you to interpret) and shares verbally with their mate the "story" behind the person.

"Oh, there's Rodger," says Player 1 about a random, middle-aged man wearing a beat-up black T-shirt and jeans, carrying a very smart briefcase. "He just came from his big meeting about this mural he'd like to paint on that wall over there." Player 2: "Oh, how did Rodger's meeting go?" Player 1: "Not so well, you can tell by the look on his face. While they liked the idea, they thought it was too radical for this neighborhood." Player 2: "What do you think Rodger will do now?" Player 1: .... etc.

The idea is to practice telling compelling, descriptive stories (as we recall, this skill can be very useful to create messages that will stick with your audiences). Also—as an added bonus—be mindful of your own unconscious biases that may be creeping into the conversation and call one another out when these occur (beefing up your own mindfulness from Chapter 3).

**ACTIVITY #3: Inventory Your Preferred Comm Ways …** We shared some ideas on the different ways in the workplace jungle you can share your stories and communicate with those around you.

Grab a pack of Post-It® Notes and write out all the ways you communicate in your respective workplace (one item per sticky note). On a wall, put them in your preferred order, left-most item is your most preferred; right is your least preferred.

Now, look at the messages and stories you get over the course of a week. Where do they typically fall? Are they supporting your preferences or disproportional to your preferred communication style? Repeat this for your team: do they have a preference? Over the course of a typical week, are you leveraging the preferred style?

In both instances, what can you do as an effective LGBTQ+ Leader to shift the delivery distribution usage to maximize your and your team's preferred styles?

**ACTIVITY #4: Listen, Listen, Then Speak …** With a partner (workwife or workhubby perhaps), practice active listening. During your next conversation (formally or informally), challenge each other to use the active listening strategies we identified; use the phrases listed, be mindful of your body language, etc. Be sure you both get a turn playing the part of the listener and the speaker.

How did that work? Did you notice a difference in what you heard from one another? In your next team meeting, practice the same strategies and see if you hear things differently. Report back to one another on how it worked.

**ACTIVITY #5: How Do You Get to Carnegie Hall? …** Practice, practice, practice (again awesomely bad Dad joke!). To become proficient at anything—especially at speaking and presenting in front of others—takes practice.

Like we suggested at the end of Chapter 5, find opportunities for you to flex your public speaking skills. Maybe it's opportunities within your workplace jungle at that next All-Hands Meeting or Department Retreat, maybe it's at an industry conference, or perhaps outside of work at a civic group, volunteer organization, or place of worship: seek out opportunities to put you on stage and in the spotlight (and oh: this also helps with that *courage* skill from, too!).

# Drone Perspective: Reflective ?'s

1) On a scale of 1–10 with 10 being "I'm the most a-maaaaaaaaaz-ing communicator" to 1 being "Meh, comm ain't my jam," where would you rate yourself?

1    2    3    4    5    6    7    8    9    10

Why would you rate yourself there?

_____

_____

_____

_____

2) Of all the communication methods we shared (and the others that are maybe in your workplace jungle), which one(s) do you prefer? Why?

_____

_____

_____

_____

Do you tend to overuse this/these method(s) of communication?

_____

_____

_____

_____

How can you get more diverse in your communication methods?

_____

_____

_____

_____

3) Is listening comfortable for you? Are you what some call a good listener, or do you tend to "listen to respond versus listen to understand?"

_____

_____

_____

_____

Is this where you want your listening skills to be?

_____

_____

_____

_____

If not, list three strategies you can take to change that.

1. _____

2. _____

3. _____

4) Being inclusive in your communication efforts—especially as it relates to silent collusion—takes courage. Have you ever found yourself NOT doing one of the MOP+SAM strategies identified when an uninclusive remark was said in front of you? What happened?

_____

_____

_____

_____

Why did you do or not do what you did?

_____

_____

_____

_____

If you could "tuuuurn baaaack tiiiimme" (thanks, Cher!) and go back to that moment, what would you do differently?

_____

_____

_____

_____

5) Review the "Comm Together: How to Be a More Effective Communicator" best practices from this chapter. Which of these are you really good at?

_____

_____

_____

_____

How could you teach others on your team or within your workplace to be better at these specific communication strategies?

_____

_____

_____

_____

# JUNGLE LOVE:
# PRIDE LEADERSHIP IN ACTION

"I never understood the power of networking until I joined a large consulting firm. When I worked for a smaller company, I always thought the idea of 'network all you can' was just some sales talk; and I wasn't in sales and didn't think it was needed for my role. I was very wrong.

As a lesbian, I slowly found my guys and gals in our community within our company. It was like this not-so-secret club. As we networked both onsite at the client as well as on our company intranet through our GLBT employee resource group, I started to grow a larger network of both co-workers and 'family' members.

Soon, I was quickly hearing about new onsite client opportunities through my network first. I was able to reach out to our staffing people and tell them about the [onsite consulting gigs] because of my gays and lesbians. Their input helped me maneuver to the most enjoyable onsite consulting jobs that I probably wouldn't have known about had it not been for our connections."

*– Amanda P., Senior Consultant*
*Large Global Fortune 500 Consulting Firm*

· · · · · · · · · · · · · · · · · · · · · · · · · · · · · · · · · · · · · · · · · · · · · · · · · · · · · ·

# MR/MS/MX GREEN JEANS: BUILDING & CULTIVATING RELATIONSHIPS

*"Early in my career, Mom gave me one of the best pieces of business advice: 'Never underestimate the power of the admin.' What she meant was that there are certain people within the business—regardless of position—who have a lot of power. As a professional secretary most of her career, Mom ran her organization; everyone came to her (and not her boss) for the answers. And, in hindsight, she's been totally right. So, build relationships—not just with those at the top of the 'food chain'—but with those who really do hold the power. Relationships at any level can be great connections; and often connections you didn't realize you need."*

– Dr. Steve Yacovelli
The Gay Leadership Dude

Proactive Communication • Relationship-Building • Integrity, Authenticity, & Courage • Developing Culture • Empathy

# From Banks to Butterflies: Transactional to Transformational

> We, the People, recognize that we have responsibilities as well as rights; that our destinies are bound together; that a freedom which only asks what's in it for me, a freedom without a commitment to others, a freedom without love or charity or duty or patriotism, is unworthy of our founding ideals, and those who died in their defense.
>
> *– President Barack Obama*, 2012 speech
> (Young, 2016, para. 18).

Regardless of where you locate yourself on the political spectrum, you recognize that the 2008 election of our 44th president, Barack Obama, was a transformational event. Drawn to Obama's charismatic personality and inspiring message of hope, a record number of Americans cast votes in the 2008 election, creating a political sea change amid a time of dire economics and pervasive cynicism. At heart a community organizer, Barack Obama championed a leadership style that valued relationships over output, togetherness over silos. In his work on the domestic and international fronts, Obama relied on the contributions of experts, surrounding himself with a team of talented professionals who were given license to make their marks on the movement Obama was spearheading. "Change We Can Believe In" became the unifying message of the movement, a mantra for citizens of all colors and contexts who were anxious to see their lives—and the national trajectory—move into positive territory.

Humans, by nature, are pack animals; we like our tribes (or our prides). Because we are relational beings, the quality and durability of our interpersonal connections contribute to the goals and objectives of the organizations we serve—or negatively impact them. While the world often measures great leadership by the leader's ability and achievement, maybe great leadership is better defined as the ability to empower people to invest in the cause. When constituents—team members—are invested in the cause, they begin to understand that their contributions to the cause matter. This movement toward investment at all levels of an organization can be transformational.

## *Déjà Vu All Over Again: What Defines Great Organizational Leadership Anyway?*

While we've already gone down the path of identifying what great leadership means earlier, let's take a revisit here. Is greatness attached to notable feats of organizational growth or crisis management? Is greatness measured by bravery (see Chapter 5 on courage)? Are the great leaders those who defy the odds, take great risks, or galvanize the people around a cause? Maybe great leadership is a pedigreed trait, passed down through the generations by some serendipitous tangle of DNA, or access to the best opportunities, training, education, and the like. Can you measure great leadership through statistical means? *The great ones lead to this percentage of growth and this level of customer satisfaction.*

What if it's none of the above? Perhaps great LGBTQ+ leadership is really all about relationships. Great LGBTQ+ Leaders are the ones who know their people, cultivate long-term relationships, and then use the connections to help all involved reach the heights of potential. This *relational leadership* builds rapport and ownership of goals and objectives, while also empowering team members to articulate ideas that inform or challenge existing goals and objectives. Relational leadership—which we'll call *transformational leadership* from this point forward—is a countermovement to the leadership model that has dominated the West since World War II. Before we explore transformational leadership, let's consider its arch nemesis, *transactional* leadership.

## Credits & Debits: Transactional Leadership

The old-school leadership style was really more transactional. Transactional leaders are the type who prefer order and structures in the organizations that they lead and lead within a clear, stable, and hierarchical structure (*What is Transactional Leadership...*, 2018). Coined by psychologist Max Weber in his 1947 study on leadership styles, transactional leadership is all about the results. First calling the transactional approach *rational-legal leadership*, Weber believed that the core to this approach was what he defined as, "the exercise of control on the basis of knowledge" (*What is Transactional Leadership...*, 2018, para. 7). Simply put, managers—a.k.a. organizational leaders—give their team members something they want in exchange for something the manager/leader wants, quid-pro-quo style. This currency, whether it be wages, in-kind services, interest in the company, promotion or organizational power, or a combo of all of these, helps the leader achieve the results they want. Sometimes, a clear incentive model is part of the currency the transactional leader presents to the leader's team. Incentive pay, for example, that rewards employees for exceeding goals keeps the business or organization moving forward. The fuel? TRANSAC-TIONS (just like a bank).

The flipside of the transactional model is the reprimand (a.k.a. the debits). As the word *reprimand* implies, transactional leaders penalize team members when goals aren't met. Incentivized pay, for example, may be reduced or zeroed if the worker doesn't meet the goals and objectives. The psychology underpinning the trans-actional model is clear: it's assumed that many of the team members under this leader are not self-motivated and "require structure, instruction and monitoring in order to complete tasks correctly and on time" (*What is Transactional Leadership...*, 2018, para. 8). The leader, on the other hand, is believed to be motivated by a higher purpose—like the growth of the organization—and is tasked with pursuing this higher purpose by breaking down the goals into bite-sized chunks that the team members can achieve through various tasks.

A military leader, for example, may have the successful comple-tion of the campaign as the higher purpose. On the other hand, the soldier on the front line may see survival as her immediate goal. The transactional leader must help the soldier achieve her immediate goal while also incentivizing her contributions to the leader's objec-tives and overarching goals, which are often short-term. Ultimately, the leader is the one to articulate the org's goals and objectives and determine if the goal was successfully met. *Did the soldier under my command meet the objectives specific to her position? Did the employee satisfy the sales goals that were earmarked for them?* If the answer to these sorts of questions or other evaluative measures is a *yaaaaasss*, then the sweet, sweet rewards kick in. If, in the alternative, the answer is *nope*, then instead of carrots there's sticks: the penalties (a.k.a. reprimand) come into play.

Personally, I've always thought of transactional leadership like a game of checkers: in every game, each piece has the same job: move forward in a diagonal manner. The goal is to take out the opponent's pieces while reaching the back of the board and getting promoted to a king with even more power. As the player (or leader), you look at each piece as having the same skills and move them as needed to meet the goal.

## The Goodness and—Ultimately, the Downfall of—Transactional Leadership

OK, so we touched on the fact that the whole transactional leadership approach maybe isn't the best approach, especially if we're to be an amazing LGBTQ+ Leader in the 21st-century jungle. But transactional leadership *does* have a few bennies that we don't want to ignore:

1. **Common tongue:** It's especially beneficial in organizations that have a workforce pulled from a variety of nations and cultural contexts. The rigid structure of the transactional model provides a common language for everyone involved in delivering results on behalf of the stated goals and objectives.

2. **It's transferrable:** A transactional model of leadership is easily disseminated across the organizational structure. "Once the structure and the requirements are learned, it is easy for workers to complete tasks successfully. This works because transactional leadership is simple to learn and does not require extensive training. The transactional approach is easy to understand and apply across much of an organization" (*What is Transactional Leadership...*, 2018, para. 21).

3. **And its biggest benefit is efficiency:** Efficiency is especially important once the leaders' team truly know their jobs and can deliver consistent results that further the leader's stated goals and objectives. Team members at Burger King®, for example, know that everyone shares in the task of delivering products "made your way, right away."

So, if I'm in, say, a first responder or military organization in an emergency or high-paced situation, these three benefits might come in handy dandy. I may need that common language or have a skill that needs to be quickly transferrable to another area. But most likely we're not operating in that world. So, there's specific downsides of transactional leadership we want to be aware of:

1. **Transactional leadership assumes that the team members are not self-motivated** ... Because of this, the entire approach is designed to motivate the individual team members to function at the highest level possible in pursuit of stated goals and objectives (as well as the currency on the other end of success).

2. **No "checker piece empowerment"** ... Because there is a sense that workers are not self-motivated, they are not empowered to act in creative ways or troubleshoot problems that extend beyond their respective swim lanes in the org. In a transactional model, a leadership pyramid is in effect: ultimate power to craft organizational vision and execute the vision rests in those at the top of the pyramid. Without the "leader" calling the shots, those at the base of the pyramid are powerless to move the organization forward because they have not been empowered to operate outside of their respective lanes. It's a pyramid scheme!

3. **Very little strategic thoughtfulness** ... The transactional model doesn't allow for significant strategic planning input from the lower levels of the org. Ironically, those working at the grassroots are probably in the best position to discern if the strategic plan is actually impactful to clients, the mission of the organization, etc. So, when the project is implemented, the checker pieces don't have a lot of buy-in on the solution, because—in this model—they didn't have a say in the solution.

4. **Trust and loyalty tend to be wickedly low** ... Trust and institutional loyalty are pretty much limited by the transactional approach. If leaders don't develop relationships with those who serve under their leadership, but instead rely on incentives for doing the job, how will the leader react when a team member's performance is negatively impacted by, say, a health issue, family troubles, etc.? If you work for a "leader" who seems disinterested and detached from your life, are you willing to put your life on the line

for the organization/cause you are serving? Personally, I've been there ... and I certainly didn't have a vested interest in the success of the organization: I was there to collect a paycheck til I found a much better j-o-b.

## Playing Chess: Transformational Leadership is About Relationshipping

When President Obama was inaugurated in January 2009, the global economy was barreling into a deep recession. Confronted with calls for austerity, Obama trumpeted a different approach, using federal spending to stabilize institutions and keep people at work. The bigger challenge; however, was convincing U.S. citizens to trust the course and look out for their neighbors. Through speeches, town halls, and frank conversations, Obama tapped into the potential of relationships. Obama realized that a community uniting around a shared vision and a shared sense of sacrifice had the power to overcome tremendous odds and obstacles. Instinctively, Obama embodied an inclusive style of leadership that relied on humanity's deep impulse to connect (humans are pack animals!) instead of a transactional model that said something akin to *do this because it's your job*. Obama saw every U.S. citizen as gifted to add their voices and abilities to the causes of prosperity and a narrative other than cynicism. Cultivating a sense of belonging among his constituents, Obama convinced the people that they could help the country move beyond its current woes. This inclusive approach to leadership is transformational, not transactional.

As noted earlier, Obama's quest to engage U.S. citizens in a sociopolitical sea change had him rubbing elbows with Americans from both sides of the aisle, as well as those caught in the old tides of disenfranchisement. Obama, also wanting to portray himself as accessible, opened his administration to critique and rigorous transparency. Using humor, parables, and "beer diplomacy," Obama helped his constituents see the White House as the People's House. He understood that transformational leaders—those tapping into the power of relationship—had to model the behaviors they sought from their others. Smart, impactful LGBTQ+ Leaders lead by example; they engage in the proverbial "talk the talk and walk the walk." And they foster collaboration through relationships and a shared vision in where we all are going.

Going back to the checkers analogy, to me, transformational leadership is now like playing chess. In chess, each piece has a specific skill/personality: Knights move in that annoying L-shape move, Bishops do the diagonal thingy, and the Queen goes wherever the heck she wants (typical queen!). As an LGBTQ+ Leader, your job is to work with each piece (team member), know their skills and abilities and needs, set the board up so they can do their jobs, and not treat each one as the same. In my career as a leadership coach, I see way too many leaders look at their team members as the same versus acknowledging each one is a unique playing piece. Together they can accomplish the team's goal: TOTAL BOARD DOMINATION (OK, just kidding).

## The $1,000,000 Business Secret: Leveraging Relationships

Psst: Here's a big, giant, crazy secret. Relationships lead to transformation, and building relationships leads to leadership success.

I'm not saying the other leadership competencies we discuss in this book aren't important (and recall what's said in the introduction: that all these so awesomely work together). I have found that if you focus on building relationships using some of the other competencies (like effective communication and being your authentic selves in the workplace), you can accomplish anything. Think about it: where transactional leadership uses the carrots and sticks—incentives and reprimands—to create desired outcomes, transformational leadership seeks to engage all stakeholders, in "a process in which 'leaders and followers help each other to advance to a higher level of morale and motivation'" (*Transformational Leadership*, n.d., para. 2).

Don't believe me? Let's pull in a few experts who truly understand the power of transformational leadership. Seeing transformational leadership as a countermovement to transactional leadership, psychologist James Burns believed that the transformational approach could change both individuals and the larger organization. "It redesigns perceptions and values, and changes expectations and aspirations of employees. Unlike in the transactional approach, it is not based on a 'give and take' relationship, but on the leader's personality, traits, and ability to make a change through example, articulation of an energizing vision, and challenging goals" (*Transformational Leadership*, n.d., para. 2). Building upon the work of Burns, Bernard Bass argued that transformational leaders cultivate meaningful connections with their teams and, in turn, team members follow their leaders in pursuit of a *shared* mission. "The followers of such a leader feel trust, admiration, loyalty, and respect for the leader and because of the qualities of the transformational leader are willing to work harder than originally expected"

(*Transformational Leadership*, n.d., para. 3). Bottom line? Transformational leaders help constituents work beyond self-gain, and instead show them how their identity connects with the mission of the organization. Under a transformational system, everyone is a stakeholder, not just a widget in a compartmentalized company with a super-secret set of goals and objectives.

In transformational leadership, LGBTQ+ Leaders lead from a place of empathy, concerned about the well-being of the peeps on the team, not just their performance (*déjà vu*, Chapter 6!). Building on a shared sense of belonging, transformational leaders tap into the potential of each person on the team, reminding the individual—through actions as well as words—that the leader is invested in the success and quality of life of the individual. In his study of transformational leadership, Jon Trevor discovered that transformational leaders tend to have two vital abilities, or, in the alternative, the aptitude to develop the vital abilities. Trevor, writes, "Leaders are selected on the basis of their potential to collegially and consensually take ownership of the change agenda" (Trevor, 2012, p. 7). Said another way, transformational leaders (a.k.a. LGBTQ+ Leaders) know how to move the needle in the org, realizing that it's the peeps who make the movement possible.

## Why LGBTQ+ Leaders Rock at Building Relationships

Turn this back to you as an LGBTQ+ Leader. I would venture a guess that the vast majority of us have had to really go and build relationships within our respective workplaces. At times, we had to work very hard to find those commonalities to build those relationships: as we were more often than not the "other" or among the minority within our teams.

There's a lot of power with being able to remain your authentic self, yet still be malleable enough to find the commonality to connect with someone very different than you in the workplace jungle. We've had to do it ever since being our authentic selves at work, and that practice of connecting with others on a genuine level is a crazy powerful skill within your work context and well beyond.

One of the lessons I've learned is the power of building rapport. It's not small talk (although that may be a strategy to build rapport), but it's the concerted effort to find commonalities and build off them. It's not becoming BFFs in 20 seconds, but it's connecting in some capacity and building a basic foundation of a relationship.

For example: over the years, I've come to realize that certain employers and corporate work cultures with which I've been a part of truly resonated with people in the world. Years ago, I happened to mention I worked at XYZ company, and people asked me so many questions about the experience; they truly wanted to know. This former employer was, and continues to be, a very popular Central Florida vacation destination, so people connected with it not just on a business/operations level but more so on an emotional level. "Ohh, that must have been magical to work there!" Sure, it was a really good work experience, but I quickly realized two things:

1. People love to connect emotionally on topics, even with a stranger (kids and animals are great examples of how people elicit visceral responses from other people: thus, Facebook posts of puppies frolicking get big-time "likes") and

2. I could name drop the work gig to quickly connect with people if I wanted to on said emotional level.

It's not manipulative, it's smart leadership. Rapport can be summarized as "like likes like," meaning we—as tribal and pack beings—like to find similar tribe members. This hits our unconscious bias for safety and security: we feel "good" with people like us; whatever that *like us* means. And, as LGBTQ+ people, we have—consciously or unconsciously—been able to tune into those small social cues that help us identify friend/ally/"family" or foe. We look for those subtle clues that allow us to connect with others and build off that. While it initially helped us find safety and our peeps, when leveraged by the savvy LGBTQ+ Leader, it is a very powerful way to connect to people naturally that many leaders have to really work at. This is relationship-building gold and you may not have realized it!

**Pro Tip:** reflect on our definition of diversity and The 5 Layers by Gardenswartz & Rowe from Chapter 3. This is a great way to think about finding a connection to someone; surely you can find at least one facet of the five layers that you have in common with someone as a starting point!

# Droppin' off the Goods: Transformational Leadership Styles

Because the transformational leadership is all about the relationships, the LGBTQ+ Leader must spend time with the various team members to build trust, rapport, and a shared passion for the work (and remember: team members aren't just those direct reports if you have them: they're peers, bosses, executives, and all those folks around you in your workplace jungle). With the relationship well established, the LGBTQ+ Leader provides supports to the team that builds the capacity of the individual and strengthen the organization's *esprit de corps* or heart and soul (*tres bien!*). Transformational LGBTQ+ Leaders believe that their team members are self-motivated. Support that the LGBTQ+ Leader offers to the team can include one or more of the following styles: (1) One-to-One Time; (2) Intellectual Development; (3) Inspiration; and (4) Normative Influence. These efforts support the basis of the relationship between the LGBTQ+ Leader and the team and become pivotal in the success (or unsuccess, a.k.a. failure) of the transformational model. Let's explore each style.

1. **Eye Focus: One-to-One Time** … This is the style in which you as the LGBTQ+ Leader attend to each team member's needs, act as a mentor/coach to them, and listen to their concerns and needs. As the Leader, you give empathy and support (Chapter 6), keep communication open (Chapter 7), and place challenges before each team member. You also encompass the need for respect and celebrate the individual contributions each member makes. The team has a hankerin' for self-development and has intrinsic motivation for their tasks (chess pieces not checkers!).

2. **Brain Focus: Intellectual Development** … This is the style in which you as the LGBTQ+ Leader challenge assumptions, take risks, and solicit team members' ideas. LGBTQ+ Leaders with this style stimulate and encourage creativity in their team. They nurture and develop their

peeps to think independently. For such a Leader, learning is a huge value, and unexpected situations are seen as "areas of opportunities" to learn. Team members ask questions, think deeply about things, and figure out better ways to execute their tasks.

3. **Heart Focus: Inspiration** … Here's the style in which the LGBTQ+ Leader articulates a vision that is appealing and inspiring to the team. LGBTQ+ Leaders with inspirational motivation challenge team members with high standards, communicate optimism about future goals, and provide meaning for the task at hand. Team members need to have a strong sense of purpose if they're to be motivated to act. Purpose and meaning provide the energy that drives the group forward. The visionary aspects of leadership are supported by mad communication skills that make the vision understandable, precise, powerful, and engaging. The team members are willing to invest more effort in their tasks, they're encouraged and optimistic about the future, and believe in their abilities.

4. **Feet Focus: Normative (or Idealized) Influence** … This style is where the LGBTQ+ Leader serves as a role model for high ethical behavior, is admired, instills pride, and gains respect and trust. Just by being their authentic selves and "walking the walk," they are influencing others around them to adhere to the same behaviors and ethics, (*What is Transactional Leadership…*, 2018).

Obviously, LGBTQ+ leadership support is personalized for each team member, and you, the Leader, can engage and interact with each team member using the right style of transformational leadership described here. And this is one of the great benefits of this model: regardless of the focus used (*Eye, Brain, Heart,* or *Feet*), trust and rapport grow through the relationship, and the relationship gives the LGBTQ+ Leader the means to hone the right skills of the individual team member receiving personalized attention.

## An Itty Bitty Bit More on Motivation

I've had Leaders ask me time and again, "How do I motivate my team?" My response: you don't. Motivation isn't something that you can thrust upon a team member, it's something that must start from within each of them.

Now, that being said, as an LGBTQ+ Leader, you can create the environment in which the team member is inspired and motivated. Creating a culture that embraces different thoughts, rewards good performance, listens to various team members' perspectives, respectfully honors diversity, is inclusive, etc., are ways in which team members will be motivated and inspired to do their best to work toward the team goals.

Your job as an LGBTQ+ Leader isn't to give those around you motivation; it's to create the context (environment) that allows their motivation to grow from within. It's like you're a gardener: a gardener doesn't tell their plants, "GROW NOW!" but rather waters the soil, ensures there's enough light, prevents weeds, etc., and allows the plant to do their thang. That's an LGBTQ+ Leader's role regarding motivation.

And how do you know what motivates someone? *Ask. Them.* It's not rocket science to find out what motivates an individual, just sit down and have a chat. Most people (especially those in higher spots within a lot of organizations) think that motivation comes from money. Actually, studies show that it doesn't. Once an employee makes a certain amount of money where they're not thinking about "making money," the person can then fully focus on the work. Dan Pink, in his awesome book, *Drive*, cites three concepts that tend to pop up over and over again in various studies focused on what drives a person to perform at their best:

- **Autonomy** ... being able to have empowerment to do the job, perform the task, and be left alone to get it done;
- **Mastery** ... becoming an expert or extremely proficient at something that you see progress and growth in your skills and abilities; and
- **Sense of Purpose** ... being part of something bigger than just getting a paycheck; being in an organization or on a team that helps make the world a little bit better (Pink, 2011).

While these may not be exactly what drives your team members to perform at their best, as an LGBTQ+ Leader striving to foster solid business relationships, ask your team what motivates them, then "create the garden" to potentially provide it. And don't assume it's just moolah.

## Influencing Change Through Inspiration: Articulating Purpose

While we dove deeper into effective communication earlier (Chapter 7, ICYMI), let's focus on building relationships as it relates to your communication style and LGBTQ+ leadership effectiveness.

There's another song in the Broadway musical *Avenue Q* (methinks Steve has an unconscious bias for this musical) where one of the main characters, Princeton, is trying to figure out what to do with his life. He starts to sing the song, "Purpose," and the beginning lyrics go like this:

*Purpose/It's that little flame/That lights a fire/Under your ass ...*

While a little crass (which awesomely describes this Tony-Award winning show), it really hits the concepts of what a purpose is all about, especially when we think about the reasons for change and how to get support from the team to head into that change.

To articulate that purpose (without lighting a physical fire ... somewhere), an LGBTQ+ Leader needs to be able to articulate the purpose of the team. Now, to be clear: you don't have to be a world-class public speaker to effectively be a transformative leader who can rally the troops toward the identified purpose. However, they must be passionate about their organization's purpose, and highly skilled at articulating that purpose (mission, goals, objectives, etc.) to others. Consider Bill Gates. Unlike his late rival Steve Jobs, Gates didn't build Microsoft based solely on his rock star-caliber computer engineering super powers; he learned how to articulate his passion for personal computing and deliver that passion in a highly personalized way. This innovator brought other inspired dreamers onto his team by connecting with gifted individuals at a personal level and convincing them that the cause was worthy of personal investment.

Relational leaders—transformational leaders—move the needle by inspiring. Inspiration, as noted by Nicole Gillespie and Leon Mann in their piece, "Transformational Leadership and Shared Values," presupposes that the leader has already done the kind of work that cultivates trust (Gillespie & Mann, 2004, p. 281). And, if you're sleeping here, wake up: because here's the big takeaway. In the absence of trust, charisma devolves into the sort of insincere sales pitch that one would expect from someone hawking used cars for a living* (*no disrespect meant to the used car salespeople in my life, but come on—you know you're a little like that).

Inspired team members feel empowered to challenge the status quo in their workplace jungles. This dynamic can be especially powerful if the LGBTQ+ Leader has successfully taught their team how to engage in strategic planning and think creatively about the products and services the organization could provide to customers (internal customers or external, interpret that how you will) in the future. This inspiring, empowering, and autonomous perspective gives team members the license to step out of their swim lanes (swim out of their swim lanes?) and dream the next big thing without judgment, fear of being chastised for using resources, or worse, fear of failure. Facebook provides a good example. The social media giant's annual "hackathon" gives license to everyone in the organization—from entry-level peeps to upper management—to articulate and pursue ideas that can strengthen the overall organization and bring innovation to the actual social media platform. That "like" button you, well, like so much? Yeah, that's the product of a hackathon. And the hackathon concept itself was the offspring of transformational Leaders who recognized that real change is possible when creative individuals at all levels of an organization feel valued for their expertise and are allowed to exercise it by those leading (Weinberger, 2017).

## Growing it Like a Weed: Forming & Sustaining Relationships

The title of this chapter—"Mr/Ms/Mx Green Jeans: Building & Cultivating Relationships"—might have been lost on you, so let me peel the onion here a bit (sorry for the plant pun). While growing up, there was a kid's TV show, similar to *Mr. Rogers' Neighborhood* (R.I.P., Reverend Rogers!) called *Captain Kangaroo*. Captain Kangaroo and his crew entertained kids through their silliness, informative segments, cartoons, and appearances from awesome puppets like Mr. Moose. One of the frequent guests stopping in was Mr. Green Jeans, a local farmer and sidekick to the Captain. Anytime I want to think of a farmer, the early childhood memory of Mr. Green Jeans sticks in my noggin.

And, when I was writing this book and when I think about building relationships, I always see the farmer and the garden: planting the seeds, tilling the soil, adjusting the water, etc., to help grow the plants to their potential (just like our story with motivation a little bit ago). And to me that's synonymous with relationships: you (as the LGBTQ+ Leader) are Mr (or to be inclusive Ms or Mx) Green Jeans; it's your job to create the right context to not just start or plant the seeds of a relationship, but to cultivate and grow it. Mystery solved.

OK, back at it. With some of the tenets of transformational leadership in place, let's take a look at what this model looks like in your real world as an LGBTQ+ Leader. Transformational LGBTQ+ Leaders, in the words of leadership writer Kim Scott, "care personally and challenge deeply" (Scott, p. 16). Transformational leaders can both honor the empathetic impulse to make everyone on the team happy and healthy, while also sharpening the inconsistent and often sterile use of power demonstrated by the leader versed in the transactional model.

Transformational leaders, well, feed the feedback loop. Trust, as established already, is the backbone of effective feedback (and heck, part of the foundation of effective leadership overall). When members of the team sense that the LGBTQ+ Leader truly cares for them, they will welcome your feedback and offer their own. Again, you're the gardener creating the environment, and that feedback-rich environment creates feedback and trust. A transformational leader MUST provide feedback, even when the feedback is messy, potentially hurtful, or could be taken negatively by the recipient (Chapter 5—courage again!). While transformational leadership emphasizes the cultivation of strong relationships, transformational Leaders have the courage to tell those they are leading:

1. Your plan didn't work;
2. Your work product didn't meet our org standards;
3. The work is incomplete as submitted;
4. The behavior you showed is unacceptable here; and
5. Yadda, yadda, yadda.

Calling this *Radical Candor*, Scott contends that effective leaders who focus on building solid relationships practice frankness with members of the team while describing and modeling replacement behaviors/expectation that move the organization and individual forward. "Here's what I need from you as we pursue this particular objective, and here's how I think you can get there" (Scott, 2017).

Remember, a team member who has faith in you, my LGBTQ+ Leader, will receive feedback and is also willing to articulate areas of your leadership style that may be holding the team back. If you aspire to practice transformational leadership, recognize that you're not immune to feedback. By all means, ask for it, receive it, ponder it, and—maybe most importantly—do something about it (even if you don't agree with the feedback, the very least you should say is, "Thank you for your feedback."). When you accept responsibility for the things that go pear-shaped (as my Aussie friends say, meaning when things go to hell), you communicate to your team, "I need you to accept some responsibility, too."

Transformational leaders share, if not shun, the spotlight. When the rewards of the work arrive, whether they come in the form of revenue, recognition, awesome swag, etc., transformational leaders highlight the contributions of individuals and share the reward. Transformational leaders also provide feedback about the successes to the whole team: "Here is how X's contribution moved our mission forward."

Transformational leaders also create rituals that honor the success, prime the pump for future success, and celebrate individual milestones and personal moments. Do you have team meals, recognition events, and outings on the calendar? If not, make it happen, LGBTQ+ Leader. But, also be mindful of how different people want feedback (positive or negative). Some on your team may want the praise-like feedback in private; while other team members are cool with sharing their missteps with the rest of the team publicly to help the greater good. An empathetic and transformational leader has already asked team members their preference and acts accordingly.

## Beyond the Immediate Team: Networking

Smart LGBTQ+ Leaders not only know to build relationships within their team and throughout their organization, they are smart enough to leverage their relationship super power to foster relationships beyond their org and out to the greater Universe (or at least outside to other businesses locally).

In her work on the intersection of relationships and leadership, Samantha Harrington asserts that relational leaders always network, that is, deepen relationships with other professionals. "An essential part of business success is having a strong network. In fact, a Harvard study found that 85% of professional success comes from people skills. Though it certainly must be easier to build a network if you're inherently part of a world of business and money, all you really need to build a good network is to be willing to meet new people and step out of your comfort zone" (Harrington, 2017, para. 1).

In order to step beyond the comfort zone, relationship-focused LGBTQ+ Leaders must be willing to connect with people from a variety of cultures and contexts (back to that darn leadership courage thing again!). An unwillingness to stretch relationships in this manner will sow bad seeds within the LGBTQ+ Leader's organization. As team members are always taking cues from the behaviors they're seeing from their Leaders, an LGBTQ+ Leader with a network of peeps who look an awful lot like them demographically speaking will nonverbally (or unconsciously) communicate to the team, "I'm unavailable to people unlike me." Inclusive leadership (Chapter 3) means including others not like you in your leadership context and building relationships with those people.

Harrington believes that transformational leaders practice give and take in healthy networks and also build inclusivity by focusing on the expertise the "other" brings to the network. "Networking can't be one-sided," she contends, "If you want help from people, you have to help them. One of the most helpful things I think that people can do is connect you with people who are experts in what you're trying to do."

The cool thing is, as an LGBTQ+ Leader, you tend to already be open to embracing the "others" within the group; you're naturally more prone to meet those not necessarily like you. Harrington's notion of not being one-sided in your professional network is probably a reality to you already. If not, there's another "area of opportunity" for you to expand that network.

Transformational leaders have lives beyond the workplace. If they are not relational outside of the proverbial cube, how do they hope to nurture relationships within it? "Regularly reach out to people in your network," Harrington says, "Ask them what they're up to and how you can help; that strengthens your relationship and makes it mutually beneficial" (Harrington, 2017, para 3-5). Personally, I've started to really leverage tools like LinkedIn to continue to build my network. Instead of constantly scrolling through my Facebook on my downtime to watch that hundredth video of cute puppies frolicking (awwww!), I open LinkedIn and find some network contact I haven't touched base with in a while and just send a quick hello! message. You'd be surprised how effective this is in keeping those relationships fresh, even in the digital sense.

## Final Thinks on Relationship Buildin'

If we get into our drone and look around, the developed world was built through the transactional model of leadership: relationships are what gets stuff done. However, as affluence, educational attainment, and technological innovation continue to tick forward, a new leadership model emerges that honors the contributions of *all* team members instead of simply incentivizing how we want people to behave. Transformational leadership affirms that organizational change depends on the team members, and not necessarily the leader. Effective LGBTQ+ Leaders must relate to their peeps, build trust, and inspire the team to embrace the organizational vision, not just the paycheck. An empowered team is a transformational team. President Obama learned this in his community development work, and later when he sought the nation's highest office; you can learn this in your jungle.

Listen, learn, and inspire... those are your prime directives as an LGBTQ+ transformational Leader.

# Tie to G Quotient

How does transformational leadership and building relationships from our Pride Leadership tie back to Snyder's work from *The G Quotient* (Snyder, 2006)? When we look at the concept of building relationships and how it connects to your LGBTQ+ super powers, it touches upon three of Snyder's G Quotient principles:

- **Principle #4: Connectivity** ... By definition, Snyder's principle of connectivity is about building relationships. Whether that be external networking to having internal awareness to fostering relationships that complement each groups' gaps in skill, smart LGBTQ+ Leaders leverage their connections to, well, foster relationships to better their teams and themselves.
- **Principle #7: Collaboration** ... Collaboration, according to Snyder, is to work with others to foster movement and advancement of the greater good. LGBTQ+ Leaders leverage their connected networks (Principle #4 above) to build and leverage resources (#7 Collaboration) to better meet results. This is ultimately the benefit of why we build relationship with those around us in our workplace jungle.
- **Principle #1: Inclusion** ... To build relationships is to be inclusive by design. As an LGBTQ+ Leader, you have the inclination to be more open and inclusive to others, and that gift makes you a more effective leader by definition. Inclusive leaders foster relationships outside their immediate circle and homogeneous demographics, and LGBTQ+ Leaders leverage that inclusiveness to build relationships both near and far.

# "Mane" Development Strategies: I'd 'Ship' It

Here are several activities you can do to increase your own relationship shippiness, LGBTQ+ Leader:

**ACTIVITY #1: Never Eat (or Caffeinate) Alone** ... There's an old saying about never having lunch alone. Take that to heart, and—at least twice a week—go to lunch or coffee with someone in your network. Mix it up: go with close allies and work acquaintances.

Don't overplan but be prepared to build rapport and ask questions to get to know the other person. Approach these events as fun and not as a work-networking-thingy.

**ACTIVITY #2: Walmart-Greet Your Way Thru the Business** ... You may not be a Walmart Aficionado, but they are (or were) known for their greeter as you walk into the store who asks, "How can I help you?"

Be that greeter and ask those in other areas of the business, "How can I (or we) help you?" Forge partnerships with other peers and departments to see how you can collectively leverage resources and open up opportunities to not only cross-pollenate among your teams but help each other succeed. "A high tide rises all ships."

**ACTIVITY #3: Meeting "Special Guest Stars"** ... If you have weekly team meetings, regularly invite a "special guest star" from another department. Allow this SGS to share what they do for the organization and prep your team to ask questions of the person (refer to the active listening strategies for help in Chapter 7).

Ask the SGS how the team can help them succeed. After any partnership or collaboration happens, allow them back to share what worked, what succeeded, and what the collective team could learn for the future.

**ACTIVITY #4: Just Me and My Shadow!** … Ever job shadow someone from another area? Follow them around, sit with them, and get down and dirty in what they do on a day-to-day basis?

Schedule some time to do just that with someone in another area. Strategically find people whose roles you really don't know anything about to share their world with you.

You'll be extremely surprised: (1) what you will learn observing their daily job interactions and their perspective; and (2) how far this will go to forge a relationship with the person you're shadowing.

**ACTIVITY #5: Are You Linking In?** … Are you using LinkedIn? If not, GET ON IT … NOW (and no, I don't get credit if you do). LinkedIn is a great way to keep business network relationships connected.

Get in the habit of finding and connecting with people on LinkedIn after meeting within your workplace, at conferences, in random meetings, at volunteer organizations, etc. Make it a habit to weekly (at least!) get on there for an hour to cultivate your LinkedIn garden.

Like your live relationships, you can garner a lot from these virtual gardens. Keep them alive.

# Drone Perspective: Reflective ?'s

1) On a scale of 1-10 with 10 being "I'm the best relationship gardener in the world!" to 1 being "Oh man, I have a relationship black thumb," where would you rate yourself?

1    2    3    4    5    6    7    8    9    10

Why would you rate yourself there?

_____

_____

_____

_____

What is one thing you could do to move that number up?

_____

_____

_____

_____

2) What do you do to create an environment that helps to motivate your team and/or those around you?

_____

_____

_____

_____

Is it enough?

_____

_____

_____

_____

What are two more things you could do to help better create an environment to foster motivation?

1. _____

2. _____

3) What are three rituals that you're doing in your workplace to build your team and build relationships?

1. _____

2. _____

3. _____

Is this enough?

_____

_____

_____

_____

What are two more you could do to strengthen the
bonds with those around you?

1. _____

2. _____

4) What's one small gesture (and to whom) you can do
tomorrow to foster a relationship that maybe you've let
wither or at least not grow like it could?

_____

_____

_____

_____

5) Inspiration is a great strategy for a transformational
leader. What are three things you can do for your team
and/or those around you to inspire them to increase
their performance and, well, be happier in the workplace
jungle?

1. _____

2. _____

3. _____

# JUNGLE LOVE:
# PRIDE LEADERSHIP IN ACTION

"The leadership approach that my current boss has followed is certainly effective. My boss is constantly pushing us to give our best and try our hardest while explaining the purpose and end goal of our actions.

Our team is large but ridiculously busy, which means that, at the end of the day, we're lean and mean. There is no time for meaningless work. Every action has a rationale supporting it, which invariably is linked to a major strategy. My boss is also very hands-on and engaged.

By giving us a sense of purpose and walking the walk with us, my boss' leadership approach has definitely done its job."

*– Dr. Felix B., Executive Director*
*Large Southeastern U.S. University*

..................................................

## CHAPTER NINE

# GETTING IN SHAPE:
# SHAPING CULTURE

*"Managing change and shaping the organization
is a powerful strategy for any leader. But I've seen
only a small number of folks really do this well; and
it's those who can balance the needs of the business
with the human aspect that make up the organizations
that succeed. Leadership is about the balance of
thinking with the head but leading from the heart, and
nowhere is this more evident than in times of change
within an organization."*

– Dr. Steve Yacovelli
The Gay Leadership Dude

Proactive Communication • Relationship-Building • Integrity,
Authenticity, & Courage • Developing Culture • Empathy

# Understanding the Realities of Organizational Culture

When we think about building relationships (Chapter 8, ICYMI), and we do that with a bunch of folks within our workplace jungle, we inherently begin to change the shape of our organizational culture. So, how do we consciously shape that culture to be more inclusive of "the other"? Through understanding our organizational culture, what it takes to contribute to that culture, and—if it's not how we think it should be—how to influence it to create change for the better. Let's explore, my Leader-peeps.

Storytime ... Imagine it's your first day on the job, and your friendly HR person gives you a pamphlet on what you should look like at work. This "look book" defined what your hairstyles should look like (men: short!), the amount of jewelry you can wear (women: very little!), what to do with body art you might have (cover it!), types of clothing style (no pants for women!), even the amount of cologne or perfume you can wear (very minimal!).

Now imagine you're a transperson sitting in that same HR office who is just starting to transition. What do you do? You don't want to potentially lose the new job you fought so hard to get, but you want to be your authentic self and who you are as a person. Or consider you're a cis- or gay man who doesn't necessarily conform to the gender stereotypes of masculinity, or a cis- or lesbian woman who doesn't conform to the stereotype of femininity. What do you do when that look book is shared with you, defining what your work self should be?

This scenario hits on a real issue that we LGBTQ+ folks face: fitting in in our respective corporate cultures. A 2018 HRC study found that 46% of LGBTQ+ employees say they're closeted at work, down just 4% over the past 10 years. Of LGBTQ+ employees, 53% said they've heard jokes about lesbian or gay people at least once in a while, and 31% of LGBTQ+ workers say they have felt unhappy or depressed at work. One in five LGBTQ+ employees report having been told (or had co-workers imply) they should dress in a more masculine or feminine way. And why don't LGBTQ+ employees report negative comments they hear about LGBTQ+ people to a supervisor or human resources? The top reason is that they (we) don't think anything would be done about it—and they (we) don't want to hurt existing relationships with co-workers (Kozuch, 2018).

Whether it's how we express our true selves or sharing whom we love, corporate cultures are a huge part of our lives and our identity. It's very American to ask, "What do you do?" when you meet someone new. We, as a society, find that where we focus our work energy is extremely important in defining who we are. So, for LGBTQ+ employees *where* we work and fitting in in that culture is of high importance—it further defines us as a person. And, as an LGBTQ+ Leader, we have the opportunity—and the natural skills—to help shape that culture to be more inclusive to us and to everyone.

BTW, the look book scenario above is real (it happened to me), and I'm happy to say this organization has since evolved to where they've changed their corporate policies on dress to be more inclusive of gender identity and individualism, while still maintaining a professional workplace. But so many businesses have not and, as LGBTQ+ Leaders, we need to be more aware of our organizational cultures and how we can help them evolve.

# Bob and Ron and Some Straight Talk (So to Speak)

Here's another story: before Bob Chapman took over leading package manufacturer Hayssen Sandiacre, there seemed to be two companies, the culture of those who worked in the admin offices, and those who worked on the factory floor. Bob didn't really like this, but wasn't quite sure what to do. Then he had a chat with Ron Campbell, a twenty-seven-year veteran of the company. First, Bob gave Ron his word that he could speak honestly about what it was like to work for Hayssen, and boy did he do just that. Ron shared how the use of bells and clocks that regulated check-ins and-outs, breaks, lunches, and going home; the use of locks on tools to be checked-out; and the company phones that were freely available to administrative and office employees gave the plant workers the impression that plant workers were less trusted than office employees. Ron even shared how he felt more trusted when he was not working onsite.

Bob immediately ordered the removal of the bells, clocks, locks, fences, and pay phones, which immediately began establishing a culture of empathy and trust that resonated throughout the company. "Preferring to see everyone as human instead of as a factory worker or office worker, [Bob] made other changes so that everyone would be treated the same way" (Sinek, 2017, p. 12). The new environment gave people a sense of belonging, and they felt cared for and respected. In turn, they began to treat each other that way by helping each other to solve personal and professional problems.

As co-workers, regardless of one's title, difference in pay, or uniforms, is it really right to treat each other indifferently or with disrespect in the workplace jungle? Our differences are more than unique; our differences make us who we are, and who we aren't. What our differences don't make us is better than each other.

Bob's leadership played a significant role in shaping Hayssen Sandiacre's culture. Once he listened to a willing employee (Ron) share the way he, and likely others felt, he didn't question whether it was true or not; he simply removed what created the problems. By doing so, Bob demonstrated not just his authority, but his trust in what he heard and his confidence that things didn't have to be that way, nor would they be. Nice job, Bob!

## What the What Do We Mean by Organizational Culture?

Bob awesomely monkeyed around with Hayssen Sandiacre's organizational culture, but what does that term really mean? As stated by the *Business Dictionary*, organizational culture is:

> The values and behaviors that contribute to the unique social and psychological environment of an organization ... it is based on shared attitudes, beliefs, customs, and written and unwritten rules ... Also called corporate culture, it's shown in the ways the organization conducts its business, treats its employees, customers, and ... the extent to which freedom is allowed in decision making, developing new ideas, and personal expression, how power and information flow through its hierarchy, and ... It affects the organization's productivity and performance (Organizational Culture, n.d., para. 1).

In short; organizational culture is all the stuff that makes up the workplace: the traditions, ways of doing the work, expected interactions, history, etc.

Regardless to how we define *culture*, when team members are disengaged as a result of workplace misery (or pain), organizational leadership (that would be you, dear reader) must address the root cause(s) to be sure that the continuation of said pain doesn't infect the culture and affect the employees' and organization's ability to thrive. In his book, *The Truth about Employee Engagement: A Fable about Addressing the Three Root Causes of Job Misery*, Patrick Lencioni identifies the three, well, root causes of workplace pain: *anonymity*, *irrelevance*, and *immeasurement* (or lack of measurement) (Lencioni, 2007).

## Woe is Me: The Workplace Jungle Misery of Anonymity

Let's look at the feeling (or perception) of *anonymity*. Lencioni says that, "People who see themselves as invisible, generic, or anonymous cannot love their jobs, no matter what they are doing" (Lencioni, 2007, p. 221). Taking a genuine interest in each other at work helps to give that sense of belonging that team members (and heck, anyone in that workplace!) needs to feel like they are part of something bigger than themselves and that really, really matters (think Chapter 8 and Dan Pink's *sense of purpose* from our chat on motivation). Although all leadership can (and should) play a role in making everyone a visible part of the organization, Leaders who work more closely with team members on a day-to-day basis are likely more equipped to engage with employees and get to know them as people.

For example, authentic engagement (there's that *authenticity* word again!) can develop when leaders ask about a team member's family, hobbies, work aspirations, or any concerns, issues, or questions that the person may be dealing with. These kinds of conversations don't require a lot of planning, preparation, or time; on the contrary, the more natural the engagement, the more likely the team member is to feel connected and secure enough to share. People are complex and their lives are wickedly dynamic. It's difficult to know from one day to the next what is going on with co-workers, so Leaders need to understand they need to keep their eyes and ears open and stay aware of what's going on with their team members and co-workers. Even if an LGBTQ+ Leader doesn't feel like it's their role to engage with their team on a personal level, it's better to make every effort to do so. As Lencioni writes, "People want to be managed as people, not as mere workers" (Lencioni, 2007, p. 231).

## Still Woe is Me: The Miseries of Irrelevance & Immeasurement

Another cause of workplace jungle misery is *irrelevance,* or not feeling that your work has meaning or a connection to a larger outcome. LGBTQ+ Leaders can recognize each team member's contribution, even in some small way, and that acknowledgment can go far with helping your peeps (or co-workers, peers, etc.) to take special pride in what they do, knowing that they do indeed make a difference (again, a sense of purpose). Take the opportunity to help a teammate to see the difference their role is making in the success of the organization. "If managers cannot see beyond what their employees are doing and help them understand who they are helping and how they are making a difference, then those jobs are bound to be miserable" (Lencioni, 2007, p. 235).

Workplace misery can exist when team members feel "*immeasurement*," or an inability to gauge their own progress and success. It's empowering and motivating to a team member when they feel they can control their own workplace destiny or fate. Having the ability to self-check and self-correct their actions, behaviors, or thoughts helps each team member improve on their own without being reprimanded by the Big Boss. So, for an LGBTQ+ Leader (like you), "The key to establishing effective measures for a job lies in identifying those areas that an employee can directly influence, and then ensuring that the specific measurements are connected to the person or people they are meant to serve" (Lencioni, 2007, p. 236).

## Managing the Misery

There are both benefits and roadblocks to managing team member engagement (and thus helping to share your organizational culture). For example, positive team member engagement can benefit an organizational culture's productivity output, recruitment and retention, and cultural differentiation from competitors. Happy peeps who are satisfied with their work tend to work with passion and purpose and consistently deliver greater productivity and quality, and without being coerced to do so.

Organizations save mucho bucks on recruitment because engaged team members stay, and they also help to spread the word about the awesome sauce of working at the organization, so that increases the pipeline of potential prospects for hiring. If leadership takes care of their team members, team members will willingly take care of their jobs, the org's equipment and resources, the customers/ clients, and each other. Basically, there is a lot riding on job satisfaction.

So, a great culture is an organization's asset, and also can be used to promote the group and set it apart from the competition who will be wondering what's being done to keep team members content and engaged. With all of the benefits of managing effective and efficient employee engagement, why do some organizations flub it up? The truth is that it's not title or compensation that keeps team members consistently and successfully engaged; it's the feeling that they're not invisible or anonymous, that their work is relevant and matters, and that they have a way of knowing how well they're doing daily so they can adjust and maximize performance, quality, or productivity. It's not so much their heads that need to be led, but their hearts (see Chapter 6 again on *empathy*). Lencioni awesomely notes that, "In order to be the kind of leader who demonstrates genuine interest in employees and who can help people discover the relevance of their work, a person must have a level of personal confidence and emotional vulnerability" (Lencioni, 2007, p. 228).

## The Case (*Dun-Dun!*) & Execution for Org Change

So, what if our organizational culture isn't where we—as LGBTQ+ Leaders—think it should be? What if it's just not as inclusive or embracing of diversity as we think it should be? Then we have an opportunity. ("*Dun-dun!*" ... that's the sound at the beginning of the *Law & Order* TV shows ... pick one of the twenty-eight versions of the show you like.) We can make the case for change.

## Building the Change Case (Dun-Dun!)

In their insightful book, *Change the Culture, Change the Game*, authors Connors and Smith write,"… the most compelling case for change always incorporates the best practices" (Connors & Smith, 2011, p. 123). They say first, make the case (*dun-dun!*) for change real. This means truly understanding the organization's business, its competitors, team members, and stakeholders. Effective change isn't done in a vacuum (that would suck … get it?). Also, making it "real" entails good storytelling (see Chapter 7). Being able to share what happens one year after the change has occurred helps people visualize how life will be better when the change is done and part of the organization's DNA.

In addition, making the case for change (*dun-dun!*) simple and repeatable helps makes it stick (again, good storytelling). Don't make it complicated. Regardless to how difficult the change might be, use the K.I.S.S. Method: *keep it simple, silly!* Also, keep it relatable, relevant, reasonable, and repeatable. This just means that the change should be easily understood and communicated to everyone. This creates a sense of belonging and increases sustainable buy-in, which is what's needed for true change.

When selling the change case (*dun-dun!*), make sure the story is applicable to your audience. Really dive deep into learning about the concerns, needs, and thoughts of the entire audience (which includes all of the aforementioned folks above), so that the change is not biased, blind, or bloated with nonessentials. Also, make sure the case (OK, I'll stop the "*dun-dun!*" because I know you are totally hearing it in your head each time) is convincing—if it's well thought-out and supported with important evidence, it is easier to convey and implement.

Finally, be sure that the case you're building isn't final; this should be a dialogue or conversation about the change. Come together and engage in productive dialogue and discussions that capture and sustain the attention and buy-in of workers and everyone the change impacts. Change can be difficult, but dialogue or conversation is a way to minimize the uncertainties and stresses often associated with change.

Approaching change with authenticity of purpose, audience consideration and knowledge, transparency, and simplicity in thought and presentation, credible support, and open communication and conversations are the best practices to engage in sustainable change that is meaningful and matters. *Dun-dun!* (Sorry: had to.)

## Make That Change: How to Execute Organizational Change

Early in my Change Management career, I came across an interesting group of folks called Prosci (pronounced *pro-sigh*) Management. They're a consulting group that is huuuuuuge in the "change" world. They've analyzed over 6,000 change leaders from 85 countries over the past twenty-plus years and found several best practices for change management. Leader Practitioners (their term for folks who lead changes within workplaces) who participated in the research included 70% with at least four years of experience and 30% with more than twelve years of experience in leading organizational change or change management (Prosci Change Management, n.d.). So, as we think about you, LGBTQ+ Leaders, and your ability to move the organizational culture forward, let's repurpose (a.k.a. borrow) the key learnings from these wicked smaaaart change people for our own organizational change:

1. **Mobilize an active and visible executive sponsor** … Participants consistently cited the need for a positive, active, and visible leader's involvement as the most significant contribution to change success. Specifically, senior leadership that supports and attends to the need for change, champions and motivates others in the organization, makes effective decisions, works with others in the organization to align priorities, communicates frequently with other leaders, and remains accessible.

2. **Dedicate change management resources** … A change team of flexible, decisive, collaborative individuals provided with dedicated resources and funding were noted as having greater overall change management effectiveness.

3. **Apply a structured change management approach** …. The structured approach should be customizable, scalable, and easy to implement and build on throughout the project. The main thing is that structure helps to create accountability and a way to monitor progress, and also leads to more effective change.

4. **Engage with employees and encourage their participation** … Employee engagement and participation was identified as a top contributor to change success. Therefore, leaders need to keep in mind that when they can

communicate how change will affect individuals and teams in the organization, the greater the likelihood of buy-in and adoption. Plus, getting to know those whom the change impacts, building positive relationships with them, and providing essential training leverages the change process. More importantly, effective change management requires consistent reinforcement combined with sustainment activities that are likely to lead to achieving project objectives.

5. **Communicate frequently and openly** … Leaders are charged with also communicating change, and participants cited cadence, consistency, transparency, and leveraging of multiple communication channels as essential to sharing what was happening, expectations, and the impact of change in the short- and long-term for employees' and the organization's goals.

6. **Integrate and engage with project management** … Change is a project, and there are many moving parts. Structuring change management activities involves continuously aligning plans, assigning roles and responsibilities, and providing essential training for leaders to ensure that they understand the process and are prepared to guide the organization.

7. **Engage with middle managers** … Being closest to employees impacted by change, participants explained that the managers' roles and communication via one-on-one or team meetings or focus sessions was to build awareness of impact of the change to those affected and provide appropriate resources and support that help managers to

navigate change successfully. Involving managers in early phases of change was cited as critical as middle managers were seen as the most resistant group to change in Prosci's research.

As you think about shaping your organization's culture (especially to be more inclusive in nature), keep the Prosci best practices in mind in order to successfully help facilitate change goodness in your jungle.

## How LGBTQ+ Leaders Can Promote a Culture (Club) of Change

Back to the two other rock stars in organizational change, Connors and Smith (2011) crafted what they're calling four ways to promote culture change within an organization:

1. **Don't Resist the Change** … As an LGBTQ+ Leader, you support and accept and don't resist the need for change to occur.

2. **Shape the Change** … You're an advocate who supports continuous open discussions that push for the urgency and necessity for the change

3. **Provide Resources for the Change** … You support or are the sponsorship that gives the time and/or resources needed to prioritize and implement the agreed-upon change

4. **Champion and Hold You (and Others) Accountable** … You champion and solicit support from every person at every level within the org to ensure they are accountable,

committed, engaged, focused, and involved, and maintain the viability and visibility of the change

Funny thing about change: it's always happening. Whether your org realizes the need to change (to be competitive, more effective, recreate best talent, etc.), or the rest of the world has moved on and changed, causing your group to re-evaluate its position; the very annoying phrase, "the only constant is change" is actually very accurate.

As an LGBTQ+ Leader, your opportunity is to lead the change. Through our awesome natural leadership skills of building relationships, effective communication, having empathy (for those being impacted by the change), and all the other facets of leadership awesomeness that we shared, you're in an amazing position to help shepherd the change within your organization.

If you look at the resources above (Prosci, Connors and Smith), one of the common *ah-has!* from these experts is the idea of someone (looking at you, LGBTQ+ Leader!) leading through the change. It's not really rocket science: shaping organizational culture requires that leaders (LGBTQ+ Leaders) participate and direct the change.

## Engaging & Coaching Your Culture

In his really good book *The Coaching Habit: Say Less, Ask More & Change the Way You Lead Forever*, author Michael Bungay Stanier identifies seven questions that can help any leader engage with their team and learn more about what it's like to do the work that they do for the organization, while simultaneously coaching the culture toward more harmonious, productive results. Below are some of the best coaching questions to consider (Stanier, 2016).

**The Kickstart Question: "What's on your mind?"** ... This is a way to focus and engage in real dialogue while setting the tone for an open response. This can reveal concerns of excitement, anxiousness, fears, etc., while creating a safe space to really discuss what matters most; and that could ultimately segue into deeper discussions about the project.

**The Awe Question: "What else?"** ... This question is useful in several ways, but primarily as an LGBTQ+ Leader, you want to use it to keep yourself in check so that you don't hijack the conversation, assuming that you know the question or problem and the answer, too (see Chapter 7 on effective listening). The "What else?" question can help you to stay curious and genuine and recognize success or move the conversation forward. Plus, you ask "What else?" to probe deeper, to challenge or question someone's course of action, to explore for better clarification, to guide check-in meetings, and to encourage new ideas (this is personally one of my favorites to use).

**The Focus Question: "What's the real challenge here for you?"** ... Digging for the real challenge is a way to redirect the potential "verbal diarrhea" some folks may spew during times of change or stress. This question validates and gets to the heart of how something is directly concerning or impacting the individual.

**The Foundation Question: "What do you want?"** ... This is a question that forces a person to dig deeper within themselves, and rather than just complaining, to actually visualize the outcome before they decide that something is impossible. This question is akin to someone asking you where you want to go. If you can only respond with, "I don't know," then it's hard to get there; that's not a destination. So, this question—though surface level—may help to lead into deeper need or must-have responses, which are often more difficult to discern.

**The Lazy Question: "How can I help?"** ... Asking this question forces the person to respond with a direct, clear request, but it also stops you, as an LGBTQ+ Leader, from assuming and jumping to conclusions with what you think is best. The danger of assuming that you think you know what the person needs is that you could be totally wrong, or you could actually agree to something that doesn't really help the person.

Just be careful to watch the tone of voice you used with this question in order to not come across as aggressive, whiny, or smothering. In fact, it's a good idea to frame the question with, "Just so I know..." or "To help me understand better..." or even "To make sure that I'm clear..." Once the ball is in your court, then there are several options to responding, which include, "Yes, I can do that," and "Nope, I can't do that...," but counteroffer with what you can do, or you can just buy yourself some time by responding that, "I'm not sure—let me check on what I might be able to do here."

The Strategic Question: "If you're saying yes to this, what are you saying no to?" … This helps the responder think about prioritization; what's most important and what's not as important. Plus, it helps folks understand the repercussions of not doing something. Some people (and professions) are horrible at sharing the cost of doing XX over YY and end up either, (1) over-stretching their resources (time, money, and/or people); (2) not meeting even their Goal #1; (3) meeting the goal(s) without key stakeholders knowing the drama and pain that meeting those goals with limited resources has done to the team; or (4) any combo of the above.

The Learning Question: "What was most useful for you?" … As an LGBTQ+ Leader, this question helps you to get a person to get things done and become more competent, self-sufficient, and successful. Leaders create the space for teachable moments that can inform the usefulness of information (from Chapter 8's create the garden), make it personal, provide feedback, draw out a specific response, or serve as an evaluative mark for you as the Leader.

So, seriously: commit these questions to memory, write them on your hand, tattoo them on your thigh, or whatevs it takes to remember them and use them as tools to not only help learn more about what's happening in your organization, but also to create a great organizational culture of openness, continuous learning, and empathy and to build trust.

As an LGBTQ+ Leader, in order to help facilitate an organizational culture shift, you can improve your skills and implement the following strategies to achieve a more unified and inclusive culture that allows every employee to thrive.

**Create the Garden** ... Imagine what it's like to be in a place where you feel like you don't have anyone to talk with, relax on break with, share laughs, or discuss concerns (and especially think about this if you have a distributed team or some team members working remotely). Having a sense of belonging is important. As an LGBTQ+ Leader, you can play a pivotal role by being empathetic (see deets from Chapter 6).

Let's return to Stanier's Seven Questions (2016). When you engage in questions and listen with empathy, you can help to create a sense of trust and belonging. Initiate conversation with, "What's on your mind?" If you get a sense that there's more or something going unsaid, then ask, "What else?" If you aren't sure what the takeaway is, ask, "What is the real challenge here for you?" Make the conversation about the team member by inquiring, "What do you want?" Show that you care by asking, "How can I help?"

Asking questions like these positions your leadership in a whole different light. Help team members decide how to balance what's possible against available capacity, needs, priorities, and resources by asking, "If you are saying yes to this, then what are you saying no to?" Allow the conversation or meeting to be purposeful and to assist you in determining challenges and changes that may be needed by inquiring, "What was most useful to you?" Moreover, these same questions should be given to your team members so that you can gather feedback about their concerns and the culture. This two-way exchange shapes and sustains culture and change.

SIDE NOTE: Years ago, I had just earned my Master's in Educational Policy and Leadership Development. A lot of our coursework was in the counseling psychology world (like effective listening strategies, etc.). One of the phrases and ideas was active listening and seeking to understand what a person had said with, "So what I hear you saying is ..." and repeating what I thought I had heard to the speaker. After graduation, I got a job working at a software company where we did both phone customer support (really strategic problem-solving using the marketing software) and face-to-face training. While I was in my cube taking calls, I'd use the, "So what I hear you saying is ..." and made sure I understood the customer's problem before going through a solution. It worked well.

However, my cube-mates would hear me use that phrase, "So what I hear you saying is ..." about fifty times a day and subsequently made fun of me (literally to this day twenty-plus years later, looking at you, Matthew!). Customers only heard it once but, based upon the feedback from my co-workers, I have come to realize I was being an "Active Listening Parrot" and overusing the phrase. So, don't be a Steve Active Listening Parrot and vary the phrasing and use of Stanier's Seven Questions. Mix up the phrasing, use different ones, and don't make my mistake and overuse them, as they can erode your perceived sincerity and their effectiveness ("Rhaaaw ... Stevie want a cracker! Rhaaaw!")

**Meeting Time = Good Time** ... I believe we all wish we had more meetings in our workday (that was a joke, my friend, but see Chapter 7 on how to make face-to-face meeting "great again!"). In all sincerity, individual employees, teams, and organizational meetings shouldn't just be used to share information, but to gather it as well. If the same people always lead and attend the meetings, that practice could be leaving out important voices and concerns. Continuously ask, "Who's not in this meeting?" Invite different team members or even department reps from across the organization. Just like with our Hayssen Sandiacre story from earlier, the floor workers' challenges were important, but they hadn't been addressed directly with leadership, or perhaps not effectively. Taking real action helps to give the sense of trust and belonging. Leadership matters because leadership can get change done. It's as simple as that.

**Back to Creating an Inclusive Organizational Culture** ... You already know this from many, many parts in this book, but it bears repeating: leadership that embraces differences helps to create a caring culture. Diversity comes with a multitude of differences and inherent biases that we all have as a result of our varied backgrounds and experiences. LGBTQ+ Leaders need to build a culture that strives to be biased toward fairness, truth, and the treatment of people the way they want to be treated. That's showing leadership, courage, and respect. As LGBTQ+ Leaders, hold yourselves accountable; you're a Leader for a reason. Take care of and protect your peeps, have the courage to do the right thing for the people who work for and with you, and share the struggle that comes with shaping organizational change (Sinek, 2011).

# Hey LGBTQ+ Leader: Should You Even TRY to Change the Org Culture?

Just because you can, doesn't mean you should.

As an LGBTQ+ Leader, you have the skill and the passion to help facilitate change. But should you? That's a wonderful and really thought-provoking question. And my first reaction: focus on that during your mindfulness exercises (see the next chapter for more). Seriously; if your organizational culture is really uninclusive to our LGBTQ+ brothers and sisters, that's a lot of work in addition to your day job. Ask yourself: do you want to fight or fly from the challenge?

I—Steve—will absolutely not answer that one for you; that's a very personal decision, weighing a lot of variables, ideas, and considerations. But I will share an idea to help you think through the situation as best as you can. This is in two parts: (1) understand what you have in relationship to an inclusive organizational culture; then (2) determine how/if you want to change it.

## Part 1: How Inclusive Is Your Org Culture?

As a consultant, I have the opportunity to glimpse into many corporate cultures (I'm sort of like an organizational anthropologist—think Jane Goodall, but in cubicles instead of the jungle, and more smartly dressed, and maybe a little less butch). I've seen businesses with corporate values like "We Promote Work/Life Balance!" yet expected employees to work 60+ hours a week. I've seen organizations say, "We celebrate diversity!" yet all senior leaders were middle-aged white dudes. And I've seen businesses say, "We want to make the world a better place!" and they do a lot of philanthropic efforts and promote employees' volunteerism to truly make the world a better place.

For me, I like to look at a corporate culture and see how inclusive it is to all people, but especially to our LGBTQ+ Community. In my experience there are 5 Top Indicators of an Inclusive Business Culture to explore when seeing if an organization is inclusive and therefor embraces LGBTQ+ people being authentic and true to themselves at work:

1. **Leadership** ... What does the leadership look like? What do they do (and not just say) to promote inclusivity? Is their language truly inclusive or is it more heterosexist? What's the demographic makeup of the leadership team and does it fairly represent the rest of the org?

2. **Corporate Policies** ... Does the organization include policies referring to same-sex couples (married or otherwise)? Does it include health care specific for trans employees? What's the company's Nondiscrimination Policy: does it include sexual orientation and gender identity and gender expression?

3. **The "Real" Corporate Values at Play** ... Using the criteria above, what are the organization's real values, the ones on display every day? Are they the ones listed on the organization's website, or are they really different? Is there obvious alignment in what the organization says it does and what it promotes to the outside world?

4. **Inclusion Support (HR, D&I, ERGs)** ... Is there a Head of Diversity & Inclusion in the organization? What do they

do? Is it their full-time gig? Does *diversity* to them really mean, "Let's celebrate _____ month!" or does it go deeper? Does the organization have an Employee Resource Group (ERG) dedicated to LGBTQ+ employees and their allies?

5. **External Efforts** … Does the organization market or communicate directly to the LGBTQ+ Community? When same-sex marriage became legal, what did your organization do to support or hinder its progress? When certain groups threaten the rights of LGBTQ+ people outside of the workplace (like at the state or federal level), does the organization (and its leadership) stand up or remain silent?

Through looking at the data of the above, you can get a really good sense as to how inclusive your organizational culture is. Now on to Part 2 …

## Part 2: Do You Fight or Flee for LGBTQ+ Inclusivity?

1. **Define** … Define what are YOUR personal values (see Chapter 4 on authenticity). Identify your top five-ish values.

2. **Discover** … Discover the true Corporate Values (step #3, above). … Do your own Nancy Drew-ing on what your organizational culture is really like.

3. **Aligned?** … Ask yourself, "How's the alignment?" between your personal values and those of the organization. Are your values reflected in the real values of the business?

4. **Is this OK?** … Comparing the two data sets, can you live with this level of alignment?

5. **What's Next?** ... Now comes the big decision: *fight* or *flight*. If you aren't as aligned as you'd like, make some choices. You can try and foster change within the organization and lobby for more inclusivity; or you can pack up your toys and find an employer who embraces the beautiful difference that is you. (And yes, it's a job, but life's too short to work at a place that won't embrace your authentic self.)

If you choose to facilitate change, use the strategies shared in this chapter to help. Also consider joining (or starting!) the Employee Resource Group (ERG) or other employee organization to be sure your LGBTQ+ voice is heard.

# Tie to G Quotient

How does influencing and helping to change the organizational culture from our Pride Leadership tie back to Snyder's work from *The G Quotient* (Snyder, 2006)? When we examine the concepts of change and how it connects to your LGBTQ+ awesomeness, it touches upon three of Snyder's G Quotient principles:

- **Principle #5 Communication** ... If you look at Prosci, or any other change management expert, one of the top ways in which to foster change in a culture is through effective communication. And it's not just the facts and figures. Inclusive and empathetic communication are skills an LGBTQ+ Leader can naturally bring to the table.

- **Principle #7: Collaboration** ... Changing organizational culture happens when people work together to foster the change; it can't happen from the top-down nor from the bottom-up. LGBTQ+ Leaders have the natural ability to leverage their relationships and collaborate with others to usher in change that minimizes the impact on the organization and specifically the individuals associated with the change.

- **Principle #2: Creativity** ... In any change initiative, the use of creative problem-solving is paramount to success. Whether that's identifying ways to maximize the resources to support the change or minimize the impact of the change on the people, creative solutions can make or break a change initiative. LGBTQ+ Leaders have that creative eye that can be used for the benefit of the change initiative.

# "Mane" Development Strategies: Culture Club (I'd Tumble for Ya)

Here are several activities you can do to increase your own effectiveness in impacting organizational change:

ACTIVITY #1: Build the Change Case (*Dun-Dun!*) ... Earlier in our chapter, we define the steps you can use to build a case for change within your workplace jungle. Identify something within your business that needs changing and make it happen.

Be sure that you thoroughly identify the change, initiate the conversation about what you think is the change with the right stakeholders, and identify the resources and plan needed to make the change happen. Have courage and present this to your leadership and see what happens ... you just might make some change!

ACTIVITY #2: Put Me In, Coach! Practice the Coaching Questions ... page 266 of this chapter shares seven coaching questions. Find a partner or workwife/workhubby. Engage in a conversation but force yourself to use one or a few of the questions during the conversation. After a few moments, switch roles.

How did that work for you? Was it awkward? Did the questions flow and allow the conversation to continue, garnering more information from the person you were questioning?

How can you ensure you use these questions and move them into your *unconscious/competence* arena?

ACTIVITY #3: I Second That Promotion! Promoting Change ... Review the steps or suggested strategies for promoting change within your organization. Now, be real: would they actually work within your business?

Why or why would they not work? If they wouldn't, what *should* you to do promote change initiatives within your respective workplace jungle?

ACTIVITY #4: Turn Your Head and Cough: Org Culture "Personality Check" ... Next time you're at work ask your-self these five questions in order to decipher your organization's personality or culture:

1.  How would you describe your organization, using only ten words?
2.  What's really important at your organization? Where do resources (time, money, people) tend to go?
3.  Who gets promoted?
4.  What behaviors or actions get rewarded or recognized?
5.  In your organization describe who fits in and who doesn't.

ACTIVITY #5: Fight or Flight? Conduct the "Should You Even TRY to Change the Org Culture?" Analysis ... In this chapter, we lay out some good steps to analyze how inclu-sive your organization's culture is and what you should (or should not) do with those results.

Conduct this analysis with your org. What do you see? What should you do?

# Drone Perspective: Reflective ?'s

1) On a scale of 1–10 with 10 being "I love change! Bring it!" to 1 being "Oh no, I fear change!" where would you rate yourself?

1    2    3    4    5    6    7    8    9    10

Why would you rate yourself there?

_____

_____

_____

_____

What are three things you could do to move that number up (even if it's pretty high)?

1. _____

2. _____

3. _____

2) Of the Seven Engaging Questions by Stanier, which one—if you were forced to pick just one—really resonated with you most?

_____

_____

_____

_____

Why?

_____

_____

_____

_____

3) Think about an organizational change you were part of in the past. How did it go? (1=Horribly ... 10=Great!)

1    2    3    4    5    6    7    8    9    10

Why?

_____

_____

_____

_____

Compare to our Prosci 7 Best Change Tips. Which ones helped or hindered your change?

_____

_____

_____

_____

4) Using the analytical process identified in this chapter, how inclusive is your organization to the LGBTQ+ Community and beyond? (1=Very 'Uninclusive' … 10=Very Inclusive)

1     2     3     4     5     6     7     8     9     10

Where do you think or want it to be? (1=Very 'Uninclusive' … 10=Very Inclusive)

1     2     3     4     5     6     7     8     9     10

What are the three strategies you can start next week to move that rating to where you want it to be?

1. _____

2. _____

3. _____

5) What is your favorite thing about where you work?

_____

_____

_____

_____

The least favorite?

_____

_____

_____

_____

If you aren't happy at work, what can you do?

_____

_____

_____

_____

. . . . . . . . . . . . . . . . . . . . . . . . . . . . . . . . . . . . . . . . . . . . . . . . . . . . . .

# ALL ABOARD!
# THE APPLICATION STATION

*"Awareness is the first step to any personal change.*
*But it takes desire, planning, resources, and above all*
*else, commitment on the part of the LGBTQ+ Leader to*
*make lasting change in themselves and their leadership*
*effectiveness. If it was easy, we'd be surrounded by rock*
*star leaders; but it's the ones who put in that courage*
*and effort who truly become the rock star leaders."*
– Dr. Steve Yacovelli
The Gay Leadership Dude

Proactive Communication • Relationship-Building • Integrity,
Authenticity, & Courage • Developing Culture • Empathy

THE SAYING GOES, "You can lead a horse to water, but you can't make 'em drink vodka," (or something like that). So, my leadership friend: consider yourself led to water.

It's now your job to drink (or apply) the concepts here to make yourself even more of a rock star LGBTQ+ Leader. But what exactly are some proven strategies that will help change your own behavior and get your leadership awesomeness to that *unconscious/ competence* stage? Let's explore!

## It's One Thing to Learn, It's a Whole Other Ballgame to Apply

Think about your last week in December. Typically, this is when people start to make New Year's Resolutions: How will I be better once January 1st hits? Some people do the whole diet thing, and/or exercise, or cut back on vices like booze or smokes, or make plans to make changes in the upcoming, shiny out-of-the-wrapper new year. Now, think about the other development books you've read or training classes you've attended in the past. How have you adopted their key findings into your life, if at all?

There's a lot of ways psychologists have studied how humans hold onto these goals successfully (or ways in which they peter out and stop going to the gym come February 1st). With that in mind, here are my top five suggestions so you can hold yourself accountable to change your leadership behavior and keep moving toward greater self-development:

1. **Keep note of your own leadership behavior and write it down** … If you've found the drone perspective/mindfulness skills are spot-on and in that *unconscious/competence* area we talked about earlier, develop your own personal diagnostic to see what happens in your own behavior.

For example, if you decided you really want to focus on improving your level of empathy (Chapter 6), then "observe yourself" in situations that require empathy. After that staff meeting, ask yourself if you did all you could do to embrace that type (and more thoughts on the "write it down" thing in a minute).

2. **Remember you're about to eat an elephant: take one bite at a time** ... You don't just try and gobble an elephant all at once (not that you should really be eating such beautiful creatures, but I digress). Sit and make out a plan of attack to meet your goals. Goals are typically made up of milestones or smaller objectives (bites) that will help you move toward the bigger goal. What are the concrete steps you'll take to meet your goal? Identify these baby steps and, before you know it, you've eaten your elephant, er, twelve-foot-long sub* (*no pachyderms were harmed in the use of this analogy).

3. **Where's that workwife/workhusband when you need them?** ... Find help from those around you. Ask for feedback from a trusted friend, colleague, mentor, or your workwife/workhusband or workplace BFF. Having someone first be aware of what you're trying to do can help be a second set of eyes and ears on what you're actually doing. Remind them of your goals and desired behavior change, and, most importantly, be open to their feedback for what they are observing.

4. **Change is hard, but definitely not impossible** ... Creating lasting behavior change—whether it be to improve your own leadership awesomeness or even stuff like "get

healthier"—takes time and effort. You can't expect to, say, be a marathoner after running around your block one day. So, remember that improving yourself is a marathon, not a sprint. Take your steps identified in Step 2 (above), break them down into realistic deadlines, and be patient with yourself; which leads us to …

5. **When you stumble—and you will—be kind to yourself**
   … We humans make mistakes, even when we think we've set out to meet those important goals. Often, when we're faced with some new way of doing things, we revert back to what is known (see our story earlier about the accountant who becomes the boss but still tries to micromanage their accountants because it's in their comfort zone—*unconscious/ competence*). As long as you're taking that drone perspective and being aware of your behavior—and what is working and what isn't—you'll be moving to foster change and growth in yourself. And, when you run into a hiccup on progress, just dust yourself off, learn from it, and move on.

# Wicked S.M.A.R.T.: Creating Goals

"I have been impressed with the urgency of doing. Knowing is not enough; we must apply. Being willing is not enough; we must do."

– Leonardo da Vinci, Italian Renaissance painter, sculptor, architect, musician, scientist, mathematician, engineer, inventor, anatomist, geologist, cartographer, botanist, and writer (1452–1519)
… and we're pretty sure he was a homo.

Once you have determined that, yes, 'tis a good idea to start to work on my leadership awesomeness, then it's time to translate that desire into goals that can be clearly communicated to those around you (see *accountability*, above) as well as allow us to measure if and when we meet the goal (of course!). Effective goals clearly state the what, the when, the how, and the who (not The Who), and they are specifically measurable. They should address what you need to do in the short-term (think one to three years) to achieve your objectives.

There're several methods out there to construct tangible goals that we can use and measure against. My personal favorite is the S.M.A.R.T. Method for Goal Setting. The concept was first mentioned in November 1981 issue of the *Management Review* and has been a staple in B-Schools and Board Rooms alike ever since (Doran, 1981). The S.M.A.R.T. acronym identifies the five parts to a solid, measurable goal:

- **Specific:** Goals needs to be specific. Try to answer the questions of how much… and what kind… with each goal you write. So, for your leadership goal(s), ask yourself specifically what do you want to get out of setting this goal?
- **Measurable:** Goals must be stated in quantifiable terms, or they are only good intentions. Measurable goals help you facilitate planning, implementation, and control (a.k.a. quality of success). For example, for non-leadership goals, a measure might be "# of new customers" or "% complete" and a target might be "500" or "100%," respectively.
- **Attainable:** While goals must provide a stretch that inspires you to aim higher and grow a bit, they must also be achievable, or you're setting yourself up for failure

(which then can lead to demotivation and inaction down the road). Set goals you know you, your organization, and your team can realistically reach.

- **Responsible person:** Goals must be assigned to a person or a department. But, just because a person is assigned a goal doesn't mean that they're solely responsible for its achievement; they just need to be the point person who will ensure the goal is achieved. So, for personal leadership goals, take a guess whose responsibility it is to make 'em happen? (HINT: look in the mirror.) For more on this, see our convo on *motivation* in Chapter 7.

- **Time specific:** With reference to time, your goals must include a timeline of when they should be accomplished. I'm a big fan of timeframes like "by end of Quarter 2" or "before my next Mid-Year Performance Review" so it puts some structure to prioritization but is loose enough should things need to take focus. Also, *time* ties in with *attainable*, too; you don't want to set a goal and expect to be an expert leadership person next Monday.

While we share the S.M.A.R.T. Method here, you may have come across other methods that work for you (or slight variations of S.M.A.R.T., where R=Realistic meaning pretty much the same as our A=Attainable and then that model's A=Assigned, which is what we call R=Responsible. Confused? Just stick to what we have above for simplicity). Regardless of which model you use, if you're to grow as an LGBTQ+ Leader, it's best to have some sort of goal-setting where you're sure it's not just a "it'd be cool if I improved my leadership skillz" to something more, well, smart.

## Action (Jackson) Plans

If you've worked in any Fortune 500 company or within an organized, well, organization, you're probably familiar with Action Planning. After you create your S.M.A.R.T. goals for improving your leadership competencies, Action Planning is defining exactly *how* you are going to make them come to life. Here's a few suggestions on actually meeting those goals:

1. **Write. It. Down.** ... Studies have shown time and again that when someone writes down a goal, they are more apt to meet it. Get out your Microsoft Word, or better yet use an actual pen and paper, or still better yet use that white board that's staring you in the face on a daily basis to identify your goals. It really is best if—even if you put it on a Post-It® Note on your computer monitor—it's literally staring you in the face as a reminder of where your focus should be.

2. **Tell someone and provide updates** ... We discussed that workwife/workhusband as being a good sounding board, but don't forget your leader or boss. If you have annual performance meetings, be sure that you incorporate your leadership goal(s) in that document. This not only helps hold you accountable (my boss knows now!), but also helps keep the goal top of mind. Consider setting up frequent meetings between you and said work BFF (or boss) to discuss goal progress say, once a month or so. This will bring your goal into the spotlight and allow you to remember that you have to take steps in order to meet said goal periodically.

3. **Still tell someone, even if you're talking to yourself ...**
   It's better to tell another about your plans to meet your goals (#2, above), but if there's no one to tell (or you don't feel comfortable telling someone) fret not: there's always one person listening: you. Set an Outlook or iCalc reminder to periodically ask yourself, "Howzit going there, LGBTQ+ Leader?" Reflect on how well you're working toward those goals—and be honest with yourself. If you can, find ways in which to tell your boy/girlfriend or significant other or bestie how much progress you're making toward your goals. If you're scared, you'll be reporting, "No movement yet," repeatedly to that person, then channel that fear into action to get 'er done.

## Lemme Think: More on Mindfulness

One of the biggest challenges I often hear from Leaders I coach is the idea of being mindful of their own behavior. And it makes sense: it's often hard to watch yourself doing something when you're doing it. And thus, our conversation of "drone perspective" and mindfulness. But I want to re-emphasize the whole concept of mindfulness.

Studies show that—aside from the benefit of helping you realize your in-the-moment behavior—mindful meditation has been proven to help increase productivity, increase morale, and provide overall health benefits.

I cannot say I'm an expert on mindfulness, but I can say I practice it as best as I can. I've absolutely seen a definite difference in my focus, and especially being able to understand in-the-moment

## :kson) Plans

Steve doing stuff that thoughtful-reflective-Steve probably didn't intend, and work to fix it. Mindfulness helps me suit up and fly in my drone.

To make mindfulness work for you as an LGBTQ+ Leader, here's some strategies to get you started:

1. **Make the time, rinse, and repeat** ... Mindful meditation doesn't require a yoga mat, a comfy lay-down couch, or a completely quiet space (but some of these might help certain folks); it does require a commitment to practice it to get it to that *unconscious/competence* state of being in you. Add it to your calendar or your daily routine and stick to it. How do you get to Carnegie Hall? Practice, practice, practice (thanks, Dad, for the awesome Dad joke!).

2. **Set your mindful stage** ... Do get yourself comfortable, usually in a seated position. Have good posture, but don't be rigid. Put your feet on the floor like a "proper lady" (no, seriously, it helps with the posture). Some folks close their eyes but really you don't have to; just adjust your gaze downward and let it soften. Breathe deep through your nose and fill up your lungs. Focus first on just your breath: maybe try five seconds of deep inhale, one second pause, and five seconds exhale* (*please consult your doctor or primary care provider before engaging in any sort of exercise or activities suggested within this book. Thanks, Legal Beagles, for that reminder!).

3. **Mindfulness loves a lot of "presents"** ... Mindfulness isn't to make your inner voice completely silent or to get to that place of ultimate Zen suspension, but really to

just focus your attention on what's happening IN THAT MOMENT and WITHOUT JUDGMENT (and yes, my caps are meant to highly emphasize that point). That's focusing on your breathing, what you're hearing, what your nerve endings are feeling, etc.

Literally—just this moment—I stopped writing and moved into a light mindful state. I felt my arms get heavier on my side. I heard my dog Ella breathing under my desk. I felt my breath slowly get deeper and slower. That's what *present* means. And that's not necessarily easy, especially for those of us whose little mind-hamster is running in that mental wheel at 90 miles per hour, but that's the goal of mindful meditation. And with that said …

4. **Don't be a Judgy McJudgenstein while engaging in your mindfulness** … Your mind-hamster is a judgy beotch and will throw judgment shade on those thoughts that go by as you're trying to be mindful. Just pull an Elsa and "Let it go!" Again, easier said than done, but the goal of mindful (as my caps in #3 note) is to be nonjudgmental with the thoughts occupying your mind. Mental Post-It® note those thoughts that bubble up and move on as best as you can.

5. **Just come back to the present, please** … As mentioned earlier, if you practice yoga, you know that it's called a *practice* because you really should never reach perfection, even if you are the most amazing yogi, you'll have that off day and not be your best. Awesome! You just come back tomorrow and try again; it's a journey and not a destination. Same with mindful meditation: if your mind-hamster

pulls you away from the present it's all good. Just let the thought pass and come back to the present and back to #2 above and just ... be.

**STEVE'S DISCLAIMER:** Again, be sure to consult your primary care provider before engaging in this type of work (but I'll bet it will be VERY beneficial to your physical self!).

Finally, note that there's a ton of online and other resources available to you to help you flex your mindfulness muscles. Aside from the typical Google search, my personal favorite is Headspace, an app that slowly guides you through being more mindful (and no, I'm in no way affiliated with nor do I get a kickback from the good folks at Headspace). There're other apps as well as a bunch of books out there, too; I've just not personally used them.

# Drone Perspective: Reflective ?'s

1) What do you think is your biggest challenge to meeting your leadership goal?

_____

_____

_____

_____

What are two ways you can overcome this challenge?

1. _____

2. _____

2) What are three ways you'll hold yourself accountable to the goal(s) you've identified?

1. _____

2. _____

3. _____

3) What was your reaction to the concept of *mindful meditation*? Come on: be honest.

_____

_____

_____

_____

For the sake of your own development, give it a try. After three days of trying, look at your response to the question above. Do you still feel the same?

_____

_____

_____

_____

OK, Now be sure you've tried it for a total of seven days in a row. See a difference? (You're welcome.)

......................................................

# LEADER-SHIPPING OUT (FINAL THOUGHTS)

*"Being an LGBTQ+ Leader takes effort, but the fabulous thing to remember is that: (1) you're not alone; and (2) you got this. Any other challenge is something that pales in comparison to the great stuff we as LGBTQ+ people have already dealt with. Resilience is part of our Community, and so is support for each other's success."*
– Dr. Steve Yacovelli
The Gay Leadership Dude

Proactive Communication • Relationship-Building • Integrity, Authenticity, & Courage • Developing Culture • Empathy

ELL, THAT'S ALL we got for this book. Hopefully you have garnered some nuggets of wisdom to help improve your LGBTQ+ leadership rock star-ness. A few closing thoughts as we literally close the book on this topic.

## One Last Li'l Steve Story

If I could pull a Cher and "turn back tiiimmme," I'd love to go back to my Twenty-Something Steve (most likely on the dance floor at a downtown Orlando club dancin' away or at a local LGBTQ+ watering hole with some friends) and tell him to start and think about building his leadership capacity so—when he does become a leader within his workplace—he'll have started the skills to get beyond that *unconscious/incompetence* stage and move a little quicker to that *unconscious/competence* way of thinking about communication, engaging in empathy, being authentic, and the other competencies we shared in this book. And the same can be said to you, my LGBTQ+ Leader friend. (Oh, and while I have you, Twenty-Something Steve: You might want to wear more sunscreen while you're at it, kid. Just a thought.)

The cool thing about self-development is that you can indeed teach an old dog new tricks and, whether you're just entering the workforce or are a seasoned professional, you have the opportunity to make yourself just a little bit better here through self-reflection, practice, and—for yourself—forgiveness when you don't necessarily stick the landing and get the leadership stuff 100% spot-on.

## Eating the Elephant & Remembering Your P.R.I.D.E.

If developing yourself is the key here, then remember from Chapter 10 that you're about to eat an Elephant: pick one or maaaaaybe two areas to focus on to develop. Get a plan (again see

Chapter 10) and work on it; don't expect it to just serendipitously fall into place without some thought, planning, and measurement with regards to your success.

One of the things that's often tough when trying to remember new or newer concepts is, well remembering them. Until it's in that automatic *unconscious/competence* zone, there's that conscious, mind-focused need to remember the key concepts, the strategies, tools, procedures, or tactics needed to move the learning into that "it's part of my DNA and how I do things" world.

Acronyms are an awesome way to remember lists, think S.M.A.R.T. from Chapter 10, or ROYGBIV from your childhood to remember the colors of the rainbow (as if you need that by now!). If we reflect on the key concepts presented in this book, they actually can fall into a nice, fancy acronym that I truly hope you can remember:

- **P – Proactive Communication** … our concepts focused on in Chapter 7, but woven throughout
- **R – Relationship-Building** … what we zeroed in on in Chapter 8, but woven within our conversation
- **I – Integrity, Authenticity, & Courage** … three concepts so tightly aligned they *could* have been just one chapter, but we split them over Chapter 4 and Chapter 5
- **D – Developing Culture** … the focus of our chat in Chapter 9
- **E – Empathy** … and last but definitely not least, our energy around having empathy, which we discussed in Chapter 6

By using the P.R.I.D.E. acronym, hopefully you'll be able to remember the key concepts of this book, and what to begin to focus on within your leadership world.

## Put Me in, Coach! Coaching, Mentoring, Counseling, & Therapy

As an awesome LGBTQ+ Leader, you may either find yourself in a position to need someone to help guide your leadership awesomeness, or you may be the one who's going to help others be the best, authentic, inclusive LGBTQ+ Leader that they can be. People often throw around the phrases, "Get a mentor," or "Be a mentor!" But is that the right term? Should it be *coach*? What exactly is the difference between *mentoring* and *coaching*?

There's a cool model I've used for years to understand the difference between these two concepts, as well as *advising* and *counseling*. Picture a blank piece of paper. Now: draw a large + in the middle; at the top of the vertical line write "Your Job: More 'Ask'" and at the bottom of that same line write "Your Job: More 'Tell'". Now: on the horizontal line on the left write "Focus: Problem" and the right of that same line write "Focus: Solution".

The upper-left quadrant—where the focus of the relationship is on a *problem* and your job is to *ask* more questions—is what we call **therapy**. If you've ever been to any sort of therapy, this is the approach of the therapist: to ask you a lot of probing questions to get to the root of your challenge or problem.

The lower-left quadrant—where the focus of the relationship is still on the *problem* but now your job is to *tell*—is what we call

**counseling.** Think of, say, a career counselor. They tell you things like, "Be sure you updated your résumé," or "Don't forget to check on LinkedIn for jobs in your area."

The lower-right quadrant—where the focus of the relationship is now on a *solution* and your job is still to *tell*—is what we call **mentoring.** If you've ever had a mentor in this sense, they were more telling you about what you should/shouldn't do to better your career, your opportunities, etc. "I would check with Human Resources to see what special projects you could get to help you advance ..." could be something a mentor says to a mentee.

Finally, the upper-right quadrant—where the focus of the relationship is on a *solution* and your job is to *ask* more questions—is what we call true leadership **coaching.** This is where you really want to be with regard to cultivating the talents of those you could help. While some are really tempted to fall into the mentoring zone ("I'll tell you what you should do..."), better LGBTQ+ Leaders who want to develop others allow them to come to their own solutions. But asking open-ended, probing questions can help the coachee come to those conclusions and action items. When anyone comes up with their own solutions and action plan, they're so much more likely to follow through versus when someone tells them what to do. As an effective Leadership Coach, your role is to guide, not tell. (**SIDE NOTE:** Remember our awesome Coaching Questions from Chapter 9!)

With that said, if you feel you've got this leadership thang, then maybe consider setting yourself up as an LGBTQ+ Leadership Coach. Becoming a coach is very rewarding, but it's not just so simple as sitting down with someone less experienced than you with a cup o' joe and dumping your wisdom onto them (again that's *mentoring*, my friend). True leadership coaching takes skill, preparation, and communication; it's like any relationship you may have. So, regardless of where you find your coachee, here's seven tips and best practices you should use to get the most out of your coach/coachee relationship:

1. **Establish expectations upfront** ... When you meet with your coachee, it's good to identify your thoughts on what you want out of the relationship, and ask them what they expect, too. There's nothing worse than entering into a relationship with completely different expectations; that sets everyone up for failure.

2. **Set a renewal date** ... It's a great idea to set an "expiration date" or a timeframe for the coach/coachee relationship to last. Like any contract, knowing the finish date helps put things in perspective, and not lock either party into something.

3. **Establish a communication strategy from Day 1** ... How will you two communicate? Method? For what reasons should you chat? Frequency? Establish these details in Conversation Numero Uno, so the expectations are crystal clear from the beginning.

4. **When meeting with your coachee, listen** ... We shared listening best practices in Chapter 7; be sure you're listening to understand versus listening to respond. Ask those open-ended questions (again Chapter 9), probe how your coachee got to their opinion and perspective, and ask and don't tell.

5. **Provide open and honest feedback, the good and the not-so-good** ... Building that coach/coachee relationship is vital to progress; and that's building trust between you both. One of the best ways—and sometimes most challenging—is to provide open and honest feedback (this is also tied to #3, above). Be honest with your feedback (the good and the not-so-good), be balanced (don't provide only the negative kind), and make sure your intent is to better the coachee and not knock them down to make yourself feel awesome (bad LGBTQ+ Leader!).

6. **Use your empathy skills and remember when you were in their shoes/pumps** ... In any coaching situation, the skill of empathy is a huge benefit. Be mindful of the emotions of your coachee when they share their situation/context, their frustration, their excitement, and overall their demeanor. They're looking to you for not just guidance, but comfort and reassurance. Don't dismiss their emotions.

7. **Let the coachee make the decisions** ... While this is implied by our four-quadrant coaching model described above, it begs to be repeated to be very careful to not *tell* your coachee what to do but *allow* them—through your use of questions—to come to their own decisions and action plan.

If you're savvy, you've probably already realized that—to be an effective leadership coach—you are utilizing the six leadership competencies we've discussed in this book (aren't I sneaky!). Again, it shows these concepts/skills/tools are valuable to you as an LGBTQ+ Leader. So, the W.I.I.F.M. for you as a leadership coach is your opportunity to practice and get even more skilled at the leadership competencies shared in this book. SCORE!

## Find Your RuPaul

Let's say you're the opposite of the folks above and you're the one who's really benefited from this book from a leadership development perspective. Awesome that we found you (or you us!). So, what do you do now that you've identified your goals (see Chapter 10)? Clearly, your first step is to execute those goals through your action plan. Another strategy is to find yourself a coach.

Think of how RuPaul has her *Drag Race*. She takes drag queen contestants under her fabulous wings and helps them become something more than when they started the competition. Yaaaaas-sss, contestants are invited to participate in the competition by their own strengths and skills. But, through participation of the show and under the guiding tutelage of RuPaul, contestants become something more, with some going on to win the competition.

If you're someone who wants to be "something more" after going through this book, I suggest you find your own RuPaul and get yourself a coach. There are many different organizations you can look for: from your local Gay and Lesbian Chamber of Commerce to the Small Business Administration's SCORE program (not LGBTQ+ focused, FYI) to any number of local organizations within your area that offer business and leadership coaches. While finding a coach who is not a member of the LGBTQ+ Community is fine, if you can, I feel there's a lot of extra value in finding someone who is part of our Community, who's faced similar situations, and who gets the "whole" you.

Regardless of where you look, here's some tips-and-tricks to make the most of your coaching relationship:

1. **Be realistic and upfront with your shiny, new coach** ... Share your S.M.A.R.T. goals with your coach very, very early on and ask their advice on achieving them (even if you've already given it some thoughts). Use these goals as the basis of your partnership and conversations.

2. **Be a human** ... Leverage small talk and sharing of your background and experiences to build rapport with your coach. Yes, this is a business relationship but—as we shared earlier in this book—relationships build trust, and trust is the golden ticket for all things business success. Also, find ways to instill a bit of fun into the relationship. All business makes for a boring relationship. Make it fun but get stuff done, too. Go for an ice cream, go bowling, grab an adult beverage or a coffee—whatever you can do to mix it up and have a little bit of fun.

3. **Leverage tech to build your relationship** ... Some coaches want some face-to-face time; others like a phone chat. But be sure that you're regularly meeting your coach in some face-to-face facet (virtual or IRT). Why? Humans want to engage with humans, and not disembodied voices. It's so much easier to build a relationship with a face than a voice. Use technology to connect rather than divide your coach/coachee relationship.

4. **You got this, and keep getting this** ... This relationship is yours to cultivate: so, gurl, you'd better work (yay! RuPaul). Be prepared for your conversations with your

coach and take initiative; they're not there to *tell* you what to do but to ask the right questions and give you advice so you make your decisions and plans.

5. **Listen to what your coach has to say** … What? No seriously: they have experience and expertise that can help you be a better leader, business person, and all-around awesome person. Listen to the questions they ask and the experiences they share and be open if it's not what you want or expected to hear.

6. **Give as well as take** … You're getting some awesome (and free) consulting/help from your coach; but understand they are doing this for some reason, too. Ask your coach, "What's your W.I.I.F.M.? What's in it for you?" It's not a rude question (well, as long as you don't say it with THAT kinda tone), but it's a sincere perspective to understand. Also, ask how you can help them get the W.I.I.F.M. and be sincere and active to help them out, too. If your coach isn't getting what they expect out of the relationship, it will just make things hard for both of you.

7. **And finally: be sure to say "please" and (especially) "thank you"** … Be grateful for the time and energy and questions and advice your coach is giving you and be sure to show it and say it. Be sure to connect with that coach after your time is over (LinkedIn is awesome this way) and set a periodic reminder in your calendar to reach out to them.

As a bonus: once you've worked with a coach and that relationship is over and you've grown from it, consider "paying (or 'gaying') it forward" and become a coach yourself (see section above for some tips, now that the student becomes the teacher). Business karma is a real thing, and when you take from the Fountain of Knowledge, it's also good to give some of that water back (and not in a weird sorta way).

## Now Go Gay, er, Pay It Forward!

Regardless of if you have leadership awesomeness before reading this book, ("Hey, Steve, thanks for the info, but I'm pretty good here!") or after ("I can't believe all the cool stuff I was able to apply from this book. Thanks, Gay Leadership Dude!"), it's now time for you to Gay It Forward.

There are many other LGBTQ+ professionals who maybe aren't as savvy as you in their leadership, well, savviness, so here's your opportunity to help a brother or sister out. Find ways in which you can share your leadership expertise within our LGBTQ+ Community. Reach out to your local LGBTQ+ Chamber of Commerce and see how you can help foster the leadership skills of someone else. Talk to any local LGBTQ+ organizations, like PFLAG, Human Rights Campaign, Gay/Straight Student Alliances, and see how you can volunteer to move our quest for inclusivity forward. Your time and expertise are honestly more valuable than a financial donation (but that doesn't hurt either).

An added bonus: you have a sandbox from which to continue to apply these leadership competencies that not only benefits our Community, but moves—and keeps—these mad skillz in that *unconscious/competence* box. Excellent!

# Closing Up Shop & Keepin' this Leadership Party Goin'!

As you go forward and apply what you've learned from *Pride Leadership*, let us know what happened, how things worked for you, and overall the awesome success you'll no doubt have as an LGBTQ+ Leader. Also, join our community of awesome LGBTQ+ Leaders on our website:

thegayleadershipdude.com

We have some ways to connect; our blog, which keeps the convo going; some free stuff; and cool resources you can use to further your own leadership awesomeness … and that of those around you. Come on down!

Welp, that's a wrap. If you liked this book, please Cher with your friends. If you didn't, well, "Byeeeee, Brittany!" LOL j/k. Now, seriously: go roar like the King or Queen that you are!

# BIBLIOGRAPHY

Here's the cool resources and references shared throughout this book. Check 'em out!

Aguilar, L. (2006). *Ouch! That Stereotype Hurts ... Communicating Respectfully in a Diverse World.* Dallas, TX: The Walk the Talk Company.

Aristotle, translated by R. Browne & H. Bohn. (1850). *The Nicomachean Ethics of Aristotle. Translated, with Notes, Original & Selected; An Analytical Introduction; And Questions for the Use of Students.* London, U.K.: Forgotten Books.

Authentic. (n.d.) In *Google.com.* Retrieved 12/05/18 from www.google.com

Banks, E., P. Brooks, & M. Handelman (Producers) J. Moore (Director). (2012). *Pitch Perfect* [Motion picture]. United States: Universal Pictures. Retrieved 02/14/19 from: https://getyarn.io/yarn-clip/14cfe10d-0ce3-46ac-bf94-ee48dae60614

Bass, B. & B. Avolio (eds.) (1994). *Improving Organizational Effectiveness Through Transformational Leadership.* Thousand Oaks, CA: Sage Publications.

Belonwu, V. (2018, May 8). "20 Ways to Communicate Effectively with Your Team." *Small Business Trends.* Retrieved on 01/02/19 from http://smallbiztrends.com/2013/11/20-ways-to-communicate-effectively-in-the-workplace.html

Bernstein, R. (2017, December 14). "Business Psychology: Golem Effect vs. Pygmalion Effect." Brescia University Online. Retrieved 10/11/18 from: https://online.brescia.edu/management-news/golem-effect-vs-pygmalion-effect/

Bias. (n.d.). In *Wikipedia.* Retrieved 01/05/19 from https://en.wikipedia.org/wiki/List_of_cognitive_biases

Brown, B. (2018). *Dare to Lead: Brave Work. Tough Conversations. Whole Hearts.* New York: Random House.

Burns, J. (2004). *Leadership.* New York. Harper & Row.

Cherniss, C., D. Goleman (ed.) (2001). *The Emotional Intelligent Workplace: How to Select for, Measure, and Improve Emotional Intelligence in Individuals, Groups, and Organizations.* San Francisco: Jossey-Bass.

Clark, N. (ed.) (2012, November 9). "10 Steps to Effective Listening." *Forbes WomensMedia.com.* Retrieved on 01/04/19 from www.forbes.com/sites/womensmedia/2012/11/09/10-steps-to-effective-listening/#2295de233891

Coleman, B. (2017, August 21). "Inclusive Leadership: Just Be Good to People." *Forbes.com.* Retrieved on 12/22/18 from https://www.forbes.com/sites/forbescoachescouncil/2017/08/21/inclusive-leadership-just-be-good-to-people/#6e2952b21d67

Collins, J. (2001). *Good to Great: Why Some Companies Make the Leap ... and Others Don't.* New York: HarperCollins Publishers, Inc.

Connors, R. & T. Smith (2011). *Change the Culture, Change the Game: The Breakthrough Strategy for Energizing Your Organization and Creating Accountability for Results.* New York: Portfolio/Penguin.

Courage. (n.d.). In *Merriam-Webster.* Retrieved 01/11/19 from: https://www.merriam-webster.com/dictionary/courage

Covey, S. (1989). *The 7 Habits of Highly Effective People.* New York: Franklin Covey.

Coyle, D. (2018). *The Culture Code: The Secrets of Highly Successful Groups.* New York: Random House.

Curtiss, P. & P. Warren. (1973). *The Dynamics of Life Skills Coaching (Life Skills Series).* Prince Albert, Saskatchewan: Training Research and Development Station, Dept. of Manpower and Immigration.

Doran, G. (1981). "There's a S.M.A.R.T. Way to Write Management's Goals and Objectives." *Management Review,* Vol. 70(11), pp. 35–36.

Duarte, N. (2010). *Resonate: Present Visual Stories that Transform Audiences.* Hoboken, NJ: John Wiley & Sons, Inc.

Empathy. (n.d.). In *Merriam-Webster.* Retrieved 01/11/19 from https://www.merriam-webster.com/dictionary/empathy

Fisher, C. (1997). "Emotions at Work: What Do Feel and How Should We Measure It?" *Bond University School of Business Discussion Papers, Paper 63.* Retrieved on 01/20/19 at: http://epublications.bond.edu.au/discussion_papers/63

Gardenswartz, L. & A. Rowe. (2010). *Managing Diversity: A Complete Desk Reference & Planning Guide (3rd Edition)*. Alexandria, VA: Society for Human Resource Management (SHRM®).

Gatling, A., P. Castelli, & M. Cole. (2013). "Authentic Leadership: The Role of Self-Awareness in Promoting Coaching Effectiveness." *Asia-Pacific Journal of Management Research and Innovation*, Vol. 9(4), pp. 337–347.

George, B. (2016). "The Truth About Authentic Leaders." *Harvard Business School Working Knowledge*. Retrieved on 01/02/19 from: https://hbswk.hbs.edu/item/the-truth-about-authentic-leaders?cid=spmailing-13138219-WK%20Newsletter%20 07-06-2016%20(1)-July%2006,%202016

Gerdeman, D. (2017, May 17). "Minorities Who 'Whiten' Job resumes Get More Interviews." *Harvard Business School: Working Knowledge.* Retrieved 11/10/18 from: https://hbswk.hbs.edu/ item/minorities-who-whiten-job-resumes-get-more-interviews

Gillespie, N. & L. Mann. (2004). "Transformational Leadership and Shared Values: The Building Blocks of Trust." *Journal of Managerial Psychology*, Vol. 19(6), pp. 588–607.

Gladwell, M. (2005). *Blink: The Power of Thinking Without Thinking.* New York: Little, Brown, and Company.

Goleman, D. (2006). *Social Intelligence: The New Science of Human Relationships.* New York: Bantam Dell.

Grasz, J. (2011, August 18). "Seventy-One Percent of Employers Say They Value Emotional Intelligence Over IQ, According to CareerBuilder." CareerBuilder.com. Retrieved on 01/22/19 from https://www.careerbuilder.ca/share/aboutus/pressreleasesdetail.aspx?id=pr652&sd=8%2f18%2f2011&ed=8%2f18 %2f2099

Gunther, M. (2006, November 30). "Queer Inc.: How Corporate America Fell in Love with Gays and Lesbians." *Fortune*. Retrieved 12/11/18 from http://archive.fortune.com/magazines/fortune/fortune_archive/2006/12/11/8395465/index.htm

Harrington, S. (2017, June 30). "How to Build Strong Relationships." *Forbes.com*. Retrieved on 12/22/18 from https://www.forbes.com/sites/samanthaharrington/2017/06/30/how-to-build-strong-business-relationships/#5a4b338a356f

Heath, C. & D. Heath. (2010). *Switch: How to Change Things When Change Is Hard*. New York: Broadway Books.

James, G. (2018, October 15). "All Great Entrepreneurs Have This." *Inc.com*. Retrieved 12/19/18 from https://www.inc.com/geoffrey-james/all-great-entrepreneurs-have-this.html

Johnston, D. (2010 March 26). "Physical Appearance and Wages: Do Blondes Have More Fun?" *Economic Letters*, Vol. 108(10–12). Retrieved on 10/12/18 from http://amosyang.net/wp-content/uploads/2012/11/physicalappearanceandwages.pdf

Keller, G. & J. Papasan. (2012). *The ONE Thing: The Surprisingly Simple Truth Behind Extraordinary Results*. Auston, TX: Bard Press.

Kotlyar, I. & L. Karakowsky. (2006). "Leading Conflict? Linkages Between Leader Behaviors and Group Conflict." *Small Group Research*, Vol. 37(4), pp. 377–403.

Kozuch, E. (2018, June 25). "HRC REPORT: Startling Data Reveals Half of LGBTQ Employees in the U.S. Remain Closeted at Work." *Human Rights Campaign*. Retrieved on 02/21/19 from: https://www.hrc.org/blog/hrc-report-startling-data-reveals-half-of-lgbtq-employees-in-us-remain-clos

Langston University. (n.d.) *Transformational Leadership*. Retrieved on 12/22/18 from https://www.langston.edu/sites/default/files/basic-content-files/TransformationalLeadership.pdf

Lencioni, P. (2007). *The Truth About Employee Engagement: A Fable About Addressing the Three Root Causes of Job Misery*. San Francisco: Jossey-Bass & Pfeiffer, 2016.

McLeod, S. (2018, October 18). "Pavlov's Dogs." *SimplyPsychology*. Retrieved 01/11/19 from https://www.simplypsychology.org/pavlov.html

Morton, M., D. Mochon, & D. Ariely. (2011). "The "IKEA Effect": When Labor Leads to Love." *Harvard Business School Working Knowledge*. Retrieved on 01/02/19 from https://www.hbs.edu/faculty/Publication%20Files/11-091.pdf

Newcomer, L. (2017, February 10). "Here's How to Get Over Your Fear of Public Speaking." *Quill.com*. Retrieved 02/11/19 from https://www.quill.com/blog/careers-advice/public-speaking-is-scary-heres-how-to-get-over-your-fear.html

Newlon, C. (2016, March 6). "The 6 Benefits of Incorporating Mindfulness at Work." *Mental Floss*. Retrieved on 11/11/2018 from http://mentalfloss.com/article/76310/6-benefits-incorporating-mindfulness-work

Northwestern University. (2006, June 19). "Obama to Graduates: Cultivate Empathy." Evanston, IL: Northwestern University. Retrieved on 01/19/19 from https://www.northwestern.edu/newscenter/stories/2006/06/barack.html

Organizational Culture. (n.d.). In BusinessDictionary.com. Retrieved on 01/13/19 from http://www.businessdictionary.com/definition/organizational-culture.html

Patterson, K., J. Grenny, R. McMillan, & A. Switzler. (2012). *Crucial Conversations: Tools for Talking When Stakes Are High.* New York: McGraw-Hill.

Petrucci, A. (2017, November 20). "Storytelling Takes Corporate Communications to The Next Level." *Forbes Magazine.* Retrieved on 01/03/19 from www.forbes.com/sites/forbescommunicationscouncil/2017/11/20/storytelling-takes-corporate-communications-to-the-next-level/#480e853a7cbf

Pink, D. (2011). *Drive: The Surprising Truth About What Motivates Us.* New York: Riverhead Books.

Project Implicit. (2011). Retrieved 11/09/18 from https://implicit.harvard.edu/implicit/aboutus.html

Prosci Change Management (n.d.). "Best Practices in Change Management." *Prosci.com.* Retrieved on12/22/18 from www.prosci.com/resources/articles/change-management-best-practices

Rauch, J. (2019, January/February). "It's Time to Drop the 'LGBT' From 'LGBTQ': The Case for a New Term That Describes *All* Sexual Minorities." *The Atlantic.* Retrieved 01/15/19 from https://www.theatlantic.com/magazine/archive/2019/01/dont-call-me-lgbtq/576388/

Schilt, K. (2010). *Just One of the Guys? Transgender Men and the Persistence of Gender Inequality.* Chicago: University of Chicago Press.

Schwantes, M. (2017, January 18). "The 5 Communication Habits All Leaders Need to Motivate a Team." *Inc.com.* Retrieved on 01/04/19 from www.inc.com/marcel-schwantes/first-90-days-communication-habits-all-leaders-need-to-motivate-a-team.html

Scott, K. (2017). *Radical Candor: How to Be a Kickass Boss Without Losing Your Humanity*. New York: St. Martin's Press.

Shepperd, J., P. Carroll, J. Grace, & M. Terry (2002). "Exploring the Causes of Comparative Optimism" *Psychologica Belgica*: Vol. 42, pp. 65–98.

Sinek, S. (2011). *Start with Why: How Great Leaders Inspire Everyone to Take Action*. New York: Penguin Group.

Sinek, S. (2017). *Leaders Eat Last: Why Some Teams Pull Together and Others Don't*. New York: Portfolio/Penguin.

Smith, Chris (n.d.). "Guide to The Seven Barriers of Communication." *Guides.co*. Retrieved on 01/05/19 from http://guides.co/g/the-seven-barriers-of-communication/37696

Snyder, K. (2006). *The G Quotient: Why Gay Executives Are Excelling as Leaders … and What Every Manager Needs to Know*. San Francisco: Jossey-Bass.

Somvanshi, S. (2016, April 13). "What Did Frank Underwood Mean By 'Tall Men Make Great Presidents'?" *Quora.com*. Retrieved 10/12/18 from https://www.quora.com/What-did-Frank-Underwood-mean-by-Tall-men-make-great-presidents

Stanier, M. (2016). *The Coaching Habit: Say Less, Ask More & Change the Way You Lead Forever*. Toronto, ON: Box of Crayons Press.

Statista.com (n.d.). In *Statista.com*. Retrieved January 29, 2019 from https://www.statista.com/topics/751/facebook/

Statista.com (n.d.). In *Statista.com*. Retrieved January 29, 2019 from https://www.statista.com/statistics/274564/monthly-active-twitter-users-in-the-united-states/

Statista.com (n.d.). In *Statista.com*. Retrieved January 29, 2019 from https://www.statista.com/statistics/293771/number-of-us-instagram-users/

St. Thomas University. (2018, May 8). "What is Transactional Leadership? How Structure Leads to Results" Retrieved on 12/23/18 from https://online.stu.edu/articles/education/what-is-transactional-leadership.aspx

Tardanico, S. (2013, January 15). "10 Traits of Courageous Leaders." *Forbes Magazine* (Online). Retrieved on 01/04/19 from www.forbes.com/sites/susantardanico/2013/01/15/10-traits-of-courageous-leaders/#51acd1ad4fc0

Tobak, S. (2013, February 15). "8 Ways to Be a Courageous Leader." *Inc.com*. Retrieved on 12/28/18 from www.inc.com/steve-tobak/the-most-important-leadership-attribute.html

Trevor, J. (2012). "Developing Transformational Leadership." *Developing Leaders: Executive Education in Practice*, Vol. 1(9), pp. 2–8.

Value. (n.d.). In *Merriam-Webster*. Retrieved 01/11/19 from https://www.merriam-webster.com/dictionary/value

Vedantam, S. (2010). *The Hidden Brain: How Our Unconscious Minds Elect Presidents, Control Markets, Wage Wars, and Save Our Lives*. New York: Spiegel & Grau.

Weinberger, M. (2017, June 11). "'There are Only Two Rules'—Facebook Explains How 'Hackathons,' One of its Oldest Traditions, is also One of its Most Important." *Business Insider*. Retrieved on 12/29/18 from https://www.businessinsider.com/facebook-hackathons-2017-6

Wilson, T. (2002). *Strangers to Ourselves: Discovering the Adaptive Unconscious*. Cambridge, MA: Belknap Press.

Young, A. (2016, July 28). "A Look Back at Obama's Convention Speeches." *National Public Radio (NPR.com)*. Retrieved on 12/22/18 from: https://www.npr.org/2016/07/28/487769331/a-look-back-at-obamas-past-convention-speeches

Young Entrepreneur Council (2015, May 18). "14 Best Practices for More Effective Communication." *Inc.com*. Retrieved on 01/04/19 from www.inc.com/young-entrepreneur-council/14-best-practices-for-more-effective-communication.html

Zauderer, D. (2002). "Workplace Incivility and the Management of Human Capital." *Public Manager*, Vol. 31, pp. 36–43.

# ACKNOWLEDGMENTS

This book wouldn't be possible without the help, support,
and love of some awesome peeps who have been in my corner
and been there for me—whether it's a word of encouragement
or a glass of vino (or both!) while I venture down this book
writin' Yellow Brick Road:

Mme Ruth Bond, my mentor and friend who's been my Dogette
and inspiration in and out of the workplace. Thanks for always
asking me the tough questions.

Laurie Brown, who has awesomely hounded me to get this
book done for years, and who's been one of my biggest
cheerleaders from the sidelines
since our days of strudel-collecting in Frankfurt.

Mark D. Gibson, my author-brother who was
not only an empathetic ear
while I was toiling away on this project, but also instrumental in
helping me "think big" to share my story with the
peeps in the world.

Debbie Drew, another cheerleader and supporter in this work
who's given me the inspiration to "think big" and be a Big Dog.

Wes Wagaman, my thinking partner and sister who was there to help
this extrovert think out loud on what should be included in this book.
Love ya like my luggage.

My biological fam—Ma and Pa Yock and mon sœur Terri:
thanks for continuing to support your favorite youngest from the
sidelines, despite the distance.

My awesome publisher Jenn Grace and the team at Publish Your
Purpose Press. You're a collectively amazing group of folks who
kept me on track from Day 1!

And of course, to my amazing and
supportive husband Richard Egan,
who's allowed me to—not just support my business dream—but
been the best partner and friend throughout this and all my
cockamamie ideas. After all these twenty-plus years
you're still my favorite ... :^)